What Others Are Saying

Hurley's debut combines a story of his personal experiences with a blueprint of the skills he currently employs on his road to mental health. Raised on a 500-acre South Dakota family farm with his fifteen siblings, Hurley absorbed the work ethic drilled into him by agricultural necessity, church and tradition. In college, however, his personal affairs began to go awry. After law school, he became a hardworking, wealthy California lawyer—his license plate read "PD2WN" (paid to win)—but he was blindsided when his first wife took their child and left. His legal battles began then and intensified after his second marriage, which gave him more children, ended in divorce. Although the author's subsequent stories of custody fights are a bit self-indulgent, his riveting chronicle of his struggles in New York City on September 11, 2001, during the World Trade Center attack, demonstrates his considerable writing skill ("Emergency lights flashed. Anguished people spilled out of the ferries"). As his chronic insomnia intensified, he was diagnosed with post-traumatic stress disorder, and soon his behavior, which included night terrors and depression, led to his being unable to practice law in the state of California.

The book's second half offers helpful advice to people who are fearful of being stigmatized as mentally ill. Hurley nimbly combines biblical teachings with sound cognitive behavioral therapy practices that he learned through research and therapy with a Dr. S. Hurley writes, "Cognitive behavioral therapy is not simply the power of positive thinking...Rather, it is the recognition that your thoughts about a situation or event...are being *automatically* interpreted and distorted in a negative way."

The author outlines seven reasonably detailed skill sets to show the way, which include recognition, reflection, retreat, renewal, recovery, rejoice, and reliance. In this book, Hurley effectively argues that "there is no happy pill," but that the brain can be trained to think constructively and positively after negative experiences.

A persuasive guide to living with PTSD that blends autobiography and advice.

—Kirkus Reviews

◇◇◇◇◇◇◇◇◇◇◇◇◇◇◇◇◇◇◇◇◇◇◇◇◇◇◇◇◇◇◇

God Is My Architect by John Hurley begins with an engaging autobiography of his formative years, his highly successful career as a litigation attorney, the pain of divorces, the trauma of being in New York on September 11, 2001, and the experience of depression and post-traumatic stress disorder. Baby boomer Hurley's description of being raised in a small town on a 500-acre farm in a large, high-achieving Irish Catholic family includes heartwarming, humorous, and challenging situations that entertain and inform. This autobiographical section of the book provides rich data for discussion of topics such as nature versus nurture, priorities, individualism vs. collectivism, grace and forgiveness, struggles associated with religious differences between family members, and attitudes about mental illness.

In the second section of the book, Hurley describes how to use the seven cognitive behavioral therapy strategies that helped heal and restore him from depression and posttraumatic stress disorder. What is new is the way he ties the seven strategies to the Bible, and what is meaningful is that Hurley was willing to sacrificially relive past traumas as he wrote this book because he is confident that others can benefit from using the seven strategies and understanding their biblical foundation. The cognitive behavioral approach may heal and restore on a certain level, but its effectiveness is enhanced by the added layer of spiritual healing provided by scripture. As Hurley puts it, the added layer brings spiritual joy that is not provided by the secular approach alone.

An added strength of Hurley's book is that it dispels misconceptions about psychology that some Christians have. These misconceptions have held some Christians back from seeking psychological help when they could have benefited from it. Thus, one of the book's major contributions is that Christian readers who need psychological help may be prompted by the book to get such help.

I recommend the book to a wide audience, not just Christian readers. I particularly encourage those suffering from mental illness, those who know someone suffering from mental illness, psychology students, professors, clinicians, feminists, antifeminists, Catholics, Protestants, non-Christians, pastors, priests, laypeople, lawyers, people who are contemplating divorce or who are divorced, and especially anyone who is put off by the title to read this book. Why? Two reasons. First, in this historical time when diversity and multiculturalism are celebrated, it is important to be knowledgeable (and hopefully impacted) by the Christian worldview that is described so clearly by Hurley in *God Is My Architect*. Second, one needs to find out why a man with an English degree and a law degree names God as his Architect.

—Susan Nakayama Siaw, PhD, California State Polytechnic University, Pomona, psychology professor

You can't help but be drawn in by John Hurley's story. His candid and conversational style puts you at ease. He offers a clear and effective approach to surviving the mental health ravages of life's challenges. A particularly important section is his discussion of forgiveness, joy, and mental health. John makes it clear what forgiveness is and is not, clarifies common confusion regarding forgiveness and justice, and highlights the fruits of forgiveness. John's message is an important one—forgiveness gives reason for joy and joy brings about the truest fulfillment of our calling in life.

—Loren Toussaint, PhD, Luther
College, department of psychology

GOD IS MY ARCHITECT

GOD IS MY ARCHITECT

A BLUEPRINT DESIGNED TO LIFT YOU UP
FROM DEPRESSION AND POST-TRAUMATIC STRESS

JOHN A. HURLEY

TATE PUBLISHING
AND **ENTERPRISES**, LLC

Published by Tate Publishing & Enterprises, LLC
127 E. Trade Center Terrace | Mustang, Oklahoma 73064 USA
1.888.361.9473 | www.tatepublishing.com

Tate Publishing is committed to excellence in the publishing industry. The company reflects the philosophy established by the founders, based on Psalm 68:11,
"The Lord gave the word and great was the company of those who published it."

Book design copyright © 2015 by Tate Publishing, LLC. All rights reserved.
Edited by Kathryn Feather
Cover design by Joana Quilantang
Interior design by Gram Telen

Published in the United States of America

ISBN: 978-1-68187-111-0
1. Religion / Christian Life / General
2. Self-Help / Mood Disorders / Depression
15.10.08

Acknowledgments

I wish to express my sincere and heartfelt appreciation and love to my wife, Janice, for her endless inspiration and support not only in encouraging me to write this book, but also in talking me off the ledge on more than one occasion. While others abandoned me, she never let go. She is my partner and my best friend. I am truly blessed to be her husband. I owe special thanks and gratitude to Dr. S, who is a brilliant psychologist. He saw through and beyond the faults and negativity surrounding my life when I could not. I also wish to thank Rick Yount, the executive director of the Warrior Canine Connection, for giving me permission to use his testimony before the Congressional subcommittee. I also wish to thank Judge Talcott and Judge Honn, who showed me compassion and understanding during a difficult time. I also wish to thank my editor, Kathryn, for all her support, encouragement, and invaluable guidance.

The Lord is close to the brokenhearted and saves those
who are crushed in spirit.

—Psalm 34:18

Contents

Prologue

For he was looking forward to the city with foundations,
whose architect and builder is God.

—Hebrews 11:10

"Mr. Hurley, I have reviewed your accomplishments. Why are you here? You seem to have lost your way." California State Bar Court Judge Robert Talcott had cleared the courtroom so he could talk privately with me, and his assessment of my situation stunned me. I couldn't hold back the tears. Judge Talcott vocalized publicly the question that privately tormented me: *John, what is wrong with you?*

As I looked up at Judge Talcott, I didn't have an answer. His years of experience and wisdom discerned something in me that I did not understand myself. Wearing his black robe and trademark bow tie, his demeanor was more pleading than judgmental. His question conveyed compassion more than condemnation. I sensed in his attitude a genuine desire to help me. It was an expression of help I had longed for and needed desperately.

However, I wasn't able to answer his question. Perhaps because he had compared my past achievements to my present situation, I only felt embarrassed and ashamed. My life seemed to be falling apart, and I didn't know why.

Judge Talcott studied me from the bench. I sat quietly, unable to speak. I felt alone and isolated. I didn't know why this was continuing to happen. I would have some good days, and then I would have some awful, frightening, and pain-filled days.

I tormented myself by assuming others also must be silently wondering what went wrong with me. With each indignity, I became more reticent and reclusive. Judge Talcott now was asking the same question—the question that defied reason and logic. He wanted me to account for myself. He wanted to know how could someone seemingly so skilled, so smart, and so accomplished continue to repeat the same mistakes. How could someone perform at such a high degree of professionalism on some cases and seemingly abandon his clients on others?

I didn't have an answer. I just remember feeling so extremely sad. I felt as if I was crumbling from the inside out. I felt like a complete failure and a total loser.

Judge Talcott interrupted the quiet stillness by stepping down from the bench. He walked over to the counsel table and sat next to me. With an understanding look I will never forget, he said, "We have a program that I think may help you." For the first time, someone was reaching out to me and offering help. I was drowning, and at last, someone was throwing me a lifeline.

Not long after that encounter with Judge Talcott, a psychiatrist diagnosed that I had been suffering for some time from a dysthymia, a prolonged chronic depression, exacerbated by posttraumatic stress disorder (PTSD). The mystery was over. I took the first long, painful step on my journey toward recovery.

This book relates my battle with depression and PTSD and recounts my recovery. It is a true story, and one that is going to be extremely painful to write. Why did I choose to be completely vulnerable and write this story? Why would I own and celebrate all the circumstances that led to my depression? Why would I rip off that scab and expose the injury and pain festering just beneath the surface? Why would I relive each excruciating experience? Several compelling reasons convicted me to summon the strength and the courage to share my story.

The first reason I wrote this book is that I hope sharing my story will help others suffering from depression or PTSD. For far too long, mental illness has been ignored, discounted, or denied. Those suffering from mental illness may not have sought treatment because they have been made to feel stigmatized, ostracized, or rejected. They also may not have sought help because, until recently, many insurance policies did not provide coverage or benefits for mental illness.

My wish is that if you are reading this because you may be depressed, or if you have a loved one or friend who has exhibited symptoms of depression or PTSD, you may take some comfort from reading about my experience. Depressed people often have low self-esteem not only because of their perception that they have failed but also because they believe they have failed themselves and others. They believe, most often from within, that their mistakes and failures somehow diminished their worth. Often, this may occur to such a degree that even their capacity for living has lost its value or meaning to the point that they can become suicidal. I hope that telling my story will encourage others to take that first painful step toward seeking help and support.

You are not alone. Approximately twenty million Americans suffer from depression. There is support and help available to you. There is hope. You can get better. You *will* get better. You just have to take that courageous first step. My hope is that your reading this book will help you take that step. As you will learn upon reading my story, I was right where you are now. Be encouraged by the knowledge that you are not alone.

Those suffering from depression or PTSD need to understand that they need not be a prisoner to their feelings, thoughts, or emotions. At the outset, I emphasize that I am not a victim. I take complete and full responsibility for all my actions, mistakes, and failings. To those whom I have offended, I offer my sincere and genuine apology and ask for your forgiveness.

However, the burden borne by guilt may not be the only cause of depression. Events can occur, or circumstances may happen, to people in such a way so as to cause them to be *victimized*. The reason may be the result of another's action or failure to act. It may materialize with a phenomenon of nature, such as a hurricane, tornado, or earthquake. It may emanate with a health-related tragedy, such as a cancer, stroke, heart attack, death, or suicide. The cause also may be a traffic accident, a drunk driver, or a train wreck. Someone may have been abused or abandoned, or someone may just have been in the wrong place at the wrong time, whether serving our country in Vietnam, Iraq, and Afghanistan or experiencing 9-11.

Each of these examples can cause sadness, grief, despair, disappointment, and discouragement. All these emotions and feelings are normal and expected; however, when they become prolonged and chronic, they can lead to depression. Witnessing or experiencing an event can be so traumatic that it can result in PTSD where a certain visual image, sound, or smell suddenly will create a flashback and transport you back into time and force you to relive the traumatic experience.

You are not meant to suffer and be sad. It doesn't need to define you or defeat you. Seek help. Get help. In this book you will learn how I lost my way. I went from being included in *Who's Who Among Practicing Attorneys in the United States* in 1989 to being unable to practice law. I lost my way when I became sick. I struggled for years, not knowing that I was suffering from depression and PTSD before finally getting diagnosed and treated. Maybe you have lost your way.

The second reason I wrote this book is to address the unique challenge that Christians face when they suffer from depression or PTSD. It is my sincere hope that sharing my story will serve as a testimony of my faith and that others who read my story may benefit from its expression of faith. Part of my story depicts the difficulty I had accepting my diagnosis and understanding that Christians can get depressed or suffer from PTSD.

I couldn't comprehend that accepting Christ could not insulate me from experiencing excruciating events, heartache, abandonment, disappointment, discouragement, and depression. I struggled to reconcile the joy that I obtained from eternal salvation on one hand with the depression that I experienced through life's struggles on the other. If God wanted me to experience peace and joy, why was I so sad? Why couldn't prayer overcome my sadness and depression? I was conflicted and confused. My faith was challenged.

If this is how you feel, remember you are not alone. As you will learn later in the book, about one-fourth of all Christians suffer from depression or other forms of mental illness—the same percentage as non-Christians. Imagine the next time you attend church that every fourth person you see is silently suffering from depression or other mental illness.

Research reveals that Christians are more likely to seek help from their pastors than from mental health professionals, but most pastors neither are trained to recognize mental health symptoms nor equipped to treat them. Most Christians who initially seek help from their pastors never thereafter seek treatment from mental health professionals. As a result, Christians often conclude they are depressed because they are not praying hard enough or because they are not praying the right way. Satan chooses such a vulnerable time to convince Christians that their faith is weak, and consequently their depression worsens. Further depressed, many lose their faith altogether.

As a Christian, I prayed that God would remove my depression and PTSD. I thought that prayer alone could heal me. However, I learned that depression cannot be "prayed away." Depression, PTSD, or other mental illnesses cannot be cured by prayer alone.

Depression and PTSD are disorders or illnesses that are like any other physical, neurological, or medical illness, disease, or disorder. They require a proper diagnosis by a trained professional, and they require appropriate medical treatment and therapy.

Although there are many recorded instances where the power of prayer has healed people when medical science could not, certain chemical, electrical, neurological, psychological, or physiological factors exist that may be the cause, and/or the perpetuation, of depression, PTSD, and other mental illnesses and disorders. Genetics also may be a contributing factor if one's family has a history of depression. As a result, mental health conditions and illnesses require psychiatric or psychological treatment, therapy, and/or medication. For these reasons, it is important for Christians to seek such medical care. It is not part of God's plan for people to stay depressed.

The third reason I wrote this book is to share the seven self-help skill sets that can help you overcome depression and PTSD. In this book, I share my story to be a blessing and an encouragement to you, and to help you understand that you are not alone. However, the focus of the book is not my story. The emphasis of the book is the collection of the seven skills that you can apply to your own situation to help you recover from depression. Each skill set includes both a practical and a spiritual application. These are the skill sets that I used to recover from depression and PTSD.

During my recovery I experienced that, as a Christian, I could not overcome my depression and PTSD simply by believing and having faith. Because prayer alone could not cure my depression and PTSD, I discovered that I needed the practical application of the skill sets to overcome my depression and PTSD. On the practical side, I needed to apply the cognitive behavioral therapy principles to unlearn negative perceptions.

The practical application of each skill set is based on sound and proven principles of cognitive behavioral therapy. These principles will help you understand depression and PTSD and help you overcome the automatic negative thoughts that trigger depression and PTSD. My application of these principles were effective in overcoming my depression and PTSD.

Nevertheless, I found that overcoming depression and PTSD was not enough. While the practical application of the skill sets allowed me to recover from these illnesses, I was unfulfilled. I needed something more. Something was still missing.

Clearly, a person doesn't have to be a Christian to overcome depression or other mental illnesses. A person can overcome depression and PTSD by utilizing the seven self-help skill sets and, when necessary, by obtaining professional psychological or psychiatric care.

While I was relieved that I no longer was suffering from depression and PTSD, I discovered that the absence of depression is not joy. The absence of depression simply mean that I was no longer depressed. There was still something missing. I just didn't want to be free from depression. I wanted joy and peace. I needed something more, a positive meaning, to replace the negative meaning. As a result, I discovered that when I combined the effectiveness of the practical application of the cognitive behavioral therapy with the power of the Holy Spirit, I was able to find joy and peace.

It is for this reason that I included the spiritual application of the Christian and biblical principles among each of the seven skill sets. On the spiritual side, I needed to apply biblical discernment so that I could act on faith. I needed to develop a renewed mind. During my journey, I learned that I obtained the best results when I combined my medical treatment program and cognitive behavioral therapy with the spiritual application of the seven skill sets.

The spiritual application of each skill set is based on biblical verses and Scripture that will encourage you and sustain you in your battles with Satan over the meaning you attach to life's events. The spiritual application of the skill sets is not a substitute for prayer but a supplement to prayer. You will learn how both the practical cognitive behavioral application and the Christian spiritual application can be used to overcome depression and PTSD, to defeat Satan's deceptions, to develop a more personal relationship with Christ, to find meaningful joy, and to secure lasting peace.

The combination of the practical approach and the spiritual approach is the blueprint designed to heal you and help you overcome depression. If my life could be healed and restored, so can yours. If I could find my way again, so can you. You will recover. You will get better. There is help. There is hope.

The last and most important reason I wrote this book is to be obedient to God's calling to share my testimony and the Good News. I am neither a pastor nor a psychologist. Rather, I am a failure and a sinner. I lost my way when I became sick and suffered from depression and PTSD. However, I didn't stay lost. With help, I once again found my way.

I believe that God asked me to write this book so that others who are suffering from depression and PTSD also can find their way. Initially I didn't want to write this book because I knew just how painful it would be to relive those hurtful events and experiences. However, I had a change of heart when I learned that so many veterans and active duty military men and women who had suffered from depression and PTSD committed suicide. My heart also ached and was filled with compassion when I learned that Matthew Warren, the twenty-seven-year-old son of Kay and Rick Warren, pastor of Saddleback Church, had committed suicide. I knew I no longer could resist God's calling. I substituted God's plan for my plan, and I finally accepted and obeyed God's calling to write this book.

It is important during your journey to give and receive encouragement to overcome the stigmatism associated with having depression, PTSD, or any other mental illness. Such stigmatism exists both within and outside the Christian community. Do not allow the perceived embarrassment and stigmatism to keep you from getting help. There is no shame in seeking help. It would only be shameful and tragic if you did not get help.

I devoted an entire chapter toward overcoming the stigmatism that prevents people from getting help. I also created a dedicated website, a Facebook page, and an e-mail address exclusively for the book so that you can share your stories and comments, and so that you may encourage and support others:

Website:	www.godismyarchitect.com
Facebook:	*www.facebook.com/godismyarchitect*
E-mail:	*jhurley@godismyarchitect.com*

Writing about your experience is empowering not only to yourself but also to others. You are not alone. Reach out and share your stories. You will encourage and comfort others.

I am confident that the skill sets will help you recover from depression and PTSD. I pray that your journey will also lead you to know Christ and that you will find a meaningful and personal relationship with Christ. Regardless of your past, God has designed a plan, a purpose, and a blueprint just for you.

Let God be your Architect.

1

The Calling

And you also are among those who are called to belong to
Jesus Christ.

—Romans 1:6

I was born in 1955 as the seventh youngest of sixteen children
to Irish Catholic parents on a 500-acre farm in South Dakota.
That single sentence tells you everything about my upbringing:
tradition, religion, responsibility, work ethic, pride, generosity,
sacrifice, competitiveness, devotion, self-reliance, obedience,
loyalty, honor, and family.

I always enjoyed that I was born the year Disneyland opened
as the happiest place on earth, but growing up, I always believed
that the happiest place on earth was our family farm. We didn't
have money, but we were rich in other ways. I developed a
genuine closeness with my brothers and sisters. We loved and
cared for each other. We had each other's backs.

We played together, worked together, and grew up together
helping each other and looking after each other. In my mind,
we were the epitome of *The Waltons*, a popular 1970s television
show about a fictional family living during the depression era. In
difficult times, the family in *The Waltons* modeled togetherness
where individual desires often were sacrificed and subordinated
for the family.

I was one of seven boys born in a nine-year span. We seven
boys had two older brothers, five older sisters, and two younger

sisters. Sandwiched in the middle of the family, we seven brothers were inseparable. During grade school, we shared a large bedroom where two of us shared one twin bed, two shared another twin bed, and the other three shared a larger bed.

Through seventh grade, I attended a one-room schoolhouse a mile and a half from our farm. Our family comprised practically half of the students in the school, who were all farm kids who lived and worked within several miles from the schoolhouse. I had one classmate. Years later, I bragged that during grade school I never finished below second in my class.

Of course, recess and lunchtime were spent playing outdoors, and the younger kids tried to keep up with the older ones. We played all sorts of games together, and our teacher would even play with us. When the weather was nice during the spring, our school's softball team would compete against several other one-room schools in the area.

During the winter, we made tunnels in the snow that formed a maze or course in which we ran and played tag. When the snow would melt, the water froze on the grass into a pond. We would run on the frozen grass and then skate across the ice.

One day in first grade, I slipped and fell on the ice. I had quite a large bump on my head, so the teacher made me sit inside the school with her while everybody else was outside playing. It seemed like punishment, so of course, I snuck back outside and joined everybody else skating across the ice. I fell again, this time hitting my temple hard against the ice. The severe concussion blinded me. I could not see for three days, but then God miraculously restored my sight.

Going to school in that one-room schoolhouse was a wonderful way to learn. The teacher's desk was in the front of the room next to the blackboard, and all the children's desks were arranged in four or five rows toward the back of the room.

The younger children sat in front, and the older children sat in the back. The teacher began each period by calling the first-grade class to come to the front of the room and sit at her desk. While she reviewed the particular subject matter with them, all the other students would watch or study quietly at their desks. The teacher would repeat this same procedure for each subject, for each class, until that subject matter was completed for all seven grades. Our library consisted of books that circulated monthly from one schoolhouse to the next. I was so excited to see what new and interesting books would arrive each month.

Younger students could listen and learn as advanced material was discussed, and older children could review and reinforce lessons previously learned. Older students would help younger ones with their reading or homework. Each time students sat at the teacher's desk, they were held accountable for their homework and assignments before an audience of the entire school. With only one classmate, it was impossible to hide! Our grade school experience was a page right out of Laura Ingalls Wilder's *Little House on the Prairie*.[1] Homework was like chores. We were just expected to get it done, but chores came first.

During grade school, we seven boys were expected to milk about twenty cows each morning before school and each evening after school. Every day. Rain or shine. Summer or winter. Every day, twice a day. The milk from the cows not only provided all the milk and cream we needed for our family, but also the income from the sale of the milk paid for all the needed groceries that we didn't produce ourselves.

We had a two-acre garden. Just think about that—a two-acre *garden*. We raised every kind of vegetable imagined. We had rows and rows of sweet corn and potatoes planted with the same farm machinery that planted the fields of corn and soybeans. The rest of the garden was planted by hand. I often would walk out into our garden on a summer day with a saltshaker in my hip jeans pocket, pick a ripe red tomato from a tomato vine, brush off the dirt, and take a luscious bite.

Our garden also produced fruit such as watermelons, cantaloupe, pumpkins, muskmelons, and strawberries. We picked apples, cut wild rhubarb, and picked chokecherries. Our mom would can everything for storage in the cool underground cellar with all the potatoes to be eaten during the long winters. She also would make jams, jellies, and preserves. Often during harvest, she would sell the produce to the local grocery store.

During the winter, we raised cattle. My uncle was a cattle buyer and lived at the west end of South Dakota in the Black Hills. Our farm was in the southeastern part of South Dakota, near the Iowa cattle feeders. My dad would broker deals with the cattle feeders and sell them the Angus and Hereford calves that my uncle bought at auctions held at sale barns near the Montana, Wyoming, Nebraska, and South Dakota cattle ranches. With the cows, we always had milk; with our garden, we always had food; and with our cattle, we always had meat on the table.

At the end of each summer, there was not much to do on the farm while we waited for the crops to ripen. My parents would drive the eight-hour trip across the state to the Black Hills where we would visit my uncle's family for a few days and stay at their home. These trips represented the only vacations my parents would enjoy during those years, and sometimes, I would accompany them. I loved seeing the Badlands, the Black Hills, Spearfish Canyon, Mount Rushmore, and the passion play.

During one trip, we traveled to a ranch located on the Pine Ridge Indian Reservation near Oglala, South Dakota, where I watched the cowboys rope and corral the calves before they were loaded on a truck to be transported to auction. One of the cowboys broke his leg when he was thrown from his horse.

Somebody tied a board to his leg and put him in the back of a pickup where he rode the two-hour ride to the nearest doctor.

I often traveled with my dad and mom to the cattle feeders' farms in Iowa. They came to know our parents like friends. We would have a visit, always have something to eat, and then they would buy tens of thousands of dollars of cattle from my dad, sight unseen. They simply would hand my dad a check, and my dad would say the calves would arrive in about a week. They did these deals simply on trust and a handshake. My dad's word was his bond.

Growing up on our family farm meant that we had a lot of work to do. Cows had to be milked twice each day. Crops had to be planted, cultivated, and harvested. Cattle had to be sorted, vaccinated, and fed. Fields had to be plowed, disked, dragged, and fertilized. Hay had to be mowed, raked, baled, and stacked. Fences had to be built, repaired, and painted. Barns had to be cleaned. Machinery had to be cleaned, oiled, repaired, and maintained. Meals had to be cooked, and laundry and dishes had to be washed. We were taught the meaning of responsibility at an early age.

This was our way of life. This was just the way it was. We were expected to work. Our mom often said that she didn't have to get a job in town because when she woke up every morning, the work was right there waiting for her. There were no complaints or excuses. We all knew that if we didn't milk the cows, we wouldn't have grocery money; that if we didn't tend the garden, we wouldn't have food to eat during the winter; and that if we didn't care for the livestock, they would get sick and die. We knew that if we didn't harvest crops or sell livestock, we would not have any money for the entire year. We often missed school to work on the farm.

Whether at school or on the farm, we knew a closeness and togetherness. We weren't just raised to care for each other; we actually cared for and loved each other. We were each other's best friends, playmates, and confidants. We served and sacrificed for each other and for our family.

However, no matter how hard we worked, we still depended on God to provide the rain and sunshine to grow and ripen the crops. Too much rain, or rain at the wrong time, could flood a crop. Too little rain, or the lack of rain at critical times, could cause a drought. While the sun seemed to shine every day and the weather provided a wonderful growing season, temperatures that were too hot or were hot for too long or at the wrong time, could burn a crop. Spring temperatures that were too cold would not allow the seeds to germinate. Either a hailstorm or a tornado could wipe out an entire crop. As a result, religion was a large part of our life.

Our family belonged to a small Catholic church in town, about four miles away where we attended mass every Sunday. I remember when I was very young that the service was still performed in Latin. Each week, we learned our catechism, and every summer during grade school, we attended a weeklong summer church camp operated by the nuns. I later wondered if the nuns were so strict during that single week of camp so that all the children would believe that their parents' discipline during the rest of the year wasn't all that bad comparatively.

At that time, there were less than three thousand people living in our town, Canton, and our Catholic church had to be one of the smallest churches there. Most of the people who had settled in our community over the years were mainly of Scandinavian or German descent. As Irish Catholics, we were in the minority compared to the Protestants who populated the Lutheran, Methodist, Presbyterian, and Baptist Churches. Although we lived less than thirty miles from the largest city in the state, Sioux Falls, where there were many Catholic churches and a Catholic cathedral, during the fifties and early sixties, we didn't travel there very often and rarely attended mass there. For the most part, our geographical world was limited at that time to Lincoln County in general and in particular to the ten-mile radius surrounding our town.

To my parents' generation, ancestry was important. Growing up, we only heard of stories about our ancestors who immigrated to America with the *O* in front of our last name (O'Hurley) or who had homesteaded the prairie. Our parents, however, actually knew those ancestors, or had known of them. My father was born in 1914. He grew up with and knew his grandparents, who homesteaded and settled the prairie land. His great-grandparents had emigrated from Ireland. My father was a young boy when World War I ended, and both of our parents lived through World War II. Ancestry mattered to our dad.

We were raised to be proud of our Irish ancestry. We celebrated Irish traditions and customs, and we proudly wore green on St. Patrick's Day. I remember traveling with my parents to the airport at Sioux Falls to meet Senator John Kennedy during his presidential campaign. We all were so very proud when he was elected as the first Irish Catholic president.

In our family, our Irish ancestry and our Catholic religion were woven into our upbringing. My dad's first cousin was a priest (Father Kelly), and the priests from our local church (Father Reagan, Father Hamel, and Father Roney) were all frequent guests at our dinner table over the years. When I became older, I actually was surprised to learn that the Vatican was located in Italy instead of Ireland.

During grade school, my brothers and I served in the church as altar boys. Not only did we stand on the altar alongside the priest, but also we personally handled many of the items used by the priest during the celebration of mass. As a young boy, I found this experience intriguing. The mass seemed mysterious.

Even after it was performed in English instead of Latin, many parts of the service were still spoken in Latin. I wanted to know the meaning behind the words and the rituals.

In our home, we had a family Bible, but it mainly was used to record our family ancestry and to house important papers. We didn't read the Bible at home. That was something that was done on Sunday in church. However, then only the priest read from the Bible. My recollection is that, at that time, the booklets that the parishioners were provided so as to be able to follow the priest performing the service did not include the excerpts from the Bible read by the priest during the service. Only later were those excerpts added to the booklets, and church members were selected to read portions of epistles or Gospels. However, even then, Bibles were not provided in the pews. I listened intently as a young child to the stories and lessons read from the Bible by the priest, wanting to read and understand more.

At Christmas 1955, to celebrate my birth, my namesake uncle (my mom's oldest brother) presented my mom with a book to give to me later. The title was *The Life of Christ.*[2] My uncle John inscribed the inside cover to me and signed it. I don't remember when Mom finally gave it to me, but I believe it was when I received my first Communion. Obviously, I wasn't able to read many of the words at that time, but I loved looking at the colored pictures and holding the red leather-covered book. As I later learned to read more proficiently, I often would read the stories about Christ, and I was thrilled at reading Christ's own words, printed in red, as they jumped off the page and spoke directly to me. I still have this book. It is one of my most treasured possessions.

Through my adolescent years, I enjoyed attending the Catholic Church, and occasionally, either our priest or my dad's first cousin, Father Kelly, would ask me if I wanted to become a priest when I grew older. I honestly told them that I would love to learn the Bible but that I couldn't become a priest because I was going to be a major league baseball player.

I loved to play baseball. I was one of those kids who slept with his glove under his pillow. I loved to read stories about Babe Ruth, Lou Gehrig, and the great New York Yankees championship teams. When I was a kid, Mickey Mantle was my favorite player and the Yankees was my favorite team.

For hours at a time, I would throw a rubber ball against the side of our house. If I threw the ball upward, I could practice catching flies. If I threw it downward, I could practice catching grounders. I practiced pitching by throwing the ball against the barn wall.

My brother Dan and I would play entire baseball games just between the two of us. He liked our "local" team, the Minnesota Twins, and had the Twins roster memorized as I had for the Yankees. We didn't collect baseball cards (we clipped those on to the spokes of our bikes), but we read the box scores. We not only knew the players' names, we also knew their respective batting orders and lineups. One of us would pitch while the other would hit. Where the ball landed determined whether it was a single, double, triple, homer, or out, which often was the subject of intense debate. We painted a rectangle representing the strike zone on the garage door, which made a perfect backstop. If the ball struck either on or inside the rectangle's boundaries, it was a strike; otherwise, it was a ball. Whoever was batting would announce each player's turn at bat.

We looked forward to each time Mom would come home from the grocery store with a large box of laundry soap because there would be a hard rubber ball hidden inside the box as a bonus for purchasing the soap. We became so good at throwing the ball so that it would strike the low outside corner of the strike zone that we eventually broke the board in the hand-built garage door. A wooden panel or board about four inches wide broke loose and came apart from the rest of the garage door. We didn't bother to fix it and, instead, just ripped it off the door. With the board gone, we had an even better target.

However, the garage was full of junk. Whenever a fastball zipped through the hole in the garage door, we had to interrupt the game and look for the ball. Sometimes, our game was called on account of darkness, and sometimes, our game was called on account of a lost ball. We then would have to wait for Mom to buy more soap before we could play another game.

It didn't matter what we were doing. We were always playing ball. If we were baling hay, the haystack would be the backstop. If we were cutting silage, the pile of silage would be the backstop. One time, the haystack was located near the feedlot and Dan hit one of my pitches all the way to the house. The ball crashed right through the kitchen window. By the time we ran up to the house, Mom was standing on the porch, holding the ball, wanting to know why we were playing ball so close to the house. We pleaded our case and told her that we were playing way out against the haystack and that Dan had hit the ball that far. She didn't believe us because she didn't think Dan could hit my pitching. Both Dan and I knew that he could.

As a result, we decided we needed a new backstop. So when Mom wasn't looking, we rolled up the largest mattress in our room and shoved it out of our second-story bedroom window onto the porch roof. Whoever slept in that bed was just going to have to sleep on the box springs. While somebody served as the lookout, we tossed it from the porch roof on to the ground, hoisted it up above our shoulders, and then carried it all the way out to the pasture, which became our new ball field. On the way home after church on Sundays, Dad often drove around the fields to admire the growing crops. Imagine our mom's surprise when we drove past the pasture and she saw the mattress propped up against the fence! We had to do extra chores after that one.

I have so many happy memories of growing up on our family farm, but one of the happiest memories of my childhood was when our dad and all of us boys played infield together. We had a large area separating the house from the barn and the machine shed. The ground was covered in gravel, but it would still get muddy after it rained. When the mud dried, we would pull the drag behind the tractor, driving in circles to smooth out the ruts. After the yard was dragged, it was nice and smooth, just like an infield on a ball field—perfect for hitting grounders.

This particular day was one of those lazy August afternoons after a soft summer shower. The sun was setting, and somebody suggested that we play ball on the freshly dragged yard. The dark-green rows of corn sprouting golden tassels framed the outfield of green grass that had just been mowed the day before. Earlier that week, we baled hay and tightly stacked the bales into a thirty-foot cube next to the feedlot. The cows had been milked, and they now stood side by side eating at the feed bunk, watching us play ball across the yard. Everything smelled farm fresh. This was our field of dreams.

It was one of those times when our oldest brothers, Jim and Brian, were home, so all nine of us boys were able to play ball together. We had our own ball team, and we each took a position on the field. Dad took turns hitting us balls until it became too dark to play any more. It was one of those perfect days.

This was how it was with all of us children growing up together. We were inseparable. We learned to work together and play together. We shared everything. We would try to finish our work as fast as possible so we could go out and play. Sometimes, I would take shortcuts with work to have more time to play, but this, of course, would land me in trouble. We had to work together to make our family farm a success.

I always had gotten along with my dad, and his authority in our family was unquestioned. I took seriously the commandment "Honor thy father and mother." Obedience and respect were a major part of our upbringing. In my view, when I distinguished myself both academically and athletically, I believed that I had brought honor and respect to my parents. They proudly attended countless basketball and baseball games. We won more than our share of tournaments. I graduated from high school near the top of my class. Among other honors, I was selected king on the homecoming royalty, president of the student council, junior class president, and was a member of the National Honor Society.

During high school, I was a good athlete. Our dad didn't let us play football because he said that he was afraid we would get hurt. I think the real reason we couldn't play football was because football season coincided with harvest. Nevertheless, I enjoyed playing basketball and baseball. During my senior year, I started on the basketball team and set the basketball record at our high school for career field goal percentage. I also was named to the all-conference team.

Baseball wasn't a school sport. We played baseball during the summer as part of American Legion baseball. I pitched and played shortstop, and nearly every year, our team competed to play in the state tournament. My claim to fame was during my senior season where I had an 11–1 win-loss record and I struck out ninety batters in the sixty innings that I pitched. That meant that of the 180 outs recorded during the sixty innings that I pitched that year, half of those outs were obtained by my striking somebody out.

As a result, I received a full athletic scholarship to attend a small college, Sioux Falls College,[3] to play both basketball and baseball. Although the full athletic scholarship may sound impressive, most of my brothers and sisters were better athletes than me. As just one example, on more than one occasion when my brothers and I were playing basketball, our youngest sister, Rita, would ask to play. We always told her that she couldn't play because she was too little. After all, she was the baby of the family. Well, our baby sister later grew to be a six-foot-one point guard who was named Miss Basketball for our state her senior year. She not only received a basketball scholarship to college, she was also a star on her college team. She sure showed us who could play!

Other than a scholarship offer from a junior college, the offer from Sioux Falls College was the only offer I received. I was thrilled to get the chance to play ball in college.

What was interesting about my scholarship offer was that Sioux Falls College was a Baptist college. As a result, my dad would not give me permission to accept the offer to attend Sioux Falls College, simply because it was a Baptist college. During high school, I dated several wonderful girls who didn't attend our Catholic church, and so I occasionally received complaints from Dad because my girlfriends weren't Catholic. This athletic scholarship offer, however, became a significant source of contention with my dad. At stake was whether I could play ball in college and whether I would have to borrow money to pay for college. I could not understand why my dad would not allow me to accept the scholarship. He would not let me attend the Baptist college, and I felt like there was nothing that I could do about it. I felt powerless and helpless. As a result, I suppressed my feelings. It was a fait accompli.

This experience lit a fire within me. I wanted to know why my dad was so antagonistic toward the Baptist faith. I wanted to know why Catholicism was different from other religions, and I wanted to know why some people who believed in one religion didn't like those who believed in another religion. How could someone of one religion hate someone just simply because he practiced another religion? Weren't they all Christian?

During the remainder of my senior year of high school, and especially during the summer after graduation, I began talking to classmates about the different Christian religions. I still attended our Catholic church, of course, but I also attended some small group meetings and Bible study meetings with friends who attended other churches. A new world opened to me.

After graduating from high school, I attended the University of South Dakota, a public university, where I selected English and history as double majors. I was thrilled at the number of courses that I could study, and I was fascinated to be able to learn how religion impacted history and literature. In my first year of college, I selected as my topic for my freshman English term paper the difference between the Catholic and Lutheran religions. As I read about Martin Luther, I began a serious personal investigation into my Catholic background and beliefs.

I loved taking as many courses as I could that pertained to colonial American history and literature. I enjoyed reading about how people seeking religious freedom left Europe and settled the colonies. I was fascinated to learn how different colonists settled different colonies primarily based on how they practiced their particular respective religions. I was not only studying history and literature, I also was studying religion.

Christianity frequently found its way into the subject matter of papers that I wrote. In a Shakespeare seminar course taught by the dean of the English department, the title of my final paper was "The Christian Morality in Hamlet." For my final paper in a contemporary fiction class studying the novels of Kurt Vonnegut, a professed atheist, I nonetheless wrote about the Christian themes that I found in his novels.

Don't misunderstand. I was still a normal college kid doing normal college stuff. I walked on and made the varsity baseball team and enjoyed the college experience. I dated and went to my share of parties. However, I was beginning to question all the rituals and rules taught by the Catholic religion.

After my junior year of college, I was invited to play baseball during the summer for a semipro (I use that term loosely) baseball team in Sioux Falls. None of the teams were affiliated with any pro teams, and the league consisted of teams of mainly college players who played college ball during the summer in a radius of about a hundred miles from the point where South Dakota, Iowa, and Nebraska intersect. Instead of playing on a team with most of my teammates from the University of South Dakota, I accepted the invitation to play on a team in Sioux Falls comprised of players from Sioux Falls College, the same Baptist college that had offered me the athletic scholarship.

Playing baseball during that summer with the guys from that Baptist college allowed me to capture a flavor of what I had missed when I had to walk away from that scholarship. I referred to the team as a semipro team because we were each paid to play ball. Although the sponsor of the team paid us to paint some houses, we really were being paid to play ball. We painted houses for a few hours in the mornings and played ball at night. I started at shortstop, and we took second place in the tristate tournament at the end of the summer. During the tournament, our team even beat the team on which my teammates from the University of South Dakota played. I had a great time playing ball during that summer as I experienced what it would have been like to have had the opportunity to attend school and play ball at the Baptist college.

That summer, I also met my future wife Cindy (not her real name), who happened to attend a Baptist church. We dated throughout that summer, and soon, I began to attend Sunday services at the First Baptist Church where her family attended. I often spent weekends with her family during my senior year of college, so I went to church with them often. I increasingly was drawn to the Bible-based messages heard in the Baptist Church.

More and more I viewed the Catholic Church as a ritualistic religion dependent upon fear-based guilt. Among other things, I could no longer blindly follow the church-ordained rules and the belief that Christ's presence in my life depended upon my ability to perform works, keep commandments, and follow rules. The Catholic Church reminded me of the words in Isaiah, "Their worship of Me is made up only of rules taught by men" (Isaiah 29:13).

I related to and identified with Christ's description of the Pharisees when Christ said, "Isaiah was right…you have let go of the commands of God and are holding on to the traditions of men."[4] These verses described the Catholic Church to me. I wanted more than a religion. I wanted a relationship. I wanted a meaningful, personal relationship with Christ.

I could not accept the Catholic belief that Christ would depart when one sinned and that He only would return after one again would be administered the church sacraments of confession and Communion. Moreover, with my knowledge of history, I no longer could defend the fallacy of the infallibility of the pope. He is just a man, just like anybody else. Only Jesus was perfect. Just as none of this made any sense to Martin Luther, so also did it not make any sense to me.

I finally understood that one was saved only by grace and not by doing good works or by following church's rules:

> For it is by grace you have been saved, through faith—and this is not from yourselves, it is the gift of God—not by works, so that no one can boast. For we are God's handiwork, created in Christ Jesus to do good works, which God prepared in advance for us to do.[5]

I was being called to accept Christ. I finally answered the calling that I had been hearing for some time. I publicly recited the above three verses from Ephesians when I accepted Christ as my personal Lord and Savior and was baptized at the First Baptist Church. I was saved by God's grace that had been given to me through Christ's death and resurrection. I knew that I could not be saved by my works or my obedience to the commandments or the church's rules. I could never possibly do enough or be good enough. No one can. Only when I believed that Christ's death and resurrection alone provided the sanctifying grace that forgave my sins and assured me of salvation could I be saved "by grace…through faith…to do good works."

2

Sowing Seeds of Depression

Fathers, do not embitter your children, or they will become discouraged.

—Colossians 2:21

As I began my last semester in college, I was accepted into graduate school where I pursued a master's degree in English. I was awarded a scholarship and a teaching assistantship to teach an undergraduate English composition class each semester during graduate school. When I told my parents my future plans, I also told them I was planning to get married at the end of summer before starting graduate school. My dad was furious. Before, I always avoided conflict with Dad. Now we were on a collision course.

In typical fashion, my dad told me that he forbade me to get married because Cindy was not a Catholic. I responded by telling him I was no longer going to be a Catholic. I told him that I respected his position, but I made it clear I would not obey his wishes. I told both of my parents this was my decision to make alone, and I did not need their permission. My dad refused to accept my decision.

During the following months, he persuaded each of my older brothers and sisters to contact me and try to dissuade me. Out of respect for my parents, I even agreed to meet with the campus priest, but to no avail. I was resolute.

As the wedding date approached, I asked two of my brothers to be my groomsmen in the wedding party. When I asked them, I warned them they would be sure to catch hell from Dad, but each one assured me that not even Dad could come between us. We not only were inseparable growing up through high school, but also we had attended the University of South Dakota at the same time. During one year, Jerry and Dan were roommates and Mick and I were roommates in rooms across the hall from each other, in the same dorm, on the same floor. The year I graduated from college, Mick was a junior in college and Dan was a freshman in medical school. My brothers told me that no matter what Dad did, they would be there for me.

As it was customary to have the wedding held at the bride's church, the wedding was scheduled to take place at the First Baptist Church in Sioux Falls, only about a half hour's drive from our hometown and family farm. I tried to do everything to include my family in the wedding. We included my parents in the wedding invitations, and I told my dad we had agreed to have a Catholic priest participate in the wedding ceremony. However, even that wasn't acceptable to Dad. He had his Irish up.

When the invitations arrived several weeks before the wedding, Dad hired an attorney to send a cease and desist letter to Cindy's parents. The letter warned them not to include my parents' names on the invitation without his permission. My dad told them that he did not approve of the wedding, he would not be a part of the wedding, and he would sue them if they included his name on the invitations.

While it was too close to the wedding date to reorder new invitations, we artistically managed to remove my parents' names from the invitations. We reasoned that Dad just didn't want to go on record as approving the wedding because it was not going to be held in the Catholic Church. We mailed the amended invitations to the guests, including my parents, my family members, and all the friends and relatives on my invitation list, and proceeded with the final plans toward the wedding date. We hoped this would blow over, and my family would attend the wedding.

However, about a week before the wedding, my brothers told me they decided they no longer could serve as my groomsmen. They told me Dad had forbidden all my brothers and sisters from attending the wedding. They said Dad had told them he no longer considered me to be his son, and any family member attending my wedding also would no longer be considered part of the family.

I felt completely abandoned. The closeness I felt growing up in my family no longer existed. Dad broke that bond. Our band of brothers no longer had each other's back. Only my sister Marcy attended the wedding. I realized we weren't like the Waltons after all.

I was reminded of Christ's promise in the Gospel of Matthew:

> And everyone who has left houses or brothers or sisters or father or mother or children or fields for my sake will receive a hundred times as much, and will inherit eternal life.[1]

While Christ's promises (also Mark 10:29–30[2] and Luke 18:29–30[3]) gave me comfort, I was tormented by my dad's decision. I respected Dad and Mom, and I kept the commandment to honor my parents. Yet Dad did not respect and honor me.

I knew my dad wouldn't understand my extremely personal decision about my faith, but I wanted him to accept my decision. I wanted him to understand this was an extremely personal decision only I alone could make. However, Dad internalized my decision and viewed my rejection of Catholicism as a rejection of him. I felt like the prophet dishonored "only in his hometown, among his relatives, and in his own house" (Mark 6:4). I was shocked. I felt betrayed and abandoned.

My dad's actions were extremely hurtful to me, but I think they had an even more harmful impact on Cindy. Before our wedding, he actually told her, "It would have been nice to have you as part of our family." His threat to sue her parents was greatly distressing to her and her family.

The greatest damage he inflicted was in creating the division within our own family. For the next three years, no one in my family spoke to us. He managed to turn my brothers and sisters against me. The irony was I felt they abandoned me, and they felt I rejected them. The next time I spoke to my family was when I was accepted to law school.

The law school public relations department sent my picture and an article about my law school acceptance to my hometown local newspaper for publication. After my parents learned that I had been accepted to law school, they called to congratulate me, and my dad signaled to the rest of the family that it was permissible to resume relations with us. In my view, my dad wanted to take credit for having another son become a lawyer or doctor.

It wasn't always this way, as dad often had talked to us while we were growing up about how we all should farm together. During that time, many farm families in that area would have sons stay on the family farm upon graduating from high school. Eventually, the family farm would grow or the sons would begin farming additional land themselves. In our family, even if we wanted to stay on the farm and continue farming, we boys understood the possibility wasn't really practical with so many sons.

We boys knew not all of us could stay on the farm, and not all of us wanted to stay on the farm and work with Dad. Naturally, each of us wanted to blaze our own trail. Consequently, we each decided that we needed to excel in school. When we were growing up on the farm, we often didn't get to start homework until nine or ten o'clock at night after all the work was done. Sometimes, we often missed school to stay home and work. We worked in the fields many times with a book on the tractor steering wheel. In school, I often listened to the teacher in one class while doing my homework for the next class.

Brian was the first of the boys to break ranks by going to medical school. Jim then went to law school after he returned from Vietnam. Dan (a year older than me) followed Brian to medical school, and Mick (a year younger than me) followed Dan. I then followed Jim to law school. Later, Will went to medical school. Our accomplishments brought our parents additional attention, and they were entirely justified to be proud of their children. All the credit they received was richly deserved. They both sacrificed for their family, just like most parents, and their hard work and sacrifice was exceptional, given our large family and such huge responsibilities.

When my parents called to wish me congratulations, they did not discuss what happened at our wedding. There was no apology. Feelings weren't shared. There was just this attitude that this thing happened and that everyone was supposed to move on without anyone talking about it. Cindy and I were made to feel that, while they reluctantly permitted us to attend family events, they never accepted us. More accurately, they never accepted Cindy as part of the family because she was the scapegoat. She felt like they blamed her, and she never felt welcome. Like Dad said, she wasn't part of the family.

Returning to the farm to attend family gatherings and holidays proved to be bittersweet. I longed for the feelings of closeness and belonging, but I grew weary of the constant tension. We endured expressions of superiority, signaling both pity and scorn. Each time family events were accompanied by attending the Catholic Church, the chasm was accentuated. When we didn't observe all the church's customs and rituals, we were regarded as the conspicuous outcasts. We weren't welcome *because we didn't belong.*

As a result, we spent less time with my family. Besides, I had started law school and didn't have the time anyway. I buried my emotions and immersed myself with studying law.

By the end of my first year, I finished near the top of my class. I competed for and was selected as one of only four members of our class chosen to the moot court team, an extracurricular competition where students write appellate briefs and make oral arguments against other moot court teams from other law schools. My older brother Jim was on the moot court team when he was in law school, and I was proud to be selected to the team.

When I was young, I idolized Jim, my oldest brother by twelve years. When he worked construction during summers in college, I would wait outside at about the time he was scheduled to get home from work. I was six or seven, and I would sit on the board fence in the front yard and watch for his car to drive down the road. When I saw his old white Buick start kicking up dust on the gravel road leading to our farm, I would run as fast as I could out of the driveway and down the gravel road to meet him. He would stop, let me in, and hand me his lunch box. I sat next to him in the front seat, enjoying the couple of cookies he always left for me as he drove slowly the rest of the way home.

When I was a freshman in college, Jim was married and a senior in law school. I enjoyed hanging out at their house, and I often babysat their oldest daughter. I liked meeting Jim's classmates and listening to them talk about law school. Now I was starting law school, and we rarely talked.

During my second year in law school, I wanted to do something that distinguished me from Jim. While I was thrilled to be a member of the moot court board, just as Jim had done when he was in law school, I also wanted to compete for selection to the law review board of editors.

The law review board of editors is a group of third year law students selected to edit and publish journal articles written by professors, lawyers, and students that analyze and critique recent legislation or court decisions. The law review editors perform this work simultaneously while they complete their third year of law school classes. Students compete for selection to the law review board of editors by researching and writing law review articles during their second year of law school. The best student articles are published in the law review journal.

During my second year, however, I already was going to compete on the moot court team, which was going to take a considerable amount of time. If I was going to be successful in my goal to be selected as a member of the law review board of editors, I knew I would have to find the additional amount of time required to research and write two law review articles. Instead of taking a break after my first year of law school, I took a major course during the summer that I otherwise would have taken during my second year. During my second year, I not only competed on the moot court team, but I also researched and wrote two law review articles.

Our moot court team did well in competition. At the end of the year, I was awarded the G. F. Johnson Oral Advocacy Award as the most outstanding advocate among my teammates. The law review board of editors selected both of the law review articles I wrote to be published in the South Dakota Law Review, and it also awarded me a law review scholarship.

To my knowledge, no one had ever before served on both the moot court board and the law review board simultaneously. My plan was to apply to be selected as a topics editor, copy editor, or lead articles editor that didn't require as much time as the editor in chief so I could serve on both boards during my senior year. To my surprise, the law review board of editors selected me to be the next editor-in-chief of the law review.

During summer after my second year in law school, I clerked for a law firm, which offered me a job after I graduated from law school. I could have clerked for a judge after graduating, but because I was anxious to begin practicing law, I accepted the offer from the law firm.

Although I had been working continuously during law school over the prior three years, after law school, I didn't have time to take a break. During the third week in May of 1982, I graduated law school, moved sixty miles into a new home, started working at the law firm, and became the father of a baby girl.

After only three years, the law firm made me a partner, but I was getting frustrated. I was spending most of my time writing discovery responses and appellate briefs for the other lawyer's cases. I wanted more responsibility. I wanted to try cases. I didn't mind working on the discovery, research, and writing that led up to the trial of a case, but I also wanted to be in the courtroom trying the case. I wanted to be a trial lawyer. I wanted to be in the courtroom, just like Gregory Peck, who played the defense attorney Atticus Finch in the movie *To Kill A Mockingbird,* or Raymond Burr, who played the defense attorney *Perry Mason*[4] in the television show by the same name. I wanted to be a litigator.

Finally, I was given the opportunity to argue a case before the South Dakota Supreme Court. I wrote the appellate brief after the trial, and I was completely familiar with the case and the issues on appeal. When the attorney scheduled to make the argument was unable to attend, I jumped at the chance to argue the case before the supreme court.

In only my fourth year out of law school, I must have been one of the youngest attorneys to argue before our state's supreme court. Most of the lawyers appearing before the supreme court are senior partners who command considerable respect. Nevertheless, with my moot court experience, I was ready.

The day I appeared before the supreme court was one of those blustery, gray, chilly, South Dakota spring days when everybody expected a thunderstorm. The supreme court is housed in the state capitol building near the banks of the Missouri River. One semester during my junior year of college, I worked as an intern during the legislative session, so I was familiar with the building, but I actually had never been inside the supreme court.

In the supreme court, gleaming mahogany covered the entire floor, all the chairs and counsel tables, the podium from which the attorneys would make their arguments, and the elevated bench from which the justices would preside. Antique golden chandeliers hung from a high white ceiling, suspended above walls painted in gold leaf. A massive colorful mural titled The Mercy of the Law, painted by Charles Holloway when the capitol building was constructed in 1910, hung on the wall directly behind the solemn justices' chairs.

Although it was late in the morning when I began my argument, the characteristic South Dakota sunshine was noticeably absent. The sky outside had become ominous. As I walked to the podium, gray-black clouds took turns tumbling over each other, summoning thunder and occasional lightning. Pushed by the prairie winds, the storm moved closer as if it wanted to be part of the audience listening to the oral argument.

Inside, the globes of frosted glass glistened against the golden arms of the chandeliers. The sound of my footsteps against the hardwood floor echoed throughout the chamber as I walked to the podium. Once I began my rehearsed opening, the small LED light peered at me from the back of the podium in a digital countdown of my remaining allotted time. The dancing butterflies and weak knees belied my cool composure.

Before I could complete much of my argument, the justices began interrupting me with pointed questions, challenging my position. As the questions flourished in frequency, the impending storm outside announced its presence with repeated claps of thunder and scattered sparks of lightning. The crescendo of questions from the justices culminated at the most important point of the appeal. I had read the entire trial transcript and researched and written the appellate brief, so I knew my material well. I also knew the justices would grill me on the key issue of the appeal. I anticipated the expected examination and rehearsed my response. Now I just had to nail the delivery and hammer home the decisive point of my argument.

Slightly raising my voice, I forcefully delivered my reasoned argument with the assurance of a seasoned litigator. For added effect, I rapped my knuckles against the podium as I confidently closed my oration. As if on cue, just then a gigantic thunderbolt exploded outside. It rattled the old windows and rocked the courtroom, reverberating like an echo chamber. The flash of lightning that followed electrified the courtroom. The nearly century-old lights flickered off, darkening the chamber and then, just as quickly, turned on again.

After several suspenseful seconds, I broke the hushed silence by announcing, "Your honors, I see that my time has expired, but I'm interpreting that demonstration of thunder and lightning as a divine sign in the righteousness of our cause. Thank you." I then walked back to my seat.

We won the appeal.

3

Cultivating a Path

In his heart a man plans his course, but the Lord
determines his steps.

—Proverbs 16:9

Later that year, I received a call from a headhunter asking if
I would interview for a law firm in Kansas interested in hiring
me. He said the firm would double my salary and pay for all my
moving expenses. More importantly, he said it was a litigation
firm and wanted to hire me to try cases. After my interview, the
firm offered me the position. Cindy and I traveled to Kansas, met
my new employer, and found a place to live. Over Thanksgiving,
we decided to accept the offer and move to Kansas at the end
of the year.

I gave notice to my current firm, and we said our good-
byes to our families over the Christmas holiday. I thought this
would be a fresh start and a new beginning. However, when
the Mayflower truck arrived as scheduled early on a Saturday
morning, Cindy told me she was not going to move with me.

Cindy had completed one semester toward her master's
degree, and she said she was going to stay until she completed
her degree. She told me she worked while I was in law school,
and now she was going to complete her degree while I worked.
I was completely blindsided. We agreed that she would move
with me and complete her degree in Kansas. The moving van

literally was parked in our driveway. I was expected to start work on Monday morning. I already terminated my job.

Cindy assured me it would only be for one semester until she completed her classes. She said she would then join me in Kansas and complete her thesis off campus. Without much of a choice, I told the movers to load the things I needed, and we would move the rest of the stuff later. Our daughter was four and a half years old.

At the time, I rationalized that the next six months would pass quickly. I reasoned it would allow me the opportunity to get to know my new partners and prepare for and take the Kansas bar exam. This certainly made sense to everyone, but I'm sure they quietly wondered why this wasn't mentioned during our visit to Kansas.

Over the next six months, I drove the seven-hour trip every other weekend back to Sioux Falls. I generally would work until nine or ten on Friday night and then drive all night. After saying prayers and tucking our daughter into bed on Sunday, I would again drive all night so I could be back to work Monday morning. The time went by quickly, and I passed the Kansas bar exam. Cindy and her parents drove down with our daughter to attend the swearing-in ceremony and to celebrate my becoming a Kansas lawyer, and we openly talked about their joining me in just another couple of months. However, that didn't happen.

Instead of working on her degree for only one more semester, Cindy told me she needed to complete another semester and would not be able to move to Kansas until the end of the year. Since she worked while I went to law school, it seemed like I didn't have any other choice but to give her the same opportunity to complete her degree. She told me moving to Kansas and completing her degree would mean she would have to start over, that she liked her professors and wanted to complete the program she started.

Once I passed the Kansas bar exam, my workload increased tremendously. I was thrilled to handle my own caseload and try my own cases. The firm was completely equipped with new computers and supporting technology. Since Cindy and our daughter weren't living with me, I totally immersed myself into my law practice.

I moved into a small studio apartment close to the office, but my real home was the office itself. There were only about a dozen of us attorneys who worked in the law firm's four separate offices across the state, but our firm tried about one-fourth of all the jury trials each year in Kansas. Our office had two sets of support staff. The first one started work at 6:30 a. m. and worked until 3 p. m. The second one started at 2:30 p. m. and worked until 9 p. m. As a result, I generally arrived to work by 6 a. m. so additional documents could be drafted or prep work completed before I left for court. I routinely worked at the office until 9 p. m., and I spent most Saturdays at the office, catching up with the workload and preparing for the next week of cases. At my first law firm, we were expected to bill on average about fifty hours each week—about two hundred hours each month. At my new firm, I routinely billed twice that amount.

The firm became my extended family and my life. The senior partner in our office was a pilot. Periodically, I would accompany him as he flew his plane throughout the Midwest to different depositions or appointments. After each trial victory, we enjoyed a celebratory dinner. As the first year rolled into the second, he moved my office next to his. I was often invited to Sunday social and political functions as his wife was active in the state Republican party.

We defended insurance companies, and with each defense verdict, I began to develop relationships with the insurance adjustors. As I won more cases, I was given other attorneys' cases to try. It was not unusual to have a paralegal enter my office on a Friday afternoon with a large file and tell me I was going to be trying the case when the trial began on Tuesday morning. We learned to try automobile accidents and slip and fall cases quickly so that the trial would finish by Friday, because another one was scheduled to being on Tuesday.

The firm operated like a well-oiled machine. The founding partner was the original member of the American Bar Association Section credited with creating the use of legal specialists or paralegals used in law firms in the United States. Each case was arranged and organized in the same order. If I were scheduled to attend a deposition on another attorney's case, I could quickly review the file and familiarize myself with the case. The firm hired a team of half a dozen nurses and trained them as paralegals so they could assist on the defense of the medical malpractice cases. Instead of junior or associate attorneys to provide assistance with our cases, we had an army of paralegals who would summarize depositions and organize all the documents. By my third year, six paralegals worked exclusively on the eighty to ninety cases for which I was responsible.

While winning jury trials was thrilling, a couple of cases haunted me. The first was a medical malpractice case where a little boy had peritonitis, an inflammation of the peritoneum or the thin tissue lining the inner wall of the abdomen. The doctor performed the surgery, and everything looked good until the second post-op day when the little boy's fever spiked to 105. About a half hour later, the little boy died. Little boys aren't supposed to die in a hospital room a couple of days after surgery. The family's lawyers filed the lawsuit against both the hospital and the doctor. Each defendant blamed the other.

While another firm represented the hospital, our firm defended the doctor. Just before the trial, the hospital settled the case, leaving our client as the only target. I assisted my partner in the trial.

The allegation against the doctor was that he must have negligently nicked the boy's intestine with the scalpel because an infection caused his sudden spike in temperature. Since statistically death only occurred in less than ten percent of these kinds of surgeries in young, healthy patients, the doctor's case was difficult to defend.

The jury returned a defense verdict for the doctor. The little boy's mother sat directly behind me during the trial, and she was there again when the jury announced its verdict.

While the doctor was congratulating my partner at the opposite end of our counsel table, the little boy's mother walked up to me and tearfully said, "You should be ashamed of yourself."

My daughter, who I missed terribly, was about the same age as her little boy.

I was confused by the mother's accusation. I was happy for our client. We had won a difficult case. I told myself I was just doing my job and fulfilling the duty owed to my client. Yet I agreed with her. I felt sad and ashamed.

The second case that caused me nightmares involved a large family whose children were killed while sleeping when their house burned in a fire during a winter night. I developed some expertise in defending product liability cases, and the late 1980s was known as the tort explosion decade because of all the large product liability verdicts making national headlines. In this particular case, the family's attorneys alleged the electrical wiring in the family's home must have been defective. The fire chief's report stated that a break in the wiring's insulation caused an arc undeniably defining the origin and cause of the fire.

After the plaintiff's attorneys presented and rested their case, I persuaded the trial judge to dismiss it. Although everyone assumed my client manufactured the electrical wiring, no one actually presented any direct evidence proving that important fact critical to establish liability. Rather than file a motion early in the case, which only would have served to educate the plaintiff's attorneys and cause them to conduct more discovery, I waited until the plaintiff's attorneys finished presenting their case. They couldn't prevent the dismissal.

There were several reasons this case caused me nightmares. First, the plaintiff's family was large, just like mine. The parents had eleven children and four died in the fire.

Second, the last name of the plaintiff's family was the same as mine—Hurley. We were not related, but I often wondered if I was chosen to defend the case for this reason. The jury clearly would be sympathetic to such a tragedy and want to make someone pay for it by awarding a large jury verdict. As I defended this case I wondered, "What if this had happened to our family?" It reminded me of the division in my own family.

Third, I was haunted by the fact that I easily could have settled the case. The insurance adjustor was afraid of the great exposure of a large jury verdict. The cause of the fire, the defective wiring, was established clearly by the fire marshal's investigation and report. The insurance adjustor was afraid of the sympathy factor represented by innocent children dying in a fire. As a result, he was prepared to settle the case. I could have settled the case. Like most cases, I held that authority and discretion within reason. The insurance adjuster left the decision up to me. I told him we were not going to settle the case, and we would win. I was right. The jury never got the chance to deliberate. The judge granted my motion and dismissed the case. Once again, I told myself I was just doing my job and defending my client.

The final and most compelling reason why I continued to experience nightmares after this case concluded was because the victims continued to talk to me and torment me long after the trial ended. In the course of handling the case, I naturally reviewed the gruesome black-and-white photos of the young children who died in the fire. I could not get those images out of my mind. I could not make them go away.

Providing the family some solace, the coroner concluded the children died of smoke inhalation during their sleep before the fire reached them. The shocking photos revealing their charred remains after the fire finished its work haunted me.

I distinctly remember a photo of one of the young boys in particular. He was lying on his left side but his right arm was extended across and in front of his body, positioned across his head in a curved position. This was the one photo the trial judge allowed the plaintiff's attorney to show the jury during the trial, probably because the boy's arm covered his face.

When I first viewed this photo with my paralegal, she said she was confused by the position of the young boy's body. She wondered if someone had arranged his body in that manner before the photo was taken so as to conceal his face. Fighting back tears, I explained to her that in a large family, it was common for children to share a bed. I told her this young boy's right arm was in this position because it was hugging his little brother while they slept. I knew this was true because this is how I grew up. This was how I often slept with my brother when we were little, sharing a twin bed. This could have happened to our family. It could have been one of us.

I began to experience flashbacks and nightmares. This case created a connection between my separation from my parents and siblings and my separation from my wife and daughter. I was like the little boy in the photograph. My arm had been around my brothers, my sisters, my parents, my wife, and my daughter, trying desperately to hold on to them, but now there was only a charred chasm between them and me. My arm was still stretching and straining, reaching out for them, but they were no longer there. In my night terrors, I became the boy in the photograph.

Anguished, I kept telling myself I was just doing my job, but I didn't honestly believe it. I wondered if I had made the right decision in trying the case instead of simply settling it. I knew I could have persuaded the insurance adjustor to settle the case to avoid a potentially damaging jury verdict, but I didn't. I wanted to win. After the trial judge announced his decision, I quickly gathered my papers and left the courtroom without even glancing at the parents.

This case was especially troubling to me because it reminded me of my upbringing and the closeness I felt with my brothers. Yet when I thought back to my childhood, I couldn't escape the painful emotions, anger, and feelings resulting from the division that now existed within our family. It reminded me of the physical division I now had within my own immediate family. I missed my daughter terribly. I felt the only course of action was to bury my feelings and myself in my work.

In one of those cases, I defended a large corporation that owned a grain elevator that exploded when grain dust ignited. Half the roof of the eighty-foot high grain elevator was blown away. The insurance adjustor and investigators provided me with the photographs, but I wanted to view the damage for myself so I could better prepare the case.

Thankfully, no one died. However, someone unloading grain was standing outside the grain elevator next to the scales when the explosion occurred. The explosion caused a fireball to shoot down the elevator shaft to the bottom of the grain elevator and explode out the side of the elevator at the street level next to the scales. The force of the blast propelled the man over the scales and across the street. Although he didn't die, he suffered third degree burns over ninety percent of his body.

Fine grain dust accumulates around a grain elevator. Grain dust is extremely combustible and can explode when ignited. An investigator reported that a cigarette butt was the ignition source of the explosion. When I arrived at the elevator to conduct my site inspection, the elevator manager had me follow him up on what he referred to as a man lift. The man lift was a series of steps and rungs inside a vertical cage that would transport a person from the ground to the top of the grain elevator and back again. Because of my experience on our family farm, I certainly was familiar with silos, grain elevators, and machinery, but I had never ridden a man lift.

The manager simply told me to follow him as he reached out his hand and grabbed on to one of the rungs that was moving up the man lift. Then as his arm began to be pulled upward, he stepped out and onto the step as it ascended upward behind the rung. I let the next series of rungs and steps move upward, and then I copied his movements. The man lift took me to the top of the grain elevator, and I stepped off onto the platform. As I stood on the roof next to the manager, we could see the massive hole from the explosion.

We soon finished our site inspection, and it was time to negotiate the descent down the man lift. I watched my guide deftly maneuver himself onto the man lift by first stepping off the platform and onto the step. As the step disappeared below the platform, he reached up, grabbed on to the rung with both hands, and then leaned forward and inward. I stepped closer to the man lift to repeat his actions.

The picture below is similar to what the man lift resembled (*see* additional images at http://www.elevatorbobs-elevator-pics.com/manlifts_p1.html). Imagine the descent below the platform to be about eighty feet to the ground below:

I began to mimic his movements to step off the platform, onto the man lift, but I suddenly remembered I was carrying a clipboard and a flashlight in my left hand. I stepped on to the step, but I worried I wouldn't be able to grab the rung with both hands. I realized instead of stepping on to the step with both feet, I only stepped on to the step with my right foot. I must have been focusing on holding the flashlight and clipboard because my left foot was still firmly planted on the platform.

The distance between the outer dimensions of the step and the edge of the platform was just several inches. I immediately recognized if I couldn't get my left foot off the platform before the next descending step reached the platform, my leg would be crushed. I couldn't pull my left foot off the platform. The step's downward descent was carrying most of my weight, preventing me from shifting my weight back to my left foot. I desperately tried to pull myself up with my right arm, but I wasn't strong enough. As if in super slow motion, I could sense my right foot and the weight of my body being pulled lower and lower. I instantly realized I was about to be crushed.

In a moment, miraculously, as if someone had pulled me up, I was thrust upward and back onto the platform just before the next step reached the platform. Although I was in excellent shape, I didn't have either the strength or the athleticism to perform that feat. I didn't have enough strength in my right arm sufficient to reverse the gravitational force of the descending step and pull my two hundred pounds back up to the platform.

God intervened. He lifted me up. He rescued me from certain disaster. Defying both the gravitational force and the mechanical downward thrust of the man lift, He lifted me up and set me back again onto the platform before the next step could crush me. Without God's miracle, I surely would have lost either my leg or my life.

I took the next several minutes to catch my breath and contemplate the miracle that had just occurred. I thanked God for saving me. I wasn't scared or fearful because the entire incident happened so quickly. Rather, I was in awe. I was perfectly fine and healthy but in a state of utter amazement. I shoved the flashlight into my back pocket, tucked the clipboard inside my jeans, and got ready to get back on the man lift. After all, it was the only way I could get down the elevator. I stepped on to the next descending step with both feet, grabbed the rung above with both hands, and rode the man lift back down to the ground.

After I got off the man lift, the manager asked me if I was all right and said my face was as white as a sheet. I said I was okay, and then I promptly vomited. The manager and a couple of workers had a good laugh at my expense, but I didn't mind because I was just glad to be alive. I said another prayer of thanks. I knew in my heart I had just experienced a miracle.

I had often read about miracles happening to people, but the only other time I had any personal contact with someone who actually experienced a miracle was during the summer after I graduated high school. I was talking with a small group of friends about the Bible and the Lord. Terry was a friend and classmate with whom I played basketball on our high school team.

After graduating high school, Terry worked for a company that did a lot of welding and steel fabricating. He told us that one day at work, he was lying on the concrete floor under a huge steel frame, performing some welding when he heard a quiet voice say, "Get out of there." He said he stopped welding and rolled the cart on which he was lying out from under the framework. However, he didn't see anyone else nearby. He thought he just imagined hearing another voice. He got back on his cart and rolled back under the steel frame to complete his welding, but a few moments later, he again heard the voice warning, "Get out of there." Again, he stopped welding and rolled his cart out from under the heavy steel frame—just before it crashed down on to the concrete where he was just moments before.

When I shared with another Christian friend my experience with the man lift, he told me, "John, you witnessed a miracle. God intervened. God chose to work a miracle in you. God stepped in and rescued you because He's not done with you. God still has work for you to do."

Just as God miraculously restored my eyesight after I was blinded by my fall on the ice in grade school, He now picked me up and safely placed me back onto the platform.

I thought a lot about my friend's statements. "God chose to work a miracle in you. God still has work for you to do." I concluded they meant I was supposed to continue to try to be the best lawyer I could be. Since my wife and daughter were still living in South Dakota, I worked even harder at my craft.

As I entered my third year of work with my firm, I seriously questioned why Cindy had not yet joined me in Kansas. I moved there in January 1986, and now it was January 1989. Over Christmas, she promised me this was the last semester she would have to live on campus, and then she would move to Kansas.

My partners were beginning to question me about my living apart from my wife, and the issue was becoming the topic of office jokes.

"Are you really married?"

"Do you really have a daughter?"

"When you bought those picture frames sitting on your desk, were those pictures already in the frames?"

While I laughed, I inwardly was embarrassed, wondering what really was going on and what was keeping them from joining me. In addition to feeling embarrassed, I once again felt abandoned. Through avoidance and numbing, I blocked out these emotions and feelings and focused even more on my work.

With each courtroom success, I became more and more confident of my abilities. I was working on a huge product liability case, defending a California manufacturer sued in federal district court in Kansas. A worker had his hand cut off when he operated a shear machine after the guard had been removed. At the settlement conference just before the case was scheduled to go to trial, the insurance adjustor told me the remaining coverage under the insurance policy limits had been exhausted and spent on the settlement of other cases.

This manufacturing company made dangerous machinery used in the recycling industry and had been sued five times during the early 1980s in different states around the country. Because each of the other cases had high exposure and the potential for huge damages, the insurance company settled them rather than risk large jury verdicts of damages at trial. The insurance adjuster told me he had just settled the last two cases, and there was no additional coverage under the policy limits available for our case. We were going to trial.

In federal court, the plaintiff's attorneys argued they should be able to inform the jury about the other five cases filed against the manufacturing company. I objected and argued that each had been settled as a doubted and disputed claim without any admission of liability.

The plaintiff's attorneys contended that the evidence of the other cases should be allowed into evidence on the issue of notice, namely that the other cases provided notice to the manufacturer that it should have changed its warnings or the design of its machine before it manufactured the machine that injured their client. The federal judge decided they could present their evidence concerning this issue before him, outside of the jury's presence. He then said he would decide whether to allow the jury to hear the evidence about the other five cases at the conclusion of the hearing.

The problem with this approach was that I now had to familiarize myself with five other cases over the weekend. Sure, I knew about the other cases, as they were discussed during depositions and other discovery. I reviewed my client's deposition testimony from each of the other five cases to make sure he didn't testify in this case in a manner inconsistent with what he had said in the other cases.

However, I didn't know the other cases like I knew this case. They involved other injuries, in other situations, in other states. Yet they all involved the same kind of machine and that is why the judge was giving the plaintiff's attorneys such wide latitude.

These types of machines were called alligator shear machines because the jaws of the machine resembled those of an alligator. They would hydraulically chomp down and crush anything placed within its jaws when the operator stepped on the foot pedal. It was the perfect name and visual image for a plaintiff's attorney. Over the next three days, we interrupted our trial and held a hearing before the judge on the other five cases. Now instead of defending just one case, I was defending six cases—all at the same time. This was not going to be a hearing where the attorneys simply filed briefs and argued the law. Rather, the judge also wanted to familiarize himself with the facts of each of the other five cases before he made a ruling. This was going to be an evidentiary hearing. His order allowed evidence to be presented and meant the plaintiff's attorneys would be allowed to cross-examine my client about each of the other five cases.

I was playing a poker game with extremely high stakes. Although the insurance company said it would pay for my firm's cost of defending the trial, if we lost the case, any damages would have to be paid directly by the client. If we lost the hearing and the jury was presented evidence about five prior cases and injuries, clearly that could impact and affect the jury's decision on damages. I knew if I lost this case, the company would be forced into bankruptcy. I don't remember sleeping at all during this trial.

Fortunately, the trial judge at the end of the evidentiary hearing ruled in favor of my client and excluded all the evidence about the other five cases. I quickly proceeded to conclude the trial and deliver the case to the jury to determine the issues of liability and damages on our case alone. The jury decided the injured worker was more than fifty percent negligent and at fault for his injuries, and as a result, it granted us a defense verdict. Kansas law provided if a plaintiff is found to be at least fifty percent negligent or at fault for causing the injury, then the plaintiff is not awarded any damages. The jury found no liability against the manufacturing company.

The owners of the manufacturing company, two brothers originally from Kansas, took me to dinner that night to express their appreciation. However, they did more than that. They offered me a job. I laughed and explained to them I already had a great job, but they persisted and said they wanted to hire me away from my law firm and hire me to work directly for them. They wanted me to become their national litigation attorney. They wanted to move me to California.

They said they were desperate because they manufactured thousands of smaller alligator shear machines and baling machines used in the recycling industry. The shear machines often were used to cut rebar in the construction industry, and the small baling machines were used by supermarkets and big-box stores to bale and crush cardboard boxes so they could be recycled. They sold machines throughout the United States.

They designed and manufactured a guard attached to every machine they manufactured to protect the operator from the point of operation. They installed warning labels on the machines, warning against the removal of the guards. They also provided warnings and cautions in the instruction and user manual provided to the purchaser with the sale of each machine. They even installed a micro limit switch (a kill switch) so if the guard were removed, as it had been in the Kansas case, the motor would not start.

However, all those precautions could not prevent them from being sued. If a guard would not close after being damaged by a forklift, for example, an employer would remove the guard from the machine and then hire a local electrician to disconnect the micro limit switch so the machine would operate without the guard. The employer would then send his employee back to work and just tell him to be careful.

My clients told me the employer would never inform them when this would happen. When an employee would become injured using a machine without a guard, the injured worker's remedy against his employer for removing the guard and allowing him to operate the machine in an unsafe condition generally was limited to collecting workers' compensation benefits. The injured employee otherwise could not bring a direct action or lawsuit against his employer.

However, that didn't prevent the injured employee from suing the manufacturer. The injured worker could file a lawsuit directly against the manufacturer for product liability defect, for breach of warranty, and for failure to warn the worker. Plaintiff attorneys argued the warning decals on the machine warning against the removal of the guard were written in English and most workers didn't speak, read, or understand English. They argued the vinyl warning decals would get damaged and scratched, often making the letters and words unreadable anyway. Finally, they argued the warnings contained in the service and instruction manual were intended for the purchaser, not the user or worker, and often were never even read by the purchaser.

In the Kansas case, the purchaser testified he didn't even know the large iron mesh guard protecting the operator was even a guard. He said he thought it was a shipping crate. He said that when the machine didn't start after he removed it, he simply called an electrician to rewire the machine instead of contacting the manufacturer. The client wanted to hire me to defend these product liability cases nationwide.

Orval, the older brother, told me they no longer could afford to buy product liability insurance. The amount of the annual premium for the last quote they received was $250,000 to obtain only $500,000 of coverage, and that included a $500,000 deductible. That meant they would first have to pay $750,000 before the insurance company would provide coverage.

Even then, the insurance company would only provide coverage up to $500,000. After that, the manufacturing company again would have to pick up the tab. Since a typical case included a demand for damages of about two million dollars or more, obtaining insurance was no longer feasible. Instead, they offered to double my salary and move me to California. They wanted me to be their insurance policy. They had another case that was expected to begin trial in Las Vegas later that year.

Although the firm offered to give me a small raise in salary, its offer couldn't compare to the company's offer to double my salary. This was an opportunity to be able to pay the bills that had been mounting. Ever since I moved to Kansas, we were paying to support two households because I was living in Kansas and Cindy was still living in South Dakota. The rent on my studio apartment was cheap, but the bills kept mounting.

The company's offer was intriguing to me because it meant I would be traveling across the country defending the company. The company's offer also was timely because my wife was finally ready to complete her degree. We no longer would be living in separate states. Cindy agreed to travel to southern California to meet everyone and to look at housing. The company paid for the cost of our travel and hosted a dinner with their wives. The California weather was beautiful.

The manufacturing company was a family corporation. We met the rest of their families at Orval's home at a party held in our honor to celebrate winning the court case. Orval's five sons and his brother's three sons worked for the company. One of the son's wives worked as the receptionist. My main reservation to accepting the offer was the issue of the longevity of my future employment. They simply said that as long as I kept winning their cases, I would have a job. Extremely confident in my ability, that seemed like a fair deal.

Cindy agreed to move to California, and we viewed the move as the opportunity for a new start. She no longer would be living locally in the shadow of my family, and we discussed how she could continue to go to school in California to obtain a doctoral degree and become a psychologist. Our daughter would be starting first grade in the fall.

Within a three-year span, my salary had doubled twice. Cindy finally was finished with classes for her degree, and we once again could live together as a family. We agreed to rent one of the houses Orval owned, and we moved to California in May. Cindy seemed to be happy. While she settled in our new home, I immediately had to start work. It reminded me of the week in May seven years earlier when I graduated law school, moved, started work, and became a father all within one week. Once again, I didn't have time to take a break.

I was confident in my abilities. During the past three years, I had won every single jury trial I tried. I had just been named as a member of *Who's Who In Practicing Attorneys in the United States*. I was the conquering hero who had just saved the company by winning the case in Kansas, and now I was going to be asked to save the company again and again each and every time I would step into a courtroom across the country. In defending all the company's cases, I was going to be its national litigation attorney.

However, I first had to pass the California bar exam the last week of July. That meant I only had two months to get ready for the exam. I knew nothing about California law. Further complicating matters, only a week after taking the exam, I was scheduled to defend the company in a jury trial in Las Vegas, scheduled to begin the first week in August.

Consequently, over the next two months, not only would I have to learn California law and prepare for the bar exam, I also would have to learn Nevada law and all the facts of the Nevada case to prepare for the trial in Las Vegas. During the next sixty days, I also would have to travel to Las Vegas to attend expert witness depositions, hearings on motions, and the pretrial conference. My summer was going to be extremely busy.

While I was not admitted to practice law in Nevada, the trial court granted my motion to allow me to practice pro hac vice (Latin, meaning "for this occasion") so I could try the case accompanied by a local attorney during the trial. I would use this procedure to try all the out-of-state cases filed against the company across the country.

However, California was another matter. I had to pass the California bar exam, commonly considered the most difficult bar exam in the country with a pass rate of only about forty percent. The exam's first and third days were essays covering California law. The second day was two hundred multistate multiple-choice questions.

On each day, I got up early around 4 a. m. and studied for the exam for several hours before I went to work. I then worked from 8 a. m. to 5 p. m., preparing for the Nevada case. After work, I drove more than an hour to participate in a bar exam review class from 6:30 p. m. to 9:30 p. m., arriving home around 11 p. m. I spent my weekends studying and preparing for the exam and getting ready to try the Las Vegas case. I no longer had my team of paralegals to assist me. I no longer had my pool of clerks to type for me. I was burdened with the responsibility of knowing I had to pass the bar exam so I could keep my job. I also was under the pressure of knowing I had to win the trial in Las Vegas so the company could stay in business, and so I could keep my job. It was a grueling schedule. I didn't have much time for my family. Although Cindy and our daughter were now with me again, I was working the same shift I worked in Kansas when we were apart. I told myself, and them, that this was only temporary and everything would calm down once I got past the next ninety days. I assured them we would have time to spend together once the trial was over.

My busy schedule was interrupted one day when I got home from my bar review class. The house was dark. When

I entered our home, there was no one there. I saw things had been taken, and my first thought was that we had been robbed. I immediately became worried for the safety of Cindy and our daughter, who I soon realized were both not there. I then saw the note on the kitchen counter Cindy left for me.

The note simply said she had returned to South Dakota with our daughter, and she would contact me later. After the shock subsided, I realized she had packed their clothes and the missing personal belongings into her car and had driven back to South Dakota. At first, I was relieved they were okay and no one had broken into our home. I also rationalized that this somehow made sense, in sort of a weird way, because she basically had been living alone while I was buried in work and studying for the bar exam for the last sixty days.

I fantasized that Cindy would spend the next two weeks with her family, who already missed her and our daughter. I imagined I would fly back to South Dakota after the bar exam and join them for a few days of vacation before I had to leave again to start my trial in Las Vegas.

That thinking, though, was delusional. Such an arrangement seemed too familiar, like the one we just lived through over the past three years. The thought then entered my mind that perhaps Cindy preferred that arrangement since I was working so much. I soon concluded that the trip was not temporary. If it were supposed to be a vacation, we would have discussed it and planned accordingly. I was totally blindsided. We had been living in California for only sixty days.

Ultimately, I decided there was nothing I immediately could do about the situation other than stay the course. Most people, including us, didn't have cell phones in 1989. Even if I called her mother, the drive to South Dakota would take about four days.

At the time, I wasn't really angry. Instead, I was completely confused and in a state of shock. I couldn't even get to a place where I could ask *why* this was happening, because I didn't even know yet *what* was happening.

A hundred questions raced through my mind. Hadn't she agreed to move to California? Hadn't she traveled with me, met everybody, selected a house, and checked out the schools? When I asked myself these questions, I was painfully reminded that she did the same thing when we were going to move to Kansas.

Because I knew so little, I decided not to say anything to Orval. Tensions already were running high with the impending trial only a month away in Las Vegas. I realized the only action I could take was to continue with my plans. I would finish my bar exam review and then take the exam. Since I had worked so hard to prepare, I told myself I might as well take the test. It was only one week away.

That weekend, I called my mother-in-law, but she told me she hadn't spoken to Cindy and was surprised to hear my news. I didn't know what to think. Was she lying to me and protecting her daughter? Was she telling me the truth? If she was telling me the truth, where did they go? Could something have happened to them? Were they okay? I was driving myself crazy with worry and anxiety. Instead, I just had to block it out and bury all those questions and emotions so I could try to relax and concentrate on taking the bar exam.

I had arranged earlier with Orval to take off the entire week for the exam. I was scheduled to take the test about a ninety-mile drive away in San Diego. Since the exam was administered Tuesday through Thursday, I arranged to travel to San Diego on Monday and get settled in my hotel before the test began the next morning.

I also arranged to take off work on Friday following the bar exam. As a result, I avoided any conversations with Orval during that entire week about what was going on at home. My plan was to finish the bar exam on Thursday and then fly to

Sioux Falls the next day to see if I could locate Cindy and our daughter. I would only have one day to find them. I then had to fly back to California on Saturday night because, on Sunday, I was scheduled to fly to Las Vegas with Orval to start the trial on Monday morning. What a way to prepare for the bar exam!

After I took the exam, I flew back to Sioux Falls and drove my rental car unannounced directly to my mother-in-law's home. After just a few questions, I knew she wasn't telling me the truth. She was protecting her daughter, and she would not tell me where she was. I only had one day to locate Cindy, so I told my mother-in-law if she didn't tell me where she was, I had no other choice but to file a missing person's report. She gave me an address to a house across town.

By the time I drove there, my mother-in-law had spoken to Cindy on the phone. Cindy was waiting for me outside in the driveway when I arrived. She, matter-of-factly, told me our daughter wasn't there and the house belonged to a friend of hers. By her demeanor, I realized she had no intention of returning to California. I guessed the house belonged to a boyfriend. Her hesitation and her immediate failure to deny the accusation confirmed it. She knew I couldn't stay and that I had to honor my commitment to Orval to begin the trial in Las Vegas on Monday. She knew I had no choice but to go back to California. Arrogantly, she said, "He's a policeman, so I would leave if I were you."

I was completely stunned. Because I was so angry, I drove straight to the airport and caught a flight back to California that same night. I kept telling myself, "John, you're an idiot! How did you not see this coming?" I tortured myself with these questions because I felt like an idiot. I missed our daughter, and I was overcome with conflicting emotions. I was furious and sad. I was embarrassed and ashamed. I was alone and lonely. I was trapped and confused. Mostly, I was shocked and exhausted.

After flying back to California Friday night, I couldn't sleep. Throughout Friday night and Saturday, I was in a state of complete confusion. It was now Saturday night, and I had to force myself to try to get some sleep. Packing my trial boxes of documents and my suits and clothes for the upcoming week of trial in Las Vegas provided a welcome distraction. After enduring this ordeal, the Las Vegas trial would be easy.

The trial was the diversion I needed. By placing all my focus there, I managed most of the time to avoid thinking about my personal problems. As an attorney, I told myself I had to bury my personal problems and focus on my client's problems. Wasn't burying my feelings, my emotions, and my problems what I had done my entire life? Wasn't this how I avoided and numbed my feelings and emotions? I began to convince myself that doing so was the definition of being a professional. Yet I was completely conflicted. How could I conduct myself as a professional and expertly control, try, and win complex court cases on the professional side of my life, but seem to be unable to manage my personal life? Hadn't I been a good son, brother, husband, and father? I could not escape these questions. They tormented me. I coped by compartmentalizing my life.

I don't know whether it was because I was so focused on the trial or whether I just wanted to finish it so I could return to Sioux Falls, but I managed to conclude the trial and send the case to the jury by lunchtime Friday afternoon. It was like when I was back in Kansas and had to finish the trial by Friday because I had to start another one the following week. I had tried a good case, and I wanted to give the jury the chance to reach a verdict before the weekend.

My guess was the jury wouldn't want to be stuck in a hotel deliberating the case over the weekend when they had better things to do with their time over a weekend in Las Vegas. I was right. The jury returned a defense verdict of no liability within only thirty-five minutes. It was a new personal record.

Orval was thrilled. After a quick dinner, we boarded his plane, and he flew us back to California. I sat next to him in the cockpit, and we talked through the headsets as we flew into the setting sun toward California. He told me he was so happy we had won the case, but the reason he was so happy was because we actually tried the case, just like the one we tried in Kansas. He said it had upset him when the five other cases in the other states had been settled because in each of those other cases, he said he had been denied the satisfaction of hearing a jury decide he had manufactured a good product and won the case.

When he heard the defense verdicts announced in Kansas and, again, now in Las Vegas, he said he felt vindicated. He had designed and built his first baling machine by hand as a young man in Kansas, and he built his company into a thriving business that supported him, his brother, and their eight sons. He was extremely proud to be making products in the USA, and he wanted people to know there was nothing wrong with them.

When one of his sons once bought a foreign-made vehicle, Orval immediately demanded to know why he hadn't bought an American car. When his son told him it was cheaper than the American car, Orval immediately gave his son the amount of the difference and told him "to take back that piece of junk and buy the American car!" Orval only drove Lincoln Continentals.

This was the mind-set of the person sitting next to me in the cockpit. He had just hired me and moved me to California to solve his legal problems. I was supposed to be the solution, not another problem. In his mind, he made a huge investment in me. He depended on me to safeguard the future of his company, his family, his brother's family, and the families for each of their eight sons. As a result, I couldn't confide in him. I couldn't tell him what was happening at home.

Instead, because we had just won the case in Las Vegas and he was in a good mood, I asked him if I could take off a few days.

He stared at me and said, "Are you kidding? You just got here. Plus, we just gave you time off to take your test!"

I felt the suspense and pressure building, and I prayed he would not ask me to give him the reason for my request. If he would have asked me, I wouldn't have been able to lie to him. We were building a relationship, one that was based on mutual trust and respect. Thankfully, he agreed to my request because within the past three months, I had won two jury trials in two states that saved his company.

The spectacular sunset gave way to millions of twinkling lights as California came into view below. I thought about how wonderful a vacation would be, and I realized that the last vacation I took was seven years earlier, before I started law school. Sadly, my thoughts turned back to my problems.

I flew back to Sioux Falls the next day and drove my rental car directly to the house where I had met Cindy the weekend before. I didn't tell her I was coming, and I don't think she expected to see me again so soon after we had briefly spoken. She told me she was not moving back to California, and she wanted a divorce. It became clear to me she planned to have me pay her both spousal support and child support based on my new increased California income. I told her that would not happen because if she were going to file for divorce, then I would move back to South Dakota.

Cindy laughed and said, "You wouldn't do that. You love California."

I coolly stared back at her and said, "Watch me."

I explained to her that if she were intent on going through with a divorce, then there really wasn't anything I could do to prevent it. However, I emphatically told her I would have no hesitation whatsoever in walking away from my job in

California and moving back to be near our daughter. I told her she already had kept our daughter away from me for too long, and our daughter was more important to me than my work.

I don't think Cindy had considered that I would quit my job and move back to South Dakota. When she was busy making her plans, she didn't realize I would not learn whether I had passed the bar exam until Thanksgiving. I only had two months to prepare for the exam, and even then, much of that time was spent learning Nevada law and preparing for the trial in Las Vegas. Cindy knew if I didn't pass the exam, I wouldn't be able to work for Orval and stay in California. More importantly to her, I wouldn't have my higher California income available to pay her spousal and child support.

At the same time, Cindy also knew that, even if I were to pass the California bar exam, I would never return to California if I now moved back to South Dakota to be near our daughter. If this were about the money, she knew she would have to go back to California at least until Thanksgiving.

I tried to persuade her to move back to California with me. I told Cindy that we could work things out with marriage counseling, and that it wasn't God's plan for us to divorce. She was angry with me and said everything was entirely my fault.

I told her she might be right, I was sorry for the mistakes I had made, and I was far from perfect. I tried to assure her it would work out, and we could begin marriage counseling as soon as we got back to California. Finally, I told her our daughter deserved to have us give our marriage another chance. We had been married for twelve years, even if the last three years had been spent living apart while she was in school.

Cindy said she couldn't decide just yet and needed more time. As a result, I had to return to California alone. We talked a couple of more times on the phone during the rest of August, but nothing had changed by Labor Day. School was ready to begin in California right after Labor Day, and school had already started a couple of weeks before in South Dakota. By the end of August, I called the school district in Sioux Falls and learned Cindy had not enrolled our daughter in first grade there, so I decided to fly back to Sioux Falls over the Labor Day weekend.

I pleaded with Cindy to move back with me to California. I reasoned that if she were completely convinced to get a divorce, she would have enrolled our daughter in first grade in Sioux Falls when school had begun there several weeks earlier. I told her the fact that she hadn't enrolled our daughter in school demonstrated she wasn't totally sure of her decision, and since she wasn't absolutely sure, the right thing to do would be to return to California where we could attend marriage counseling and give our marriage another chance.

Cindy finally relented. We agreed to leave in the morning so we could enroll our daughter in school in time for her to begin first grade in California.

4

Waiting for the Harvest

The kingdom of heaven is like a man who sowed good
seed in his field. But while everyone was sleeping, his
enemy came and sowed weeds among the wheat, and went
away. When the wheat sprouted and formed heads, then
the weeds also appeared.

Both grow together until the harvest.

—Matthew 13:24–26, 30

After we returned to California, we tried to resume life as a family after the six-week interruption. Our daughter began first grade. My work hours were eight to five. We began marriage counseling. We tried our best to work things out over the next several months. Since my trial in Las Vegas was over, and since I had completed taking the bar exam, I had considerably more time to spend with Cindy and our daughter. We finally began to get out and do things like going to Disneyland and the beach. Cindy met new neighbors and other parents of our daughter's classmates at school. We fell into a comfortable routine until Thanksgiving, the first major holiday after her return to California. The day after Thanksgiving also was the day I would learn whether I passed the bar exam.

I was so relieved to learn that I passed the exam. After being admitted to practice law in three states, I didn't plan to take another bar exam. Orval was so happy for me, knowing I could now stay in California and defend his cases. Technically, even if

I had not passed the California bar exam, I still could represent him on a given case if his company were sued in another state on a pro hac vice motion since I already was licensed in both South Dakota and Kansas. However, his company had recently been sued in northern California on several baler cases, and he needed me to be licensed in California to be able to defend him continuously on those and future cases. As a result, he was extremely pleased.

Orval, his brother, and their wives took Cindy and I out to dinner on Saturday night to celebrate my passing the bar exam. Although Cindy was cordial and friendly, she seemed agitated, and she acted anxious and restless the entire weekend.

The following Monday afternoon, I had a funny feeling at work that I needed to leave and go home. I called our house, but no one answered. When I called our daughter's school, I was told Cindy had not taken our daughter to school that day. She had called the school and said our daughter would be absent. I immediately knew something was wrong. I left work and raced home.

When I drove up to our house, I saw Cindy had again packed her car and was planning to leave. She had to wait until I left for work that morning, but she now was nearly finished packing the car. I parked immediately behind her car, blocking her retreat and preventing her from leaving. As I helped our daughter out of her car, Cindy ran into the house and called the police. Incredibly, the police told me that if I didn't move my car, they would arrest me for false imprisonment! Cindy told the police officers that her boyfriend was a policeman, so they seemed intent on helping her. I was ready to get into it with one of them, but there were two of them and they had guns.

Once I calmed down, I objected and said they couldn't possibly arrest me for false imprisonment for blocking my own car in my own driveway. Without answering, the police officer simply handed me something that literally made me take a step backwards. He handed me a copy of a Summons and Complaint for divorce that had been filed in South Dakota against me.

The policeman also told me I could not prevent Cindy from leaving with our daughter. He said the divorce action filed in South Dakota meant that South Dakota had jurisdiction unless I could produce a California court order stating otherwise. The police officer reminded me that his handing me a copy of the divorce meant I had been served. I knew there was nothing I could do to stop Cindy from leaving with our daughter.

I was enraged. I knew the attorney Cindy hired to file for divorce in South Dakota. His office was located down the street from my old office. Since it had been filed for several months, surely all the attorneys in Sioux Falls knew about it. I wondered if my family knew. I noticed the divorce had been filed about the same time my wife had moved back to South Dakota. She must have told her attorney not to have me served until after we learned whether I had passed the bar exam. The plan surely was not to have this policeman serve me because that's not what they do. That's a job for the sheriff's department. However, now that he handed me a copy of the divorce, I had in fact been served. It was official and real, and I had to deal with it.

I immediately called an attorney who practiced family law and rushed over to her office. Because it was now late in the afternoon, she told me we would have to wait until the next morning to file any documents in court.

We filed our divorce petition as soon as court opened the next morning and asked for an emergency hearing. Cindy was not in court, but to my surprise, an attorney announced that he had been retained by Cindy to make a special appearance and represent her at the hearing. After listening to both attorneys, the judge ruled that the emergency relief we requested would be denied because the court lacked jurisdiction.

I wasn't allowed to say anything because the judge did not entertain any testimony. Rather, the judge only heard from the attorneys, first in the judge's chambers and then later briefly in the courtroom before announcing the ruling. I wanted to say something because I was upset. I didn't believe the judge had all the facts. When I started talking, the judge cut me off immediately. When I continued to speak, the judge ordered the bailiff to escort me out of the courtroom. I continued to protest to my attorney in the hallway. She told me to try to wait calmly while she finished talking to the attorney who appeared on Cindy's behalf. I just couldn't believe what was happening.

I paced and I listened to the attorneys talking. I heard Cindy's attorney tell my attorney that Cindy had not yet left California, but planned to wait for his phone call before she would leave. She hired him because she wanted someone in the courtroom in case the judge might enter an order against her.

When I heard this, I sprang into action and grabbed my attorney's arm and said, "Come on."

Before she could protest, I pulled her back into the courtroom, interrupting the next case being discussed before the judge. My wife's attorney quickly followed us into court.

"Your honor, she's still in California," I yelled at the judge as we entered court. The bailiff took a step toward me, but then stopped when he saw the judge's raised hand.

Everybody was staring at me.

"Your honor," I pleaded, "Her attorney said she's still in California and she has our daughter with her—you have jurisdiction. You can serve him with your order."

The judge looked at Cindy's attorney and said, "Is that true?"

When Cindy's attorney said it was indeed true, the judge recalled our case.

She looked at me and said, "I don't want to hear another word from you, or I'll have you thrown in jail for contempt."

After just a few more questions to the attorneys, the judge entered an immediate emergency order that Cindy was not allowed to leave the state of California with our daughter, and the judge ordered her attorney to tell Cindy she had better bring our daughter to court the next morning at 9 a. m.

The next morning, Cindy's attorney argued that the court still did not have jurisdiction. He said that, while the court had jurisdiction to hear our motion, it did not have jurisdiction to enter any child custody orders pertaining to our daughter because the South Dakota divorce and custody case had been filed first before we filed our papers in California.

My attorney and I spent the previous afternoon researching this issue and drafting a declaration and legal brief for the court. We were only going to get this single opportunity to make our case before the judge. I didn't want to litigate the divorce back in South Dakota.

My detailed declaration described the factual basis for our legal position. It provided the date in May that we had moved to California. We had rented a house pursuant to a one-year lease. Both Cindy and I had California driver's licenses and registered and licensed both cars in California. We enrolled our daughter in school in California, and we listed our home address in California on all the school documents as our permanent residence address. Cindy participated in all these decisions and, more importantly, had signed many of the related documents. Because of the number of pages and because we had just provided it to the judge and to Cindy's attorney, the judge ordered a recess to have the opportunity to read everything and recall our case after lunch.

Over the objections of Cindy's attorney, the judge ruled that California would exercise jurisdiction over our case in general, and, in particular, it would exercise personal jurisdiction over the custody of our daughter. Cindy's attorney argued that the exercise of jurisdiction required continued residency for a period of six months under the Uniform Child Custody Jurisdiction Act. He argued that the California court lacked that important requirement since Cindy had returned to South Dakota and had lived there for six weeks over the summer with our daughter.

The judge, however, adopted our argument that Cindy's return to South Dakota was only temporary and was not intended to be a permanent change of address. The evidence supported our legal position. Cindy had not enrolled our daughter in school in South Dakota in August when school began there. She had not changed her mailing address to her boyfriend's home address or to any other South Dakota address when she went back. She had not obtained a new South Dakota driver's license or registered our vehicle in South Dakota. The judge ruled that Cindy's acts, or failure to act, was proof that she still regarded California as her permanent residence.

The judge ruled that all parties, and especially our daughter, had lived continuously in California for at least six months prior to the filing of our motion, which was the legal requirement for the Court to retain jurisdiction over our daughter under the Uniform Child Custody Jurisdiction Act. The judge ordered that California would be deemed the home state concerning the custody of our daughter.

The judge recognized that only one state could have jurisdiction in an interstate custody battle under the Uniform Child Custody Jurisdiction Act. There could not be two separate and competing divorce cases concerning child custody. When one state court determined the child had lived continuously for at least six months in that state, making that state the home state, the divorce case in the other state would have to be dismissed, even if it had been filed first.

As a result, the judge entered the order that Cindy was required to dismiss her South Dakota divorce case. The judge concluded the hearing, looked directly at Cindy, and said, "You can move back to South Dakota if you want to, but your daughter stays here in California."

Things quickly became complicated. I learned that Cindy's boyfriend was divorced with two young children, and he was unwilling to leave his children in South Dakota and move to California. Cindy was unwilling to move back to South Dakota and leave our daughter with me in California while we waited for our case to proceed to trial. I was unwilling to allow Cindy to take our daughter with her to live in South Dakota. The only point on which we could agree was there would be a trial.

I wished we could have worked things out and stayed married. I didn't want to be in court, but it was the only means by which the California court could acquire jurisdiction, and it was the only means by which I could make sure Cindy wouldn't be able to take our daughter with her back to South Dakota. I now realized reconciliation was out of reach. Cindy wanted out, and we were beyond the point of no return.

The hearing in California exposed Cindy's entire scheme. It was clear to me that her move to California had been a charade. She had hired an attorney in South Dakota to file for divorce even before she returned to California. By the time of our hearing in California, she had an attorney in South Dakota and another one in California. She was determined to win custody at trial so she could move back to South Dakota with our daughter. She blamed me for having to remain in California. She knew she could not move back to South Dakota now, because if she did, the judge would grant me temporary primary custody of our daughter.

We soon had another hearing to determine who would have primary custody of our daughter while we waited for our case to proceed to trial. Because Cindy was not working and because Orval's cases often required me to travel, the judge granted temporary custody of our daughter to Cindy pending the trial. The concept of joint or shared custody had not really been uniformly adopted at that time. Where the child was young and the mother was not working, the mother routinely was granted primary custody of a child in a child custody case unless the mother was determined to be unfit.

Cindy did not want to give up temporary custody of our daughter. Her attorney undoubtedly told her that, absent compelling reasons and all other considerations being equal, the court often made the temporary order a permanent custody order at the trial. With the slow progress of family law cases and the congested court calendar, our case wouldn't finally reach trial until almost three years later.

This was an extremely difficult time for me. At the first hearing, the judge ordered I could exercise visitation with our daughter for only two nights each week and every other weekend. Our daughter was only seven, and the court wanted to keep her routine as stable as possible.

I missed our daughter terribly on the days I wasn't able to be with her. After she began tennis lessons, I would leave work and drive twenty miles to watch her half-hour lesson and then drive back to work—just to get the chance to see her and maybe say "hi" and give her a hug from her daddy. On my visitation days, I left work early so I could pick her up after school. On our days together, I would work late at night or early in the morning while she was asleep so we could spend as much time together as possible.

On the days I wasn't scheduled to have visitation with her, I mostly reverted to my old full-time work schedule from my Kansas days. I scheduled my travel to avoid any visitation conflicts and, fortunately, didn't have any trials scheduled.

However, Cindy soon began taking trips back to South Dakota, leaving our daughter with me on her custody days. As the trips became more frequent and of a longer duration, I was able to spend more and more time with our daughter. Cindy's weekend trips sometimes lasted a week at a time. I hired the mother-in-law of Orval's brother to stay at my apartment during the afternoons to be with our daughter after school until I could get there after work. Eventually, I went back to court to have our temporary custody and visitation order reflect what was happening in practice. The judge agreed and modified our order to provide that we each would have joint equal custody on alternating weeks pending the trial—shared equal custody!

I now knew I would have an equal chance to obtain primary custody at trial. Although Cindy didn't work, she really wasn't a stay-at-home mom either. She didn't have to work because I was paying her both spousal support and child support. She didn't have to pay income tax on the child support payments, and she was free to vacation and take trips back to South Dakota. I was caring for our daughter more than half of the time.

When our case finally went to trial, the court awarded me primary custody of our daughter, and Cindy now had visitation.

About a year after our divorce case was filed, our divorce judgment was entered, legally ending our marriage. Now two additional years later, our custody battle also was over. The court's final custody order should have marked the end to this fight. However, I soon learned that this was only the beginning.

About a year after our divorce became final, I started dating. I eventually met someone with two children (a boy and a girl) who were about the same age as our daughter. Cindy was angry that she lost custody and was compelled to stay in California. Her plans to take our daughter to South Dakota to be with her boyfriend and his children were ruined. She became even angrier now that I was dating someone else. Even though it was the court that made the decision, she blamed me, and I clearly was the target of her scorn.

"Heaven has no rage like love to hatred turned, Nor hell a fury like a woman scorned."[1]

Cindy didn't want to appear to her family and friends that she had done anything wrong or that she otherwise somehow appeared unfit to justify the court's final decision regarding custody. She did not want to return to South Dakota alone and leave our daughter with me, because doing so would mean the amount I paid her for child support would be substantially decreased. As a result, Cindy took me back to court—constantly. After she would file a request to have the court modify its custody order, we would be in court for about six months before the matter could be resolved. The judge would rule she had not provided any evidence to show there existed a substantial change in circumstances to justify a modification of our custody order. As a result, each time, the court would deny her request. But after a respite of another three or four months, she again would file another request to try to modify the court's order.

I contemplated getting remarried, and my hope was that I could have a stable marriage and home without all the drama and conflict I had experienced during my first marriage. Carmen (not her real name) and I eventually married.

Unfortunately, there was no peace, as Cindy's court filings were continually interrupting my second marriage. Cindy now was even more upset after I remarried. I still had to pay her spousal and child support, and I still had to pay for both of our attorney's fees. Even though she lost each time we went to court, the court ordered I had to pay for her attorney's fees because California law provided that both parties should have an equal opportunity and access to the courts in family law matters. Consequently, Cindy had no deterrent whatsoever from continually refiling motions to modify custody.

Cindy's constant interference soon became a source of contention in my second marriage. It also created a financial drain Carmen resented. I was supporting my new family of five, but I also was paying Cindy. More importantly, Cindy's interference had become a source of contention concerning our daughter. Carmen not only resented the constant interference and financial drain caused by Cindy's repeated motions, but Carmen also eventually began to resent my daughter. Because Carmen couldn't do anything to Cindy, Carmen began to take her frustrations out on my daughter. We fought a lot.

To further complicate matters, I started getting extremely busy with work, and I soon began traveling extensively to defend cases filed against Orval's company. At first, I managed to turn my work travel into a nice diversion, by scheduling depositions and hearings so Carmen could accompany me on a number of the trips. Carmen also was divorced, so we reconciled our custody schedules so our children were at our home at the same time. I could schedule a hearing or deposition in San Francisco on a Friday or a Monday so we could get away for a long weekend when the children were visiting their other parents. On trips to the east coast, Orval would have me fly on a Saturday and return the following Tuesday so he could get a cheaper fare and pay less for my airline tickets. As he already paid for my flight, meals, hotel, and rental car, I didn't have to pay much more to have Carmen join me on the trips. I even scheduled our family's summer vacation one year around a trip to New York so I could have our entire family join me on a work-related trip and family vacation for a week.

Most of the time, though, I had to travel alone for work to Alabama, South Carolina, Florida, Michigan, New Jersey, and New York. A number of cases also took me to Oakland and San Francisco. While I would be away from my family for only a few days at a time for the hearings and depositions, I would be gone for at least a week at a time for the trials. And we tried every case. Carmen resented having to pick up or drop off our daughter at Cindy's house when I was out of town.

Because Orval didn't have insurance, I knew that every case would result in a trial. Orval didn't want to settle anything because he believed he made a good product, and any settlement payment would reduce his profit margin. He thought that settling a case meant he was admitting there was something defective about his products. Most importantly, his experience in the Kansas case taught him that plaintiff attorneys would try to use past settled cases against him in future cases. As a result, Orval wanted to try every case. I knew that each time I stepped into a courtroom at the start of a trial, I had to win the case so the company would be able to stay in business and so I would continue to have a job.

I prided myself on being able to walk in another courtroom, in another town, in another state, and in another jurisdiction and win a case. Even though we would retain a local attorney to be with me in the courtroom, I had to learn the civil procedure and the substantive product liability law for every new state where I tried a case. I had to learn the local customs and practices to be able to identify with the jurors. For example, when I tried a case in Alabama, with adversaries named Payton and Sawyer, I learned to talk slower and develop a little bit of a drawl and end my sentences by speaking in a slightly higher pitch as if asking a question? I read the local papers so I could converse with the court clerks about the community's current events. To make sure I wouldn't get hometowned and to create some predictability, as often as possible I would remove the case to the federal district court.

Probably my most difficult case was in the federal district court for the southern district of New York in lower Manhattan. From the twenty-seventh floor windows, I could look out across the Manhattan skyline. Every time I entered the building, I hummed the tune to Frank Sinatra's song "New York, New York." I told myself if I could make it here, I could make it anywhere.

It was a complicated case, and much of Orval's future work depended on the outcome. Years before I met Orval, he had been hired to build a plant in Florida that would convert waste into electricity through a process called pyrolysis. He already manufactured machines that could crush, cut, and compact trash so that it could be recycled. However, whatever wasn't able to be recycled would be taken to the landfill or stored on barges. Orval's pyrolysis system would heat the waste that could not be recycled in a controlled environment at a thousand degrees to create by-products of fuel oil and electricity.

He had built most of the plant and actually had begun selling electricity to the electric company. However, the people who hired Orval's company could not account for all the investor's money. The project was over budget, behind schedule, and eventually terminated.

The people who took the money were prosecuted and went to prison. As a result, the investors filed the case in New York to recover their lost investment against Orval's company. To save time and money, the parties agreed to use the evidence from the criminal case. I had to examine boxes and boxes of documents, investigative reports, scientific reports, technical data, expert reports, and depositions that had been filed away in storage in Florida. Most of the testimony that would be presented in the trial would be offered as deposition testimony, without having the benefit of a live witness on the stand that I could cross-examine.

My adversary was a former US attorney who had appeared many times before the federal judge. He argued that the investors had not been told about all the risks inherent with the project. No plant like this had ever been built before. He argued that his clients didn't know this was a high-risk, experimental enterprise.

At the pretrial conference, I was successful in arguing that we did not want to try this case before a jury. Most of the time, I wanted to be in front of a jury. In Kansas, I bragged that if I could get the case to the jury, we would win the case. Here, however, the case involved complicated, scientific data. I knew that the federal judge and his team of highly educated law clerks would follow the evidence better than a jury.

Moreover, the trial would be heavily based primarily on the documentary evidence. The plaintiff introduced about 200 exhibits and I introduced about 450. Only one investor testified as the representative for all the investors, and Orval was my only witness. The investor testified for only one day, but Orval's testimony took place over the course of the two-week trial, interrupted by the court's other business. The remaining witnesses' respective testimony was introduced by depositions, and the federal judge reviewed the expert's testimony through their respective expert reports.

At the trial's conclusion, the federal judge relied on his law clerks to marshal the evidence and all the exhibits, but he relied on us trial attorneys to crystallize the case into trial briefs. The judge ordered each of us to submit our trial briefs to summarize the case, limiting the briefs to twenty-five pages.

I immediately objected. I told the judge I could not possibly condense the case into a trial brief of only twenty-five pages. I pleaded it would take that many pages just to write the statement of facts. The judge overruled my objection, and he ordered that each of our trial briefs would be due only two weeks later. Again, I objected, but the judge again overruled my objection. The judge said that he would review the briefs and provide us with his decision regarding liability in about six months.

So much depended on this case. Whereas each of the baler or shear cases sought damages of about two million dollars, this case requested damages of tens of millions of dollars, and there was no insurance company to pay any of the damages. Orval's company had now grown beyond simply manufacturing baling and shear machines. His company now was designing and manufacturing entire recycling systems for communities. He had submitted his bid to design and manufacture a recycling center for the entire city of San Francisco, and a large liability verdict would jeopardize the job in San Francisco.

Although six months passed, we still had not received the judge's decision. As each week went by, I told Orval not to worry, but I was worried. Everything was riding on the brief.

We finally received the federal judge's decision that we won the case, and we had won in spectacular fashion. Whereas my trial brief was twenty-five pages, the federal judge's written decision was twenty-five and a half pages. The judgment tracked my trial brief and then added the judge's decision of no liability at the end.

Orval was vindicated, and I was celebrated as the conquering hero. Like the Sinatra song, I had made it there in New York. I told myself I could make it anywhere.

Life at home was not so successful. Carmen was getting increasingly frustrated with Cindy's constant interference. I could see the impact it was having on our daughter. She was caught in the middle. On one occasion, I returned home from work to find that Carmen told my daughter to call Cindy and have her come and pick her up because Carmen didn't want her there when I wasn't there. Naturally, this made me furious because now Carmen gave Cindy another reason to file another motion.

On another occasion, I returned home from an out-of-state trip to find Carmen had moved out of our house. Her parents had hired movers, and she took everything she wanted out of our house and moved it into storage. She had taken the children and was living with her parents. I managed to patch things up, but some months after that it happened again. All Carmen's stunts not only impacted our marriage, but they also encouraged Cindy to rush back to court to file additional motions.

Incredibly, one day, Carmen gave me an ultimatum. She said, "Either your daughter goes or I go." It would have been easy to choose my daughter over Carmen, but my decision was not that simple because Carmen and I now had two little children of our own. Once again, I found myself in an impossible situation.

That summer, we took a vacation to Colorado where Carmen's relatives lived near Colorado Springs. Carmen's dad was a wonderful Christian. His sons attended Biola University, a Christian college in southern California. He operated a large bed and breakfast that doubled as a retreat for Christian pastors. He suggested we move to Colorado.

I was intrigued by the idea of moving. I could live just about anywhere and still defend Orval's cases. Also, the price of a house in Colorado was less than half of one in California. Since I had been paying for two households for so long, I hadn't been able to save enough money to be able to buy a house.

However, while moving might save my marriage, it would mean giving up my oldest daughter—again. After having spent so many years apart from her, was I now going to have to be apart from her again? I resented Carmen for giving me this ultimatum.

Once again, I felt stuck. Carmen and I had a three-year-old daughter and a one-year old son. I didn't want to leave my oldest daughter, but I felt I didn't have a choice. I was walking an emotional tightrope. I wondered if this was a sacrifice God was asking me to make. I felt like the mother of the living baby who appeared before King Solomon in the story told in the book of Kings in the Bible.[2]

In the story involving King Solomon, two mothers delivered their babies a few days apart. They were living alone in the same house. One night, after one of the mothers rolled over in her sleep and smothered her baby, she took her dead baby to where the other mother was sleeping and exchanged the babies.

When the mother of the living baby awoke, she, at first, thought her baby had died during the night, but she soon realized the dead baby lying next to her was not hers. Realizing the other mother had switched the babies, she ran to the other mother, picked up her baby, and went directly to King Solomon to plead her case.

Although the mother of the living baby told King Solomon the entire story, the other mother said, "No! The living one is my son; the dead one is yours."[3]

King Solomon called for his sword and ordered, "Cut the living child in two and give half to one and half to the other."[4]

The mother of the living baby was horrified and immediately cried out to King Solomon. She "was filled with compassion for her son and said to the king, 'Please, my lord, give her the living baby! Don't kill him!' But the other said, 'Neither I nor you shall have him. Cut him in two!'"[5] By this exchange, King Solomon knew which one was the living baby's mother.

He ordered, "Give the living baby to the first woman. Do not kill him; she is his mother."[6] King Solomon knew who was the living baby's real mother by her compassion.

After anguished prayer, I decided to move to Colorado. I decided to let my oldest daughter live with her mother full time. My oldest daughter was going to start high school in the fall, and I told her that it wasn't fair for her to have to live in the midst of all this turmoil. Cindy continued to take me to court, even though she always lost, and Carmen resented my daughter for Cindy's interference. This situation was extremely difficult and hurtful for my daughter. I told myself that, if I truly loved my daughter, my love for her would set her free. I would bring an end to the chaos by letting her live full time with Cindy. Carmen also would leave her two children with their father, and we would move to Colorado with our two little children and begin a new life.

However, Carmen decided not to leave her two children from her first marriage with their father. Instead, she decided to take them with us to Colorado. She was not willing to do the very thing she demanded of me. She wanted to move to Colorado and take her two children away from their father, who naturally did not want that to happen.

As a result, we began yet another custody battle. At the outset of the ensuing custody, Carmen's daughter said she wanted to move with us to Colorado, but her son surprised Carmen and upset her plans when he announced he wanted to stay in California with his father. Carmen continued to fight that custody battle after we moved. During our entire time living in Colorado, we had to make repeated trips to attend court in California. The court eventually granted her son's wish and ordered that he stay in California with his father.

Once the court ordered that Carmen's son could stay in California and live with his father, Carmen no longer wanted to live in Colorado. While I had agreed to move to Colorado to save my marriage, now I was going to have to move back to California to try yet again to save my marriage. We ended up moving back to California in less than two years after moving to Colorado.

I was so sick of family court! I missed our home in Colorado. It was in a beautiful forested development in the Rocky Mountain foothills between Denver and Colorado Springs, about eleven miles north of the Air Force Academy in the Black Forest. Many retired air force officers lived there, and it included an eighteen-hole golf course and clubhouse. Our backyard fronted a twenty-acre meadow surrounded by homes tucked in and among the pine trees.

We often sat on our deck and watched fox jump in the meadow with the Colorado Rockies in the background. I didn't have to travel as much for Orval's cases, and I enjoyed spending full time with our two young children. Carmen's father and family lived only about five miles away at their Black Forest retreat. I missed my talks with Carmen's father.

However, I left that paradise, and I hoped we finally were going to be finished with family court. Orval was happy I was returning to California where I could work with him daily, and we moved into a new house in California that Orval was going to help me purchase. The custody fight with Cindy had ended when we moved to Colorado, so upon returning to California, I now could see my oldest daughter more often, even though she did not live with us. The custody fight between Carmen and her ex-husband also was over with our move back to California. I hoped and prayed for peace.

However, Carmen blamed me when she lost her custody fight over her son. Before we moved to Colorado, her two children lived with us most of the time. However, once we moved back to California, the court ruled that both of her children should live half time with their father.

By the time we moved back to California, I began defending another case for Orval on the East Coast. This time, in New Jersey. As the weeks turned into months, Carmen kept asking me whether Orval and I had signed our contract to purchase our new house. I told her we were busy defending his cases and that we eventually would get around to finalizing the contract. Orval bought the house, and we were renting it from him.

In reality, neither Orval nor I were willing to rush to transfer the title to me because Carmen was so volatile. She had already moved out of our home on two separate occasions before we moved to Colorado. Now that we were back in California, I began to acquire a strange sense that Carmen was only biding her time until Orval transferred the title of the house to me. After all, she had moved out twice before. I felt I was reliving the time when Cindy had agreed to return to California only until she learned whether I passed the bar exam. History was repeating itself.

My instincts were right. Carmen got tired of waiting. When I had to travel to New Jersey for a deposition, I left on Saturday as usual, expecting to return on Tuesday. However, the deposition went well, and I returned home late Monday night.

When I drove into our driveway, it was almost midnight, and the house was dark. As I opened the front door, I was surprised to find practically all our belongings were gone. While I was in New Jersey, Carmen and her mother hired movers and cleaned out the house. As I walked through the house, I was somewhat in shock, but mainly I was angry.

After walking around the empty house for only about ten minutes, I picked up the phone and called a twenty-four-hour locksmith. Although it was after midnight, I had enough. I changed the locks on the house. This was the third time Carmen had moved out of our home. No more. I was having flashbacks to those times in my marriage with Cindy where Cindy refused to move with me to Kansas and then moved out of our house twice. Carmen had now moved out of our home for the third time. I felt like Job in the Bible.

In the morning, I called Carmen, who was staying with the children at her mother's home. When I told her I had returned the night before and was calling from our house, to my surprise she told me she already had filed for divorce. Sure enough, later that day, I was served with a copy of the divorce, and the court had already scheduled a hearing just a few days away. True to the playbook, Carmen wanted me to pay her spousal and child support, and she wanted me to be able to visit the children only every other weekend.

I couldn't believe this was happening to me again. When we went to court, the court ordered that I should have joint physical custody and the children would be able to live with me half of the time. I was so relieved and thankful. The court reasoned that our house was their home. Also, the court reasoned that Carmen revealed her priorities when she moved out of the house. She took all our expensive furniture, but she didn't take the children's furniture or toys. The court stated if the children were her first priority, she would have moved their furniture and toys first.

It was now 1998, and I was now going to have to be entrenched again in yet another custody battle. I called Carmen's father in Colorado and pleaded with him to talk to his daughter. He and I each knew divorce was wrong and not part of God's plan, but he told me there was nothing he could do. I was convinced divorce was the devil's cancer created to cause chaos. It divided families, upset childhoods, and drained finances. I didn't want to be divorced, but there was nothing I could do to prevent it. I was an unwilling participant and litigant.

Worse, it was déjà vu. Cindy refused to move to Kansas with me and moved out twice. Carmen moved out three times. Cindy returned to California only until she learned I passed the bar exam. Carmen returned to California only until I would sign the contract to buy the house from Orval. Having to repeat these events was taking its toll on me emotionally.

Once again, I told myself I should have seen it coming. Shortly after we moved back from Colorado, Carmen announced one day she had an opportunity to take a trip to Hawaii with one of her girl friends. Because we had been fighting so often, I thought the time away might do us both good and improve her outlook. Oddly, she didn't suggest that we get away and take a trip together, spend time together, and work things out.

Not long after that, she said her girl friend invited her to accompany her on a trip to France during that summer.

My comment to her was, "What, we're going to have separate vacations now?"

She was determined to go, and I was looking forward to having the quiet time alone with our children. By that September, she filed for divorce.

After the divorce was filed, Carmen often would travel during my week with the children. She wasn't working, and I was paying her spousal support and child support. On some of those trips, she would be gone for her week of visitation, so it was not unusual for me to have the children living continuously with me for three or more weeks at a time.

One day, Carmen announced she needed me to have the children exclusively again because she was going to travel to Europe. When I asked her how long she was going to be gone this time, she said she was going to move there to be with another man! I now suspected that this individual was probably who accompanied her on her previous trips to Hawaii and Europe. Our divorce was now final, and she said they were going to be married. The only problem with her plan was that the other guy evidently didn't want to get married as much as she did, and she returned to California.

After awhile, I started dating again, and I thought I finally was going to be able to live somewhat of a normal life. However, I soon was embroiled again in another custody fight after Carmen returned to California. The court appointed a psychologist to conduct a custody examination, and both children told him they wanted to live full time with me. However, the court ordered it would leave the custody arrangement just the way it was, with the children living one week with me and the alternating week with Carmen, so as not to disrupt the arrangement. By now, I only had a couple of cases I was defending for Orval. Instead of giving me a raise in salary, he agreed I would be free to work on other cases for other clients in my free time. As a result, I again was taken back to court in an effort to make me pay more money in spousal and child support.

Sadly, under California law, generally the more time children spend with one parent, the more child support the other parent has to pay. Consequently, divorcing parents who fight over the children often really wage a war over money. If my ex-wife could convince the court to reduce the amount of time I had with the children, she would get more money. I was reminded of an old expression that people sometimes decide to stay married for the money. In my situation, it seemed to me that both Cindy and Carmen decided to divorce for the money.

Carmen's motive became even more evident when she remarried. Under California law, when one spouse remarries, the other spouse's obligation to pay spousal support automatically ends. In my case, I learned Carmen remarried when our daughter returned one weekend and said, "Guess what, we have a new brother!" Carmen remarried several months before but had not told anyone.

The reason Carmen kept her marriage a secret was because Orval was automatically deducting the monthly spousal support and child support payments directly from my check and sending it to her. By not telling anyone she had remarried, she was able to continue to get the spousal support payments. She and her new husband went to Hawaii that summer at my expense.

When I learned Carmen remarried, I asked Lewis, Orval's controller, to stop sending her the spousal support payments. However, he said he couldn't because he had to follow the court's order. I then sent an e-mail to Carmen asking her to sign a standard stipulation so I could change the order to reflect that she had remarried, so I would no longer have to pay her spousal support. My finances were draining because I still was paying child support to Cindy.

To my surprise, Carmen said she would not sign the stipulation, so I had to go back to court to have the court enter its order. At the hearing, she then announced she needed more time to hire an attorney to defend her. To my astonishment, the court continued the hearing, which meant she would continue to collect more weekly spousal support checks until the next hearing date. Unbelievably, the court also ordered me to pay her more money so she could hire an attorney, who simply came into court and agreed that the court should enter its order ending the spousal support payments.

As additional years went by, additional requests were filed to have me pay more in child support or to modify the custody order. As the children became older, circumstances changed, so the court ordered another custody evaluation and appointed another psychologist to evaluate custody. Once again, both children said they wanted to live full time with me. However, once again, because the children were doing so well in school, the court ordered the custodial arrangement should stay the same.

The day before the beginning of the school year after Carmen remarried, she unilaterally went to the children's school, obtained copies of their school records, and enrolled them in the new school district where she now lived with her new husband and his son. Carmen had done this without any notice to me or the children. She unilaterally was going to take our children away from their friends and the only school they had attended. I had to go to court and reverse that procedure.

However, the court noted she and her new husband were living in his two-bedroom condo and that his son lived in the other bedroom. Consequently, the court stated it would change custody and enter its order that the children would live full time with me unless she and her husband changed their living accommodations. While the court reasoned that our son could share a bedroom with Carmen's husband's son, the court ordered that our daughter should have her own bedroom there.

Carmen knew such an order would mean that the amount of child support she received would be drastically reduced. As a result, Carmen rented a separate house in our neighborhood so she could live there during the alternating weeks she spent with the children. However, only Carmen moved into the rented house. Her husband and his son did not move into Carmen's rented house. Rather, he and his son continued to live in his two-bedroom condo, which was thirty miles away. She lived in the rented house with the children during her custodial week and then lived with her husband at his condo during the week she did not have custody of our children so she could continue to receive child support payments from me.

After about a year or so, the facade fizzled. Carmen ended her lease on the rental house and moved back full time into her husband's condo. She didn't even tell me she was moving. I came home one day to find about a dozen boxes of all the children's stuff at my front door. For the next two and a half years, from 2002–2005, the children lived full time with me.

After Carmen filed for divorce, I eventually began dating again. I also had been spending less time working for Orval's company and more time representing other clients. Over the seventeen years I worked for Orval's company, I defended cases for him in about a dozen different states. Each time we went to trial, and each time, we won. We never lost a case.

As a result, Orval's company now once again had liability insurance, and the insurance company paid for insurance defense attorneys to defend the cases. I had worked myself out of a job. I had accomplished what I set out to do. In my three years in Kansas and the seventeen years working for Orval, I never lost a case that went to trial. As a result, I had developed a sense of arrogant pride in my accomplishments to offset the difficulties I encountered in my personal life. I took all the credit myself. I even had a vanity license plate that said "PD2WN" (paid to win).

As I began to represent other clients exclusively, I found myself ironically handling divorce and custody cases. I clearly knew family law with all my personal experience, but in most of my cases, I represented the father. I even began to handle cases for a law firm that advertised itself as a father's rights law firm. In those cases, though, sometimes I would handle a case I just didn't seem to be able to finish or complete. Something would happen that would remind me of my own past. Something would happen that would make me just want to shut down. Something would happen that would take me back to the painful memories of my own custody cases. I was at a loss to explain why.

By 2006, I was hired by a construction company to defend its construction defect cases. What happened with product liability cases in the 1980s now seemed to have happened with construction defect cases. More and more cases had been filed alleging construction defects. The company that hired me wanted me to defend all its construction defect cases.

Eventually though, I began working more and more on the development projects the company was pursuing. Near the end of that year, we began a development project in Arizona. Carmen was divorced again and now wanted to relitigate custody. Carmen was content to have our children live full time with me for the prior two and a half years, but she now was determined to have our daughter live with her during her senior year of high school.

While both children had been living full time with me for the prior two and a half years, I no longer paid Carmen any child support. However, I never went to court to file a motion to change the order because I did not want to invite more litigation.

Just as I had predicted, Carmen wanted to litigate the issue to collect more money. Not only was Carmen seeking to change the order so our daughter would live full time with her during her last year of high school, she also was seeking to have the court enter an order that I pay her for all the child support for the past two and a half years, even though the children had been living with me full time! The total amounted to over forty thousand dollars. An action was even filed to have me held in contempt of court and put me in jail, alleging I had willfully failed to pay child support, even though the children lived one hundred percent of the time with me.

The court ruled that our daughter could live full time with Carmen because that was what our daughter said she wanted to do. Since she was seventeen, the court went along with her wishes. The court also ruled our son would continue to live full time with me, which is what he said he wanted to do. The court finally let him live where he wanted. Now Carmen was going to split our family once again by having our daughter live with her while our son continued to live with me.

While the court concluded the custody aspect of the case, the part about the money languished. Finally, in 2012, that part concluded as well. The court ordered I only owed Carmen about $1100. I argued that I shouldn't even have had to pay that amount because I paid more than $5000 for my daughter's college tuition before she turned eighteen and graduated from high school. However, since I paid that amount to the college instead of directly to Carmen, the court did not give me credit for those payments. Unbelievable.

Nevertheless, by 2012, my custody battles finally ended. What began in 1989 was finally over more than twenty years later. Carmen fought me the last fourteen years, even though we only had been married six years. Carmen collaborated with Cindy to try to create havoc in my life. She tried to embarrass or demean me in court because I also practiced before those same judges while representing other clients.

Carmen also did her best to assassinate my character. As I began to answer complaints before the state bar court, Carmen tried to use my disciplinary record against me. I coached both of our children's softball and baseball teams. Even though Carmen had not attended a single practice or game to watch our daughter play softball, just before we were scheduled to play in a national tournament in Southern California in 2005, Carmen appeared at a practice and provided copies of my discipline record to all the parents. For good measure, Carmen also told them the reason she had lost custody of her son to her ex-husband when we moved to Colorado was because the court had ordered I had been found guilty of child sexual abuse—which allegation, of course, was totally false.

Nevertheless, because we were coaching twelve-year-old girls, the other coaches immediately told me that I no longer could be a coach on my daughter's team, based solely on Carmen's accusations and lies. When I arrived at the national tournament to watch my daughter play, not one of the parents on the team would speak to me. It hurt not being in the dugout with my team and wondering what the other girls had been told about me. I told our daughter just to do her best and not worry about all that other stuff. She played her heart out. Our team won the national tournament, and our daughter was selected as the most valuable player in the tournament. Even though the tournament was only forty minutes away from where we lived, Carmen never even attended. She never saw our daughter play. That entire season, Carmen only attended one practice—the practice where she appeared for the sole purpose to ruin my reputation.

The week after this tournament, my daughter was invited by another team to play a few weeks later in the ASA Nationals held in Tulsa, Oklahoma. The ASA Nationals were a weeklong tournament held from Sunday to Sunday. While most of the tournament would occur during my regular week of custody, attending the tournament meant our children would not return by Friday, the beginning of Carmen's regular week of custody.

Accordingly, prior to our leaving, I provided Carmen with all the information relating to the trip, including all the flight information for both the outgoing and the return flights, and the name and phone number of the hotel where the team would be staying. My e-mail stated we would be returning the following Monday and Carmen could add the three days on to her vacation time when she planned to take the children with her on vacation at the end of the month.

We flew to Oklahoma City on Sunday with the rest of the team. When we returned to the hotel late on Friday night after another day of softball games, I received a phone call from a detective in southern California. The detective said Carmen had filed a criminal complaint against me for kidnapping! He said she claimed she didn't know where "her" children were. I explained to the detective that Carmen was lying and we were attending the ASA Nationals, and that I had sent her an e-mail earlier in the week providing her all the details. He concluded Carmen was lying, and no charges were filed against me. Unfortunately, however, the children heard the conversation.

I thought the situation was over, but the next night, our team again played a late night game. We lost the game, which meant we were going to have to play the first game on Sunday. Because it was so late, we arranged to have all the girls leave immediately after the game so they could be taken back to the hotel in the team van to take their showers and get ready for bed instead of stopping first to eat dinner. I got back to the hotel later because another parent and I picked up dinner for each of the girls at the drive-through.

When our daughter arrived at the hotel in the team van, it was late, and she saw the hotel security officer in the hotel lobby dressed in his full security uniform. She thought he was a police officer. She immediately panicked because of the phone call from the detective the night before and became distraught, crying and thinking the police had come to the hotel to arrest her daddy. She thought she and her little brother were going to be taken from me and put on a flight back to California and I was going to be put in jail.

By the time I got back to the hotel with the girls' meals, I learned our daughter was crying and upset and was in another room waiting for me to return to the hotel. Upon hearing this, our son, who was with me, now also became extremely upset and frightened asking, "Dad, they're not going to take you away and put you in jail, are they?" I immediately went to the lobby to talk to the police officer, but I soon learned the person there simply was the hotel security officer. Assured that everything was okay, the children settled down, ate dinner, and went to bed.

Clearly, this stunt by Carmen was her attempt to try to create chaos and sabotage my time with the children. She clearly was trying to embarrass me with the other parents and coaches on this new team, just as she had done on our daughter's previous team. She succeeded in doing this only a couple of weeks before, so now she was attempting to do it again with our daughter's new travel softball team.

Once again, Carmen was playing the part of the false mother who lied before King Solomon. Similarly, Carmen didn't care how her actions hurt our children as long as she was able to inflict harm or pain upon me. Of course, it hurt me personally to have to endure these challenges, but what hurt me the most was having to watch our children suffer. It hurt me to see the children caught in the middle. I couldn't understand how a mother would use and hurt her children to try to exact revenge.

In California, it is a felony to make a false report of child sexual abuse or a false kidnapping report. It is also a felony in California to commit perjury. However, I could not file criminal charges. I could not put my children's mother in jail for the children's sake. Once again, I was in an impossible situation.

Unfortunately, Carmen didn't stop there. Emboldened because there were no repercussions for her behavior after this ordeal, Carmen refused to allow the children to participate in their sports and activities during her alternating custodial weeks. She would not let our daughter participate in practices or games on her new travel softball team, even though she was such an exceptional player who played on a team that competed in national tournaments, and even though her teammates were her friends. She also would not allow our son to participate in soccer practices or games on his custodial weeks. I tried my best to offer compromises by offering to pick them up from Carmen's residence, to take them to all their practices and games, and to return them to her residence during each of her custodial weeks. However, she wouldn't cooperate.

My daughter was invited to play on her new travel softball team the next year, but because of Carmen's interference, she could only play half time. During my custodial week, our daughter would practice with the team on weekdays, but then Carmen would not permit her to play in the games on the weekends when she went back to Carmen's residence. During Carmen's custodial week, our daughter missed practice during the week. Even though she attended games on the alternating weekends, when she was with me during my custodial weeks, her coach made her sit on the bench for missing the games and practices during Carmen's custodial weeks. Eventually, the coach dismissed our daughter from the team, saying the situation was bad for the morale of the team and wasn't fair to the other girls.

I wanted to scream that it wasn't fair to our daughter. She was the one suffering. I had to go back to court. I had to go back to court to get a court order to force our children's mother to allow them to play sports with their friends on her custodial weeks.

Even though the court granted the order, our daughter wasn't allowed to return to her former team. She wasn't allowed to play the sport she loved with her friends and teammates. We had to move to yet another new team. My daughter would now have to play on her third team within a year just because of Carmen's interference.

On Carmen's custodial weeks, I had to pick up the children, take them to their practices and games, and return them back to Carmen's residence. Often, I picked them up somewhere else such as at Carmen's parents' house, and the children wouldn't have their gear because it was back at Carmen's residence. Our daughter's team had a rule that a player would not be able to play in a game if she arrived late for practice or a game or wasn't in full uniform. As a result, I eventually resorted to having to purchase two sets of uniforms, running shoes, cleats, and gear for each of the children, just so Carmen couldn't sabotage and interfere with their opportunity to play sports.

Carmen knew I played sports in high school and college, so she wanted to interfere with this bond that I shared with our children. It didn't matter to her that the children wanted to play sports with their friends. Rather, Carmen wanted to alienate me from the children during her custodial weeks as if I didn't exist for alternating weeks at a time.

Their mother didn't attend any of their practices or games. She attempted to discourage our daughter from participating in softball by playing mind games with her and reminding her she was missing parties and fun activities by playing softball on weekends. Carmen often deliberately scheduled events directly conflicting with games, trying to force our daughter to choose between softball and an "exciting event" with her. Once she scheduled a trip to Hawaii, knowing our daughter wanted to go, at the same time that our daughter's team was scheduled to play in a qualifying tournament for nationals. Carmen showed up in the middle of the game, walked right up to the dugout (where I and the other coaches were coaching the game), and demanded to pick up our daughter so they could leave for Hawaii early the next morning.

I never wanted to be divorced. In each marriage, I tried to work out our differences and reach a reconciliation. I know God doesn't want people to get divorced. However, no matter how hard one spouse may try to hold a marriage together, that spouse cannot control the other spouse. If that other spouse is intent on going forward with divorce, unfortunately, there is nothing that can be done to prevent or stop it. At least with a divorce, there is supposed to be some finality, some closure so the two divorcing people can at least move on with their lives.

However, that doesn't happen when children are involved. In those cases, a divorce doesn't end the relationship. Ideally, if a divorce must happen and there are children involved, both parents should realize they will continue to be parents to those children for the rest of their lives and they should commit to co-parent together and get along for the benefit of the children. In my case, unfortunately, that didn't happen. In my case, the children were used as pawns to attempt to create havoc and chaos and to attempt to exact revenge and retribution against me.

The destruction of divorce not only affects the husband and wife, but it also affects each of them as a father and mother. More importantly, divorce affects the children. I think it affects them the most. The children just want their parents to get along and stop fighting.

In my case, sure, I could have just capitulated and walked away. I could have just went on with my life and seen my children every other weekend, at least when they were still living in the same state. I could have allowed both of my ex-wives to alienate me from my children. This is what each of my ex-wives selfishly wanted and fought to obtain. However, I didn't think that would have been fair to me, and I certainly didn't think it would have been fair to our children.

A father should not have to be alienated from his children. Children should not have to be split up. So I did what I thought was the right thing to do. I stood in the gap. I held my ground and fought against being alienated from our children and against having my relationship with them destroyed. I fought against having my character assassinated and destroyed. I also fought for the children so their lives and their relationships with me weren't compromised.

After more than twenty years of custody battles, I was exhausted. I hurt inside. It hurt me even more to see our children suffer. I ached for our children.

It is written in Proverbs, "If a wise man goes to court with a fool, the fool rages and scoffs, and there is no peace" (Proverbs 29:9). I didn't know if continuing to fight for our children was wise. I didn't believe it was fair for their mother unilaterally to remove them from one school district where they enjoyed attending school with their friends and enroll them in a new school district. I didn't think it was fair for their mother to interfere with and sabotage their playing sports with their friends. I didn't know if I was wise in defending against these actions. I just knew there was no peace.

I tried to bury my feelings. However, those hurts kept coming back. As I handled other divorce and custody cases for other clients, I began to experience flashbacks. Events in those cases took me back to hurtful events that happened to me in my own custody cases—in my own marriages. My personal life suffered and now, eventually, my career also suffered.

Carmen knew I practiced and appeared in front of the same family court judges in those other cases for those other clients. As a result, she tried to embarrass me by making outrageous allegations against me in our case, knowing I would likely appear again before our judge on another case for another client. At every opportunity, Carmen tried to use my disciplinary record with the state bar against me. She also spread gossip and lies to other parents and teachers at the children's school to try to hurt or embarrass me without regard for the children. I became sad. I withdrew. Even though I had never lost a jury trial, Carmen delighted in the fact that the family law court didn't let our children live full time with me, even though they said they wanted to on two different occasions.

I just shut down.

5

Road to Recovery

Trust in the Lord with all your heart and lean not on your
own understanding; in all your ways acknowledge Him,
and He will make your paths straight.

—Proverbs 3:5–6

State Bar Court Judge Talcott suggested I talk to someone at
the State Bar about the Lawyers Assistance Program, a program
designed to help attorneys experiencing problems relating to
mental health, substance or alcohol abuse. I began attending
group therapy one evening each week.

I soon was referred to a doctor who diagnosed my depression
and PTSD and prescribed medication to help me. The first
medication was to help level out and control my mood so I
wouldn't get so sad, or so that when I got sad, I wouldn't stay
sad. The second medication was to help me sleep.

I had been experiencing night terrors. I often would scream
out in my sleep and wake up in a cold sweat. My T-shirt would
be soaked, but I wouldn't remember anything at all about why
I was having night terrors. My doctor said I was experiencing
night terrors because I suffered from PTSD.

In 1998, Carmen filed for divorce, which became final about
a year later. I began dating again, and by 2000, I began a steady
relationship with a wonderful person, Janice, who had a son
about the same age as mine. I had been so sad with the move
to Colorado and back again to California and the continuous

fighting with Cindy and Carmen in family court over the custody of the children. Janice was the ray of sunshine that burst into my life when it seemed the darkest. She understood my feelings of abandonment when I said I did not want to get married again anytime soon, and she accepted that I had trust issues. We were happy just being together and spending time with the children.

By September of 2001, I needed to travel to New Jersey to attend a hearing on one of Orval's cases. I again was scheduled to fly to New York on Saturday and return to California on Tuesday. Both Janice and my oldest daughter decided to accompany me on the trip.

Janice wanted to go with me to New York because that was the weekend of the Mercedes Benz Fashion Week, and she had never been to New York. Our daughter also wanted to go since it was the last week of summer before she would return to her second year of college, and she also had never been to New York. I thought it would be a great opportunity for us to spend some time together before she went back to college. I had been to New York about a dozen times on Orval's cases and was looking forward to their joining me this time.

We stayed at the Crown Plaza Hotel in Midtown and, on Sunday, enjoyed Central Park and the Metropolitan Museum of Art. I did my best to show them a flavor of Manhattan. On Sunday night, we went to a Broadway show, and after the show we had reservations to eat dinner at Windows on the World, the restaurant on top of one of the World Trade Center buildings. Since we ate late after the show, we were one of the last guests to leave the restaurant. One of the chefs came over to our table and took his picture with us because Janice purchased his cookbook, which he autographed for her. I wanted to be able to take them to the observation deck on the 107th floor to view the New York skyline at night, but by the time dinner was over, the observation deck was closed. Janice and our daughter planned to return to the observation deck on Tuesday morning while I was going to be in court in New Jersey.

That Tuesday morning, the world changed when two groups of terrorists flew two planes into each of the twin towers on September 11, 2001.

I reserved a rental car to drive to court in New Jersey, but since I always seemed to get lost whenever I would drive, Janice and my daughter persuaded me to take the train instead. My train left Penn Station around 8 a. m. By the time the first plane hit the first tower, the train already made a couple of stops as we traveled south in New Jersey headed toward my destination near Long Branch. As it made its third stop, some people boarded the train and excitedly said that a plane had flown into one of the twin towers. By the time the train stopped again, the conductor entered our car and announced that we all had to leave the train because the trains were being shut down. We could not take another train back to New York.

I immediately hailed a cab and began the drive back north toward New York. I was worried about Janice and my daughter. They were getting ready when I left the hotel, and they planned to be on top of the twin towers at the observation deck that morning before they went shopping. As we drove north on Highway 9, the cab driver and I listened to the devastating news on the radio. We drove up the 95 turnpike and headed east on the 78 toward New York. Once the 78 turned north, I could see the twin towers across the Hudson River as I looked out the cab window.

I could see smoke billowing above one of the twin towers. The news announcer on the radio said a plane had been flown into the north tower at about 8:45 a. m. I still could not reach Janice on her cell phone. I only got a busy tone. The cab driver told me he also could not use his cell phone, and he heard on the radio that all the satellite cells were jammed because everyone in New York was trying to make cell phone calls at the same time. Just about then, I heard the announcement on the cab radio that another plane hit the south tower.

I was distraught. I had encouraged, even insisted, that Janice and my daughter visit the observation deck. I told them how they would take the elevator to the 107th floor, where there was an indoor observatory, and then they would be able to go up a series of escalators to an outdoor viewing deck on the 110th floor. On a clear day, people could see for fifty miles. Even the name was alluring. It was called top of the world.

The observation deck was in the south tower, the one hit last. The person on the radio said it was hit shortly after nine. I had left before eight. That gave them an hour to finish getting ready and take a cab from the hotel to the twin towers. That was more than plenty of time not only to get to the twin towers, but also to make it up to the observation deck. Did they leave right after me? Were they there?

With the first plane, everyone thought that it was a tragic accident. However, with the second plane, people began to fear America was under attack. I still couldn't reach them. I repeatedly redialed, only to get a busy tone.

As the cab came closer to New York, we heard the announcement that both the Holland Tunnel and the Lincoln Tunnel were closed. We also heard the announcement that all traffic on the bridges to New York had been halted, and no one was allowed to enter the city. I told the cab driver to take me as close to Manhattan as he could. As I exited the cab, I saw that concrete barricades had been placed across intersections so vehicles couldn't drive right up to the New Jersey shoreline along the Hudson River. I got out and walked east to the Jersey shore of the Hudson River.

When I reached the shoreline, I found I was at the Newport section of Jersey City near the Holland Tunnel. I could see the smoldering twin towers just across the Hudson River. Ferries transported people off Manhattan. I heard that lower Manhattan was being evacuated.

Chaos reigned everywhere I looked. There were a half dozen ambulances parked near the shore. Emergency lights flashed. Anguished people spilled out of the ferries. Some were bleeding, but everybody was covered in gray, grimy dust. People were crying. Fear and confusion had its grip on everyone. Many seemed dazed and in shock.

Instantaneously, people were homeless. Countless apartments and condos in lower Manhattan had been evacuated. All those people were being brought across the Hudson River to New Jersey. Where would they all stay? Where would I stay? Next to me was a hotel, so I quickly walked inside and asked if I could rent a room. I thought that, if Janice and my daughter were at the twin towers and were going to be evacuated with everybody else, they would be coming across the Hudson River on one of these ferries. This, then, would be a good place to rent a room, especially if we all wouldn't be allowed back into the city. However, there was no vacancy.

Someone said to no one in particular that no traffic was allowed into New York. The trains were shut down. Busses were not running. No cabs or vehicles of any kind were allowed into the city. I couldn't just stay where I was, not knowing whether Janice and my daughter were safe. I couldn't just wait there, hoping to see them walk off one of the ferries. I had to do something, anything.

I decided to try to get back to the Crown Plaza to see if they were there. Maybe they didn't get to the twin towers before the planes hit. I had to believe that. I had to hold on to something.

I had to believe in something. I said a prayer. *Please, God, keep them safe.* Trying to get back to the hotel in New York gave me a plan and a purpose.

I heard a rumor that people were being allowed to walk across the George Washington Bridge and enter the city on foot. When I asked how far that was from where I was near the Holland Tunnel, I was told the distance was about twelve miles.

I began walking north, along the shoreline, with thousands of other people. We all were walking on the street, going north. From one curb to the other, the street was filled with people walking in unison. It was like when fifty thousand people all leave a football stadium at the same time, and they all are walking down a ramp toward the parking lot. No one said anything. There really wasn't any noise. There was just an eerie silence.

The streets around New York and New Jersey are usually very noisy. However, the hustle and bustle of the city had been silenced that morning. There were no honking cabs or any of the other distinctive sounds of the city. As we walked, I imagined if prisoners of war must have felt like this. It was as if we were in a war zone and we were all prisoners of fear and terror. By now, we all had heard another plane had crashed into the Pentagon and a fourth crashed somewhere in rural Pennsylvania. Although we were all walking in the same direction, I didn't know where I was going. I wondered how many of those people knew where they were going or where they would sleep at the end of the day. The only sound we heard was that of an F16 circling the city.

By now, it was getting hot outside. I was wearing a wool suit and a tie. I was carrying not only a large litigation briefcase full of documents, but also a bankers box of documents and exhibits. Orval proudly packed the box. As an engineer, he had sealed the box with duct tape and fashioned a handle out of duct tape so it could be carried like a suitcase. When I left California, I told him the box looked terrible and I was not taking that box with me. He said I had better take it just the way it was, and he was going to call our local attorney after I arrived to make sure I had done as he wished. The problem now was that policemen were stopping me at every intersection, wanting to know what was in the box sealed with duct tape.

By the time I reached Hoboken, my tie became a headband, and I had given a homeless guy twenty bucks for his shopping cart. After I loaded my heavy litigation case and the heavy duct-taped box into the shopping cart, I threw my suit coat over them and continued to push the shopping cart down the middle of the street among all the people. After the police stopped me for the third time because of the duct-taped box, I chucked it into a nearby dumpster, exhibits included.

As we walked, we all were aware of the smoking twin towers to our right across the Hudson River. Whenever I saw a pay phone, I would stop and try to call Janice on her cell phone. I also tried calling the hotel. Each time, I only got a busy signal. My cell phone battery already died because I had been trying to call continuously.

I soon reached Weehawken and the Lincoln Tunnel. I again tried calling Janice and my daughter from another pay phone. I also tried the hotel, but I still could not get through. I was worried sick and feared the worse. Each port was like the others, a triage of rescue and emergency personnel treating and helping people as they exited the ferries. As I walked, I prayed continually that Janice and my daughter were okay.

I kept walking north toward the George Washington Bridge so I could then walk across the Hudson River and into New York. This was my sliver of hope and focus. I was driven and determined to reach our hotel to see if my loved ones were there and safe. I passed Union City and then West New York. I continued walking past North Bergen and then Cliffside Park.

By the time I reached Edgewater, it was getting dark. I still had a ways to go to reach Fort Lee and the entrance to the George Washington Bridge. Along the way, I saw stores and offices that had been repurposed into makeshift shelters so people would have a place to sleep. I had been walking since ten o'clock that morning, and it was now after seven at night. I was worried I might be homeless later that night. As I pushed the shopping cart, I thought of the homeless guy who gave me the cart for twenty bucks. I wondered whether I was going to be just like the homeless guy that night without a place to sleep, but my concern for my welfare paled in comparison to my anguish about Janice and my daughter. I kept praying they were alive.

Dejected, I walked slowly away from the pay phone. Someone asked me where I was going and whether I needed a place to stay that night. Throughout the day, I witnessed random acts of kindness during my odyssey where people shrugged off the aloof and distant Big City attitude and extended genuine warmth and caring concern for complete strangers. Now someone was extending that kindness toward me.

I thanked him, but explained I was going to keep walking to the George Washington Bridge. I told him I was going to walk across the bridge and enter the city so I could be reunited with my family. The person looked at me with a surprised expression. He matter-of-factly told me no one was being allowed across the bridge. He said the George Washington Bridge had been closed hours before, and the city had been quarantined. He told me that anyone attempting to enter New York after dark would be arrested and fined five thousand dollars.

I was shocked upon hearing this news, and struggled to sit down on a nearby bench. I became extremely discouraged. I was praying Janice and my daughter were still alive and safe. I was worried I might not have a place to sleep. I had been walking, stopping to call, and walking almost nonstop for more than nine hours. I hadn't eaten. I had been determined to reach the George Washington Bridge, and now that I had almost reached it, I was told that crossing the bridge no longer was an option. My purpose, my plan, had been extinguished. I didn't know what to do. I had nowhere to go.

By now, I heard the twin towers had fallen. I was so sad. I prayed Janice and my daughter were safe, and I prayed for a miracle. Crossing the Hudson River for me was what crossing the Jordan River was like for the Israelites. I was not going to be able to cross the river without a miracle from God.

Just then, a small voice whispered, "Follow them."

As I looked up, no one was there. The person talking to me had left. When I looked toward the shore, I saw the same sight I had seen all day—emergency vehicles, flashing lights, and a mass of people exiting ferries. There wasn't anybody else around me, but I distinctly heard a voice. It was a soft voice, but I had clearly heard it.

"Follow them," it said.

Then something caught my attention as I looked toward the shore. There was a small group of people going in the opposite direction, toward the shore. They were walking against the tide of people getting off the ferries.

I grabbed my litigation case and suit coat and left my shopping cart. I walked quickly over to the area where they were walking. I asked a young lady in the group where she was going. She said she worked for a newspaper and her editor had sent her into New York to cover the story. She and the others heard a rumor someone from this shore, a place called the Grand Cave Marina, would smuggle people into the city for fifty dollars per person. Before I could ask if I could join them, the small group started walking toward a boat. I quickly followed.

Standing next to the boat was a small, slender man who perhaps was of Vietnamese descent. Orval's controller, Lewis, was Vietnamese and had immigrated to America with his family. This person looked like Lewis. Without saying a word, each of the people handed him fifty dollars and climbed down into the hold of the boat. I was the last one to board. With a leap of faith, I handed the man fifty dollars and climbed down into the boat. I heard the hatch slam shut behind me. It was completely dark inside the hold of the small boat. It was so quiet that I could hear the stranger next to me breathing. The sound of the engine starting startled me, and I soon heard the engine roar into gear as the boat thrust forward.

The Hudson River was extremely choppy. When the boat hit the first whitecap, I hit my head against the ceiling. At that moment, all I could think of was this little boat was going to crash and sink. I couldn't swim, and I was traveling across the Hudson with complete strangers. Absolutely no one in the world knew I was riding across the Hudson River, inside this little boat, late at night, in the dark.

Within a short period of time I heard the loud drone of the engine get quieter. The boat slowed and then came to a complete stop. The engine was shut off, and for a period of time, we all sat there in the quiet darkness. No one spoke. I didn't know if the boat had reached the other side of the Hudson or if it had been stopped somewhere in the middle of the river. I hoped we crossed over to the other side. In a moment, the hatch opened, and each of us silently and quickly climbed up and out of the hold and onto the deck of the boat. Through the lights, I could see we had reached the New York shoreline. No one said good-bye, thanks, or anything to each other. We all just quickly walked off the boat and disappeared into the darkness of the night—thankful to be on the New York side of the Hudson.

I soon realized I had entered New York at the West Harlem Pier. I knew I was considerably north of Midtown where our hotel was located, as I had been walking north on the Jersey side all day. I began walking south along the Henry Hudson Parkway, determined to reach the hotel. There were no cars anywhere. After awhile, the Henry Hudson Parkway turned into the Joe DiMaggio Parkway. I kept walking until I reached the point where I could turn left and head east through Central Park toward our hotel. Finally, I was there.

When I entered the hotel, the lobby was empty. I didn't stop to call our rooms and instead just proceeded to the elevator. I was in a hurry to get to our rooms. As the elevator took me up to our floor, I again prayed that Janice and my daughter were safe in our rooms. When the elevator opened, I quickly walked down the hallway to our door, but I was afraid to knock. What if no one answered? What if they weren't there? I said a little prayer and then knocked on the door. After what seemed like a long time, the door quickly opened. There were Janice and my daughter, smiling and crying at the same time.

"Sweetheart!"

"Daddy!"

All the prayers I had been praying all day had been answered. I thanked God for another miracle.

After tears and hugs, they told me that after I left that morning on the train, they decided to go for a jog before traveling to the observation deck at the twin towers. They were still getting ready in their hotel rooms after their jog when the first plane hit the tower. I was so thankful they were safe. So many others died that day.

The next morning, we had to change our scenery because I was so anxious and sad. I couldn't tolerate the television news any more. We spent the day at Central Park. Absolutely everything in New York was closed. We walked outside the hotel at eight o'clock that night, on 49th and Broadway, and there wasn't a single car on the street. We took a picture of Janice and our daughter standing in the middle of Broadway.

My heart ached for all the people killed and hurt in the tragedy of 9-11.

On Thursday morning, we heard the airports were going to be reopened in the afternoon, so we packed, checked out of the hotel, and took a cab to JFK Airport. As we were ready to board our plane to Los Angeles, we heard an announcement that the airport was being closed and evacuated again. At the same time we were getting ready to board our plane, additional suspected hijackers had been caught trying to board a plane—our plane to Los Angeles.[1] We heard the airports at La Guardia and Newark were also closed, and the suspects arrested were found with box cutters.[2] I was being forced to reexperience the event.

Rather than check back into the hotel, we decided to rent a car. Because of the huge rental car demand by people wanting to leave New York, our rental car company announced it would rent a car only to those customers who had reserved a rental car before September 11.

Because so many flights were cancelled, the rental car company also said it would permit one-way rentals. I had reserved a rental car before September 11, so we were able to rent a car and drive back to southern California. My daughter wanted to return in time to begin her second year of college.

Driving back to California was something positive we could do. Up until that point, I felt totally out of control and completely vulnerable and helpless. Deciding to drive home gave me the feeling I was taking back a small part of the control over my life that had been taken away. As we drove west across the Hudson River, we drove under a gigantic American flag suspended from the top of the bridge against the setting sun—a reminder that our spirit and our country's spirit was not broken. It was 5:30 p. m. Thursday. We arrived home at 2 a. m. Sunday morning.

I drove the 2,800-mile trip nonstop. Periodically, Janice drove for a couple of hours when I took a nap, but I couldn't sleep because I was still so anxious and agitated from the ordeal. My daughter wanted to be able to arrive on campus on Sunday to start college, but I also wanted to get home to see my two youngest children who were in first and third grade. They knew we were in New York. I didn't know if they would have been told something at school or may have overheard something on television about the terrorist attacks. I tried to call them on the phone to let them hear their daddy's voice, but each time I called Carmen over the past several days to talk to them, she never answered the phone, and she never had them call me back.

We originally scheduled our return flight back to California on Thursday so I would be able to pick up the younger children to begin my week of shared custody on Friday. At that time, they spent alternating weeks with me. As we drove home, I called Carmen and left messages to have the children call me back. I also left her a message that I would be at her residence by 10 a. m. Sunday morning to pick them up for my custody. However, when I arrived Sunday morning to pick up the children, they were not there. Carmen had left me a note saying she had left because she had "plans." She took the children with her to the swap meet.

After desperately trying to get back to our hotel to reach Janice and my daughter and after driving for about fifty hours nonstop, Carmen refused to let me see our children until after she received a phone call from the police. When she and the children were not home, I experienced another flashback and reexperienced the shock and anger I experienced previously during each of those times in the past when I had arrived home only to discover Cindy and Carmen had left with the children.

After awhile, my routine returned to normal, but I was anything but normal. I was not the same. I would get sad and start crying for apparently no reason. More disturbing though, I couldn't sleep. Just about every night, I would wake up between two and three in the morning. Some nights I would scream out loud in my sleep. Each time I awoke, my T-shirt was soaked with perspiration. Sometimes I would remember the night terrors, but most of the time, I wouldn't. I was constantly exhausted.

About a year later, I thought I was over my trip to New York, but then all the networks aired an anniversary program. I remember at the time wanting to watch the program, but after only about ten minutes, I turned it off, sobbing. I couldn't take it anymore.

I increasingly couldn't complete work or even simple tasks. I worked out of a home office, so I spent most days by myself working. There were days where I couldn't bring myself to walk to the mailbox. On some days, I would manage to walk out to the mailbox and get the mail, but I then wouldn't be able to open it. On other days, I would just sit and stare at my computer for hours, unable to turn it on.

Janice and the children brought me happiness, of course, and I enjoyed participating in the children's sports and activities and school events. We took vacations and celebrated holidays. We shared many, many happy and joyous times. However, without warning, I then again inexplicably would become sad.

What was most perplexing to me about my situation was that I didn't know what was happening or what was wrong. Some of the time, I would get sad when someone died or when something happened, but other times, I would get sad by just being alone. Something would happen, or I would hear a sound and a flashback would occur, forcing me to relive a prior traumatic experience.

I understood what the doctor told me about my PTSD symptoms from having experienced September 11. When something reminded me of that experience, the sight or sound would take be back to New York. It was as if I were there again. I could understand why that would happen. What I found harder to understand was how the shocking and traumatic collective experiences relating to the custody and abandonment issues had profoundly affected me. They were connected in a perplexing way. In both experiences, I was trying to rescue and protect those I loved. I was trying to insulate them and keep them from being harmed.

Early in my treatment, one of the stress tests I was administered was a test called the Holmes-Rahe Life Stress Inventory, also called the Social Readjustment Rating Scale (SRRS).[3] In completing this stress test, a patient is asked to indicate which life stressors he has experienced within the prior twelve months. Each individual life stressor is assigned a value. At the test's conclusion, the points are added to determine the level of stress experienced by the patient in an attempt to predict the probability that the cumulative stress experienced from the sum total of those life experiences will result in a health-related illness.

If the total is less than 150 points, then you have a low susceptibility to encounter stress-induced health issues. If the total is between 150 and 300 points, then you were predicted to have a fifty percent chance of experiencing a major stress-induced health breakdown within the next two years. If the total is more than 300 points, then the probability of experiencing a major stress-induced health breakdown within the next two years is increased to eighty percent.

The following is a copy of the SRRS:

The Holmes-Rahe Life Stress Inventory
The Social Readjustment Rating Scale
INSTRUCTIONS: Mark down the point value of each of these life events that has happened to you during the previous year. Total these associated points.

Life Event	Mean Value
1. Death of spouse	100
2. Divorce	73
3. Marital Separation from mate	65
4. Detention in jail or other institution	63
5. Death of a close family member	63
6. Major personal injury or illness	53
7. Marriage	50
8. Being fired at work	47
9. Marital reconciliation with mate	45
10. Retirement from work	45
11. Major change in the health or behavior of a family member	44
12. Pregnancy	40
13. Sexual Difficulties	39
14. Gaining a new family member (i.e.. a birth, adoption, older adult moving in, etc)	39
15. Major business readjustment	39
16. Major change in financial state (i.e.. a lot worse or better off than usual)	38
17. Death of a close friend	37
18. Changing to a different line of work	36
19. Major change in the number of arguments w/spouse (i.e.. either a lot more or a lot less than usual regarding child rearing, personal habits, etc.)	35
20. Taking on a mortgage (for home, business, etc..)	31
21. Foreclosure on a mortgage or loan	30
22. Major change in responsibilities at work (i.e. promotion, demotion, etc.)	29
23. Son or daughter leaving home (marriage, attending college, joined mil.)	29
24. In-law troubles	29
25. Outstanding personal achievement	28
26. Spouse beginning or ceasing work outside the home	26
27. Beginning or ceasing formal schooling	26
28. Major change in living condition (new home, remodeling, deterioration of neighborhood or home etc.)	25
29. Revision of personal habits (dress manners, associations, quitting smoking)	24
30. Troubles with the boss	23
31. Major changes in working hours or conditions	20
32. Changes in residence	20
33. Changing to a new school	20
34. Major change in usual type and/or amount of recreation	19
35. Major change in church activity (i.e.. a lot more or less than usual)	19
36. Major change in social activities (clubs, movies,visiting, etc.)	18
37. Taking on a loan (car, tv,freezer,etc)	17
38. Major change in sleeping habits (a lot more or a lot less than usual)	16
39. Major change in number of family get-togethers ("")	15
40. Major change in eating habits (a lot more or less food intake, or very different meal hours or surroundings)	15
41. Vacation	13
42. Major holidays	12
43. Minor violations of the law (traffic tickets, jaywalking, disturbing the peace, etc)	11

Now, add up all the points you have to find your score.

150pts or less means a relatively low amount of life change and a low susceptibility to stress-induced health breakdown.

150 to 300 pts implies about a 50% chance of a major health breakdown in the next 2 years.

300pts or more raises the odds to about 80%, according to the Holmes-Rahe statistical prediction model.

When I took the test, my total wildly exceeded the 300-point threshold. With the custody battles spanning more than twenty years, the stress factors seemed to repeat themselves and overlap relentlessly and incessantly year after year.

I was trying my best to manage things. I would have good days, or I would be able to get by for a period of time, but then things again would seem to fall apart. At times, I felt like I was in a fog, without direction, simply surviving. As if this wasn't bad enough, over a period of four years, a number of deaths of family and close friends made me extremely sad.

During September and October of 2004, my friend, client, and neighbor had two of his children die within a month of each other. Scott died in his sleep at college from an allergic reaction to prescription medication. Shari was killed when another vehicle crossed the median and hit her car. Their youngest sister, Kate, was my daughter's best childhood friend. Shari sometimes babysat the children. Losing one child was tragic, but losing another child only a month later was devastating for them. I was extremely saddened for their losses because we lived several houses away from them and knew them so well.

Then in March of 2005, Dad died. Since he was ninety-one, I expected it, but when I got the news, I was devastated. Over the Christmas holiday, a few months earlier, I took my family back to South Dakota and spent a few days with him and Mom. I knew it was probably going to be the last time we spoke to each other and saw each other. We had a nice time visiting, but we never talked about what happened almost thirty years earlier. When it came time for us to leave, it was snowing hard outside.

My parents wanted us to stay longer, but we had to leave so we could get back for work and school. After everyone said their good-byes, I walked up to Dad and shook his hand as I said good-bye. We shook hands like we had done countless times before, but then he gave me a hug and said, "I forgive you." I looked back at him and said, "I forgive you too." Actually, I had forgiven him years before. This was our way of telling the other we were sorry. We both seemed to know this would be the last time we would ever see each other.

I tried my best to cope with my feelings, but there were just too many memories, hurts, and heartaches. If someone is suffering from depression, most people may just think they are sad or have hurt feelings or moods that keep them down or from feeling happy. However, depression is much more than that. Depression is *painful.* The sadness *hurts.*

My doctor prescribed Lexapro to help me feel better and Ambien to help me sleep at night. I did notice an improvement, and I was less irritable and impatient. However, I felt the medication worsened the situation. I hated that depression was considered a mental illness. I hated taking medication because it made me feel weak and broken. After I would start feeling better, undoubtedly because the medication was helping me, I decided just to stop taking it. I told myself I really didn't need it and I just needed to try harder.

However, quitting cold turkey was probably the worst thing I could have done because it caused my moods and feelings to become even more unpredictable. Eventually, I followed my doctor's advice and took the medication as prescribed. During the fall of 2005, I was accepted into the alternative discipline program, which was offered by the state bar and recommended by Judge Talcott. This was a program designed to help attorneys who encountered problems in their practice because of mental health issues or substance abuse issues.

My progress during the next year could best be described as sporadic. I would do well and then I wouldn't. There didn't seem to be any steady improvement in my recovery.

However, beginning in 2007, I entered a period of about eighteen months where there were times I just crashed. In

January 2007, a friend who also coached softball suddenly died of cancer, leaving his little family behind. His daughter and my daughter played against each other on different teams in the youth recreation league, and later, they were teammates on the all-star team. Walter was only thirty-seven. It was so sudden. He was told he had cancer in December and had begun feeling better after Christmas. However, within a couple of weeks, he was gone. I didn't know him particularly well, but his death left me feeling so sad because of the connection with our daughters.

Later that summer, two more deaths broke my heart. I had become friends with a group of guys who all played tennis together at a neighborhood tennis club. We played in a doubles tennis league in a round-robin format on Wednesday nights, and then on Saturday mornings, we played doubles King of the Hill. If a doubles team kept winning, it kept the court against all challengers. Our group often enjoyed sitting around late on Wednesday nights, just talking and having a beer after we finished playing tennis. We also enjoyed playing in club tournaments with and against each other. I wasn't a very good singles player, but I was a pretty fair doubles player. This means I don't have a very good backhand. To compensate, I played the side of the court that allowed me to hit forehand shots on balls down the middle.

Michael, however, was a very good player and coached a local high school tennis team in his spare time. He was left-handed, so he played the other side of the court, which meant he also had a forehand shot on balls in the middle of the court. We had a lot of fun together, and we even played together in a number of countywide tournaments, winning those where Michael carried me. Michael was the kind of guy you loved to play with and play against. Michael also owned a restaurant, and I had the privilege of representing him in court on a matter concerning the restaurant.

Michael's oldest daughter was seven years younger than my oldest daughter. Like me, he also had a younger daughter. At the end of the summer of 2007, Michael, his wife Diana, and their youngest daughter, Sydney, drove Michael's oldest daughter to college to begin her freshman year at the University of Arizona. As they were driving back from Tucson to southern California, a truck crossed the median on the freeway and hit them. Michael, who was driving, was killed. Sydney, who was sitting behind him in the backseat, was also killed. Sydney was just six years old. I was crushed by their deaths. They were just so sudden and so senseless. I was reminded that just six year earlier, I drove back from New York to southern California after 9-11 so my oldest daughter could start her second year at college. I felt so terribly, terribly sad for their family. It also made me so extremely sad.

Within a year after Michael and Sydney died, Mom died.

No words exist to describe the loss I felt when Mom died.

6

Steps to Healing

I will praise you, O LORD, with all my heart; I will tell of all your wonders. I will be glad and rejoice in You; I will sing praise to Your name, O Most High.

—Psalm 9:1–2

When hurtful, tragic, or disappointing events occur in our lives, we are supposed to feel sad. It is natural for us to need to grieve over a loss. We have hurt or sad feelings because something happened that we didn't expect. We expect things to turn out. We expect or hope that people will be kind. We make plans. We hope for the best. We look to the better angels in people. There is a cadence and pace to life that we strive for and call normal.

When we are young, our parents care for us. They do almost everything for us. Then as we enter school, our teachers act as surrogates in place of our parents to teach us about the things we will need to know to be successful later in life. We soon gain our own independence and begin to do and think for ourselves, even while our parents are still there to nurture and encourage us. Eventually, we begin to plan our own lives, make our own decisions and our own plans.

Perhaps when we were younger, we didn't appreciate or agree with the decisions made for us. Perhaps parents or teachers disappointed us, let us down or even abused or abandoned us. Perhaps those childhood events and decisions impacted our ability as adults to make decisions for ourselves and our children. When life doesn't work out the way we plan or even the way we would like or our decisions don't produce the intended results, how we react may depend on what we learned or experienced in our youth.

Despite our best-laid plans, stuff happens. Maybe someone gets hurt or injured. Maybe a parent or loved one disappoints us or abandons us altogether. Someone contracts a disease. Someone else loses a job. Love disappoints or perhaps even breaks our heart. Someone may have disappointed you or let you down or even straight-out lied to you or deceived you.

In each of these situations, it is entirely natural to feel disappointment. You are expected to experience sadness. We are supposed to grieve. However, when the disappointment turns into despair, when our sadness turns into depression, and when our grief over a loss translates into our becoming lost, we need to get help. We cannot possibly overcome the situation alone. We are not meant to be alone. We are not meant to have to solve all our problems by ourselves.

The Internet is a wonderful resource. Electronics each year become more and more amazing. However, the danger with the Internet, in my view, is that people don't interact with other people. Let me explain what I mean by this. We use the Internet and our electronics to engage socially through Facebook, Twitter, and text messages. But that is not the same as speaking to someone face-to-face, having direct personal contact, reading one's body language and facial expressions, and listening to one's tone of voice. Even Skype doesn't allow you to shake hands with someone, give somebody a hug, or wipe away a tear. While the easily accessible Internet allows us to read, research, learn, and entertain, it generally means we do all those things while alone and isolated.

If you are suffering from depression, PTSD or any other mental disorder or illness, you probably don't know it. You only know something is different, and something has changed. When that occurs, you need to get help.

The Holmes-Rahe Life Stress Inventory or Social Readjustment Rating Scale (SRRS) is a good place to begin your awareness. When it was devised in 1967, it was considered groundbreaking because, before then, social studies and tests merely confirmed what had happened. In other words, after someone became ill, studies and research were conducted to determine the cause and explain the reason. Holmes and Rahe's Stress Inventory was one of the first studies of its kind that attempted to predict stressors or life events that could be expected to cause illness before they occurred. In this sense, it was more than simply an inventory of what is happening in one's life. Rather, it was an attempt to provide recognition that events that we experience can impact our physical health.

The same can be said for mental health. When you are sad, angry, irritable, or depressed, you are experiencing symptoms that may describe a mental illness or disorder. Your behavior is symptomatic of something bigger. Your mind and your brain are trying to tell you something. You are exhibiting warning signs that you need to get help before things get worse.

In my case, that help was my therapist, Dr. S. He was able to help me understand that cognitive behavior can impact mental health. He helped me understand we cannot control life's events. We can only control how we respond and react to those life events by exercising certain behavioral skills in response.

In my view, Dr. S is a brilliant psychologist. I would recommend him to anyone. I had seen other psychologists, but their approach was from a different perspective. There was nothing in and of itself wrong with their perspective, but it just wasn't right for me or what I needed. Dr. S approached my situation from the perspective of cognitive behavior by helping me understand how to think differently about my present environment and past events. He taught me cognitive behavioral skills that helped me focus my mind on the present without cluttering it with past mistakes or clouding it with future anxieties.

Cognitive behavioral therapy is based on the principle that cognition (our thoughts or what we think) affects our behavior. When we are depressed, our thoughts are mostly negative. As such, those negative thoughts impact our decisions and, ultimately, our behavior. With cognitive behavioral therapy, the goal is to understand the negative attitude and thoughts and then disconnect and separate those negative thoughts so they don't affect or impact how the present is viewed or experienced. Once those negative thoughts are displaced, the present can be evaluated and enjoyed without the distortion of judgments about the past or anxieties about the future.

The interaction between therapist and patient in cognitive behavioral therapy is entirely transparent. While the therapist is the expert in treating your emotions, you the patient are the expert in how the emotions feel or, to state it more accurately, how you feel about your emotions. At the outset, the therapist describes the process for the patient and explains to the patient that they will interact together.

What sets cognitive behavioral therapy apart from other treatment therapies is that it goes beyond simply having the patient describe the feelings, emotions, and moods. In cognitive behavioral therapy, the patient acquires a general knowledge about depression and a specific awareness about his own negative thought process.

The patient in cognitive behavioral therapy learns that depression basically is the result of negative thoughts automatically being applied to experiences. The patient is then equipped with skill sets or tools used to disassemble those negative thoughts. In small increments and steps, the patient practices using those skill sets upon new experiences so past judgments or future anxieties don't unduly influence those new experiences negatively. During the process, the patient often must unlearn existing thinking patterns and behaviors.

Cognitive behavioral therapy is the realization that the way the patient thinks about a situation, event, or problem often is distorted and not based on reality. This is not a bad thing; it is just a negative thing. All situations, events or problems, are not negative, but a depressed person often views them negatively or, to state it more accurately, automatically thinks about them in a negative way. The patient is then able to take his skill sets and tools in his toolbox and use them in real time to change his thoughts, perceptions, decisions, and behavior. With small, short-term goals, the patient uses the skill sets and tools to be able to exercise discernment and gain confidence in his ability to control how he responds or reacts to new stimuli by thinking differently. By controlling how he thinks about new events, the patient understands he is able to gain control over his thoughts, decisions, and behavior.

Following is my list of seven effective skill sets or tools I learned through cognitive behavioral therapy that helped me defeat depression and overcome PTSD. The labels are my labels, and each description of each skill set is my attempt to describe them in terms you easily might be able to apply to your situation. Therapists may have clinical names for each skill set or tool that differ from my labels, so my list is not intended to be clinically correct or exhaustive. The name of each skill set is not necessarily important. What is important is the application of each of the skills in overcoming depression or PTSD. The following skills worked for me, and I hope they will work for you.

That said, this self-help list of skill sets is not provided to replace treatment or therapy. If you are suffering from depression or PTSD or if you have any of the symptoms of depression or PTSD, you should seek the consultation and treatment of a professional psychologist for evaluation. Each patient and each situation is different. You need a correct diagnosis and an effective treatment program tailored for you.

What I found is that mental health is an ongoing and continuing process. Even after I got well and overcame depression and PTSD, I would continue to experience sadness at times. There were times that I would experience conditions that would cause me to reexperience traumatic events from my past. When that occurred, I simply would return to my toolbox of skill sets and practice what I learned.

I cannot overemphasize this point. Just like a cancer can go into remission and then return, you can and will have setbacks and relapses in your recovery of depression and PTSD. Even with professional treatment, you will again become sad or reexperience trauma. However, by continuing with your recovery program and by practicing your skill sets, your sadness will not spiral into another depression. You will learn how to manage and control it and let it pass. You will learn how to manage and control PTSD so a reexperience of a prior trauma will be allowed to wash over you. All this is part of the wellness program. You overcome depression or PTSD or other mental illness by becoming a survivor. One way to think about it is to compare mental illness to cancer.

Just like someone who has survived and has overcome cancer, you can survive and overcome depression and PTSD. Becoming sad again or re-experiencing a prior trauma doesn't mean you have failed or that you are going to spiral again into a period of depression. Rather, it simply means you have to treat those emotions and experiences by using your treatment program and by practicing and exercising your skill sets.

Stuff will continue to happen. That's life. That fact about life will never change. However, what can and will change is how you deal with and handle it. You cannot control what happens in life, but you can control how you react to and manage life's events. If you get physically sick or hurt, you go to the doctor and get a prescription or appropriate treatment that will make you well again. Why should your approach be any different in the care and treatment for your mind than it is for your body? When you experience a setback or a relapse, don't panic. Realize that a setback or a relapse is a normal part of your recovery.

Think of it this way. Perhaps your vehicle doesn't work properly or it was damaged in an accident. When that happens, you take it to a professional for a diagnosis. Maybe it needs to go to the body shop for repairs. The same is true for our bodies. Similarly, maybe there is something in your car's computer that needs adjusting. The same is true for our minds. Just like our car needs a proper diagnosis when it breaks down, when we break down, we need a professional diagnosis.

Sometimes we need body work for our physical injuries, and sometimes we need to work on our body's computer system—our mind. Just as there are specialists and neurologists who treat brain injuries, there also are specialists—psychologists and psychiatrists—who treat injuries to our mind. Those mental illnesses have been ignored for too long.

Even after your vehicle is repaired, it is easy to understand and comprehend it will continue to need to be serviced and repaired so it can work effectively. In the same way, when we continue to add miles to our bodies and when life's experiences continue to take their toll on our minds, we need to accept that we will need periodic treatment and adjustments, both physically and mentally. The treatment program and the skill sets are the adjustments we can make to the way we think about things.

Think of the skill sets as routine maintenance or service work for your mind just as your vehicle needs regular service or maintenance. Practice your skill sets, get regular checkups, and when necessary, seek professional help. Just as it is advisable to obtain annual or regular physical checkups or examinations, we also should get regular mental checkups.

My hope is that my story will encourage you to feel better and to get the help you need just like I had to get the help I needed. Often, people know they need help, but they don't know why they need help, and they don't know what kind of help they need. I want you to know you're not alone. I hope that by reading my story, you will obtain an understanding of how the following skill sets or tools have helped me in my battle with depression and PTSD so that they also may help you.

I learned the practical application of the skill sets, together with the spiritual application of biblical truth, created the most effective treatment program for me. They were designed to work in a natural progression so one skill set prepares you to utilize the next skill set. The more you use them, the more confidence you will achieve so you can overcome your depression or PTSD.

I also believe that many of our negative thoughts and meanings are planted by Satan to deceive us. For this reason, I provided both a practical application and a spiritual application for each skill set. The practical application of each skill set is based on principles of cognitive behavioral therapy that will help you understand and overcome depression and PTSD. The spiritual application of each skill set is based on biblical verses and Scripture that will encourage you and sustain you in your battles with Satan over the meaning you attach to life's events. You will learn how both the practical cognitive behavioral application and the Christian spiritual application used together can overcome depression, defeat Satan's deceptions, and develop a more personal relationship with Christ.

Recognition

The prudent see danger and take refuge, but the simple
keep going and suffer for it.

—Proverbs 27:12

The first skill set to learn is recognition. Just like the Holmes-Rahe Life Stress Inventory, you have to get an assessment or inventory of your symptoms. While the SRRS is a place to begin, the most important first step you can take is to seek out professional help. The only thing you know for sure is that you don't know what's wrong with you. You need someone to help you diagnose the situation, the condition, the problem.

A mental health professional will assess your mental health by talking to you to learn your symptoms. Each of your expressed emotions and feelings are factors used to determine your diagnosis. Additional tests can be administered that search for personality disorders or other behavioral conditions that may exist and that may affect the diagnosis and treatment plan. By explaining what is happening, you will be able to allow your mental health professional to determine why it is happening. Only a trained professional, a psychiatrist or psychologist, can do this effectively.

In the past, people may not have sought professional help because insurance did not pay for the cost. Generally, insurance companies were not required to provide insurance coverage for mental illnesses. And until 1996, insurance companies were not even required to pay for all the mental illness benefits provided under a plan. In 1996, Congress finally passed legislation requiring insurance companies to provide the same amount of mental illness benefits as provided for medical and surgical benefits in plans offering mental illness coverage. However, the 1996 Act contained loopholes used by the insurance companies to avoid paying for mental illness benefits under group insurance plans.[1]

Congress did not close the loopholes until 2008. It then required all group health plans offering mental illness coverage to provide the same parity of mental illness benefits that the plans provided for medical, surgical, and hospital benefits.[2] Even then, the insurance companies were not required to provide coverage for mental illness or substance abuse. The 2008 Act only applied to insurance companies already providing coverage for mental illness benefits within existing plans. The 2008 Act did not actually require insurance companies to offer coverage or provide benefits for mental illnesses or for substance use disorders.

The Patient Protection and Affordable Care Act (Obamacare) finally ensured that insurance companies would be required to provide insurance coverage for mental illnesses and behavioral disorders. In June 2012, the United States Supreme Court upheld the constitutionality of the Affordable Care Act, and on February 20, 2013, insurance companies finally were required to provide insurance coverage and benefits for mental illnesses, behavioral disorders, drug addiction, and alcohol abuse.[3]

You can now finally obtain health insurance and use that health insurance to pay for mental health treatment. No longer can insurance companies discriminate you because you seek treatment for mental illnesses or substance use disorders. No longer can insurance companies refuse to provide you with insurance coverage and benefits by claiming you had a preexisting condition. No longer can insurance companies arbitrarily set cap limits on occurrence or lifetime coverage. Get to a psychologist or a psychiatrist and get a diagnosis of your symptoms.

Often, we experience sadness, anger, or other secondary emotions when disappointed by an event's outcome. When that happens, the first skill set to employ is recognition. We need to be able to recognize what is happening. We need to be able to exercise discernment to distinguish and disarm our feelings and emotions.

Sometimes when people explain their experience or situation, they may describe their frustration by stating that an event or their life is out of control. We have an inherent desire to control our surroundings because we feel better when we feel we are in control.

Recognition is the realization that we are in actual control of virtually nothing. Sure, we make plans but someone once said the way to make God laugh is to tell Him your plans. The only thing we can control is our reaction or response to what happens. Recognition is this realization. Dr. S described recognition with a metaphor about a storm. The gray clouds come in, the rain falls, and the storm rages in our lives. When that happens, most of the time there isn't anything that can be done to prevent it. You just have to take shelter.

Storms also happen with our emotions. A flood of emotions may suddenly and unexpectedly rush over us. It may be a flashback related to PTSD or an event that makes us sad.

The key to recognition is to be able to acquire an appreciation and awareness of your feelings and emotions and to make sure your emotions don't last. Dr. S calls it "putting up your umbrella." When it starts raining, you need to get out of the rain. When you find yourself in a situation from which you are unable to extricate yourself and you cannot get out of the rain, the only thing you can do is put up your umbrella as a shield to protect you from the storm of feelings and emotions, and let them wash over you and subside. Instead of trying to control and stop the storm, just put up your umbrella to protect yourself until it passes.

Sometimes we believe the emotions we experience, such as anger, are being caused by someone else. We often use the expression that someone "makes me so mad." When we do that, not only are we admitting we are not in control, but we also are relinquishing to someone else the control over our emotions. Sure, there may be times where someone does something that causes you to react in a certain way. We may even suspect the other person is our antagonist and does it intentionally. They just push our buttons.

The secret is to recognize the trigger that evokes such emotions. You need to recognize what the other person is doing or what is happening that triggers you to overreact. Dr. S describes this as taking the energy out of the emotion. Imagine trying to use the television remote control when the batteries no longer work. If you continue to push the button, nothing happens.

Recognition is the same principle. The reason nothing happens even though you continue to push the button on the remote is because the batteries no longer have any energy stored in them. If you remove the batteries altogether, the remote no longer has an energy source.

The same technique can be applied with people. Even when someone is deliberately trying to push your buttons to elicit an intended reaction, you can avoid reacting or overreacting. Upon recognizing the trigger, you recognize what is happening so you can remove the batteries from the remote and prevent the other person from pushing your buttons.

You can take the charge or energy out of the situation so you don't overreact or let the situation escalate. So many of us get hung up on wanting to control or change the situation or wanting to control or change the other person. Sometimes we may even want to control the storm. We think if we can just remove the storm or eliminate the problem or if we can just control the situation or the other person, then our life will get back to normal. We end up trying to change or control the other person, or we end up trying to eliminate the problem. We may as well try to control the weather.

We can't control or change the weather. We can't control or change other people. We can't control or prevent the stuff that happens in our lives. We only can control how we react or respond to people and events. By exercising control over your response and reaction, you can control your emotions.

In a sort of strange way, you then are also able to affect a corresponding change in the other person's behavior. Notice that I didn't say you would be able to control or change the other person or the other person's behavior. However, you can affect a change in the other person's behavior by first controlling your own behavior. Have you ever noticed what happens if you remain calm when someone else starts yelling? The result is the other person begins to calm down. If you begin to let the situation escalate, then you both soon will be yelling.

Dr. S calls this behavioral tool "being the thermostat instead of the thermometer." A thermometer is filled with mercury. A key property of mercury is that it will expand when heated and contract when cooled. For this reason, it is perfect for thermometers. When the temperature surrounding the thermometer is raised, the mercury rises in the thermometer, and when the temperature cools, the mercury settles down. This is why volatile people are called *mercurial*.

When we are the thermometer, we become mercurial and react to whatever is happening around us by letting ourselves be controlled by our environment or events. When it starts to get hot and a storm begins raging around us, we become hot like the storm. We become the same temperature as the storm around us. We are reacting and sometimes overreacting as if we were the thermometer. As a result, the situation escalates.

When we become the thermostat instead of the thermometer, we get to control the temperature around us. When we literally stay cool instead of letting our emotions become inflamed, then we are able to lower the temperature in our environment. This is what professionals are trained to do. Firemen, policemen, doctors, and nurses are trained to handle an emergency. Military personnel are trained to stay calm during battle. In the same way, professional athletes undergo mental training to slow down the play, hyper focus, and block out distractions so they can get in the zone and perform to their optimal abilities.

Just like all these professionals train their minds, you can train your mind. You can learn how to block out the distractions. You can learn how to stay calm during the storm. You can learn how to stay cool under pressure.

Ernest Hemmingway defined courage as "grace under pressure."[4] John Kennedy, in the preface to his book *Profiles in Courage*, said, "This is a book about that most admirable of human virtues—courage. 'Grace under pressure,' Ernest Hemmingway defined it."[5] You can train your mind to be courageous so that you can exhibit grace under pressure.

Often when we find ourselves in a situation where someone or something has disappointed or hurt us, we react by getting angry. However, this is a selfish response. When you react this way, you are giving in to temptation. Just like when people eat comfort food to make themselves feel better, people also fall back to comfort emotions to make themselves feel better. Anger is one such comfort emotion.

It is easier to become judgmental or angry and blame someone for whatever is happening than it is to remain calm. It takes courage or grace under pressure to resist the temptation to react in such a negative way. You can cultivate the courage to control your reaction and response even when you find yourself in a situation where you feel you are being attacked.

It is the only thing you can control. Train your mind. Put up your umbrella. Remove the batteries. Be the thermostat. Turn down the temperature. Exercise courage. Demonstrate grace under pressure.

The spiritual or Christian part of the recognition skill set is mercy and grace. Even when someone or something disappoints you or is the reason or fault for something happening and rightfully deserving of blame or judgment, the Christian principle of recognition is to respond with mercy and grace instead of with anger and judgment. Instead of being quick to condemn, the Christian response is to provide mercy, grace, and love.

Mercy is the spiritual principle of not receiving the blame or judgment we deserve for our faults and mistakes. We rightfully deserve punishment or retribution, but instead, we receive mercy. Grace is the spiritual principle of receiving the blessings and love we haven't earned and don't deserve. As a Christian, when we find ourselves in the middle of a storm, we would do well to exercise the skill set of recognition in such a way to show mercy and extend blessing and grace toward the other person.

This is what Jesus did for each of us. While we were still sinners, He died for our sins on the cross. "But God demonstrates his own love for us in this: While we were still sinners, Christ died for us" (Romans 5:8).

When we find ourselves in a situation where we have been hurt or disappointed, our sense of fairness and our sense of right and wrong sometimes gets the better of us. We want justice. At least that is what we think we want. Satan may be telling us someone deserves to be blamed to satisfy that sense of justice within us. When we get angry, we selfishly give in to that temptation.

I remember a situation at our farm where Dad extended mercy toward me after I made a mistake. Dad had just purchased a new tractor. It was the new John Deere model and cost more than a hundred thousand dollars. I stayed out of school that day to help him get the planter ready to begin planting that year's corn crop. We spent the entire morning getting the machinery ready to begin planting, and we were going to begin planting corn right after lunch. The last instruction Dad gave me before he walked into the house for lunch was to tell me to fill it up.

On our farm, we had our own gas pump, just like the ones at the gas stations with an underground gas tank under the pump. A large above-ground storage container for diesel fuel also was located nearby the gas tank. When dad told me to "fill it up," I drove the new John Deere tractor over to the tanks and filled it up—with gasoline. But, our new tractor required diesel fuel.

I was probably daydreaming or thinking about something else when I made my mistake. I knew the tractor needed diesel fuel instead of gas. But I filled our brand-new hundred-grand John Deere tractor with gasoline. I think I even topped off the tank just for good measure.

After filling up the tractor, I walked to the house to join Dad for lunch. Just as I entered the kitchen and closed the door behind me, I realized I had put gasoline in the tractor. I just stood there.

Dad was already eating lunch, and he looked up at me from the kitchen table. I was still holding on to the doorknob (maybe it was my instinctive reaction to the mistake I had just made, just in case I needed to make a quick exit).

Dad said, "What's wrong?"

I looked at him and said, "I just realized I put gas in the new tractor."

He studied me for a second and then said, "Did you start it?"

I responded with a weak "no," not understanding the significance of his question. The distance from the gas pump to the house was just a short walk, so I simply walked to the house after I had filled the tractor with gas instead of starting the tractor and driving it up to the house.

As Dad looked at me, he must have seen the regret on my face. He could have gotten angry with me, but instead he just said, "That's okay. We'll take care of it after lunch."

We spent the rest of that afternoon draining the fuel line and removing all the gasoline from the tractor. Had I started the tractor, I could have damaged the engine.

Dad could have exploded. He could have yelled at me for being so negligent. He could have screamed at me for being so careless with such an expensive tractor. If he had done any of those things, I certainly would have deserved it. But instead of getting angry, he showed me mercy. I didn't get the punishment I deserved.

When our sense of fairness compels us to inflict deserved retribution instead of mercy and grace, consider the story in the Gospel of John where the Pharisees took a woman caught in the act of adultery to Jesus, stating that under the law her punishment required her to be stoned to death. When they questioned Jesus whether she should be stoned, Jesus said, "If any one of you is without sin, let him be the first to throw a stone at her" (John 8:7).

When you use the skill set of recognition, you can resist the initial reaction to act out in anger, especially when you feel justified or when the voice in your head is telling you to feel justified. Once you recognize the trigger that may cause you to react in anger, instead of acting on it, seize the opportunity to show mercy and extend grace. It will have a multiplier effect, not only for the other person but also for you.

Reflection

For the word of God is living and powerful, and is a
discerner of the thoughts and intents of the heart.

—Hebrews 4:12

Reflection is the skill set in the exercise of discernment, which means to distinguish mentally. The word *discern* is derived from the Latin word *discernere.* The prefix *dis* means "off or away" while the root *cernere* means to "distinguish, separate, or sift." To *sift* means "to sort and then discard what is undesirable or not needed or wanted."

Discernment is the perfect word to describe the process of sorting out your thoughts and emotions. It is not enough just to recognize the threatening thoughts or confusing comments that you hear inside of you. Not only must you distinguish and separate those thoughts, but you also must discard them off and away.

The skill of reflection is mindfulness. It is being mindful that you need to be still and reflect upon what is happening before you react. Once you recognize the trigger or event, you need to reflect and exercise discernment. Before you react to the trigger or event, practice mindfulness.

One way of doing this is through meditation, which helps you focus your mind on the present and prevent it from drifting to past regrets or future anxieties that may steal your joy in the present. Instead of allowing your thoughts to take you somewhere else, focus and train your thoughts on the immediate present. Rather than focus on intrusive thoughts about the past or future or about negative meanings or judgments, use your senses to experience only the present moment. Relax and slow your breathing. Let go of tension. Release the strain in your muscles. Remain still and calm.

When you become anxious, simplify. Avoid multitasking. In our technological age, we tend to do too many things at once. We check e-mails or text messages or tweets while in meetings, doing chores, or even listening to friends or family. We allow ourselves to become bombarded with an overflow of stimuli. The act of being mindful is to focus totally on the present moment. When you find yourself becoming agitated or frustrated or overwhelmed, unplug and unwind. Refocus your thoughts.

If you find your thoughts wandering or misdirecting you to negative thoughts or anxieties, refocus or redirect your thoughts to the immediate, present moment. Don't allow your mind or your thoughts to be misled or distracted. If your mind starts to race with negative thoughts or emotions, slowly focus again on slowing your breathing and your pulse rate. Breathe slowly through your nose, taking deep breaths, and then exhale out your mouth. Close your eyes and use your senses of touch and smell to experience the moment. Then open your eyes and focus only on what you see in the present moment. By doing this, you deliberate, appreciate, experience, and savor the present with all your senses.

When you practice mindfulness with your thoughts, you exercise discernment and sort your thoughts. Ask yourself which thoughts bring you joy and which cause you to be angered or frustrated. Reject negative thoughts or those that assign blame or judgment. Focus instead on positive thoughts. By staying mindful, you will learn how to accept those negative thoughts or emotions and then release them. Rather than get anxious about them or try to avoid them, through reflection, you learn to accept them for what they are—simply negative thoughts, emotions, or judgments that aren't real.

Practicing reflection and mindfulness is crucial when you experience intrusive negative thoughts or emotions. However, you also can practice reflection and mindfulness throughout the day. Schedule times for meditation. Practice staying calm and relaxed. Some people who are depressed may avoid this quiet time because they think they can avoid the negative thoughts by staying busy or preoccupied. They may think that the negative thoughts may come precisely when they are alone or quiet. If that happens, just redirect your thoughts and your focus back to the present. Don't let your mind wander. Don't let those negative thoughts take your mind captive. Don't be a prisoner to those negative thoughts. Meditate. Stay mindful.

You can also apply the spiritual side of reflection. God is not the author of confusion.[6] Just as another person can push your buttons, the devil will push your buttons. The devil is the great accuser. He will deceive you into believing that something is your fault. He will make you feel guilty. He will make you feel like you failed. Just when things are happening, he will lie to you and plant messages in your mind to deceive you, mislead you, and try to get you to behave or react a certain way.

The devil's tools are blame, doubt, fear, confusion, distrust, criticism, gossip, negativity, despair, guilt, regret, prejudice, hopelessness, suspicion, fatalism, depression, ego, vanity, pride, deceit, insecurity, selfishness, temptation, indifference, anger, lust, envy, greed, and lies.

Satan's tools are innumerable, as he can use anyone or anything to deceive us. His toolbox has a bottomless pit called hell. His tools are limitless because he knows exactly what fears, temptations and weaknesses exist inside each and every one of us.

As Christians, the devil has no authority over us. The victory over Satan was already won with Christ's death and resurrection. During our time on this earth, Satan will continue to skulk about in his efforts to deceive, divide, and destroy. We can defeat and crush Satan with the full armor of God and with the love and saving grace of Jesus Christ.[7]

As Paul instructed in his letter to the Ephesians:

> Be strong in the Lord and in his mighty power. Put on *the full armor of God* so that you can take your stand against the devil's schemes. For our struggle is not against flesh and blood, but against the rulers, against the authorities, against the powers of this dark world and against the spiritual forces of evil in the heavenly realms. Therefore put on the full armor of God, so that when the day of evil comes, you may be able to *stand your ground,* and after you have done everything, to stand. Stand firm then, with the belt of truth buckled round your waist, with the breastplate of righteousness in place, and with your feet fitted with the readiness that comes from the gospel of peace. In addition to all this, take up the shield of faith, with which you can extinguish all the flaming arrows of the evil one. Take the helmet of salvation and the sword of the Spirit, which is the word of God.[8]

The belt of truth is Jesus, who said, "I am the way and the truth and the life; no one comes to the Father, but through me."[9]

The breastplate of righteousness is "not having a righteousness of my own that comes from the law, but that which is through faith in Christ—the righteousness that comes from God on the basis of faith."[10]

The shield of faith is able to overcome Satan's attacks.

> For every child of God overcomes the world; and the victorious principle which has overcome the world is our *faith.* Who but the man that believes that Jesus is the Son of God overcomes the world?[11]

The helmet of salvation is Jesus. God has provided that Jesus himself is our helmet to shield and protect our mind. In Hebrew, *Yeshua* (Jesus) means "salvation."

Finally, the sword of the spirit is the Word of God, the Bible.

Among all the above elements in the armor of God, the sword is commonly considered an offensive weapon. During Roman times, the sword was called *gladius*, from where we get the word *gladiator*. The Word of God is our best weapon against Satan, but it is even better than a sword.

> For the word of God is living and powerful, and sharper than any two-edged sword, piercing even to the division of soul and spirit, and of joints and marrow, and is a discerner of the thoughts and intents of the heart.[12]

Let me repeat that truth promised in the book of Hebrews. "The Word of God…is a *discerner* of the thoughts and intents of the heart." The Word of God will help with our discernment against Satan's tools. God's Word, which is "living and powerful and sharper than any two-edged sword" can pierce "even to the division of soul and spirit and of joints and marrow." It is not enough just to understand the conflicting thoughts and emotions. We have to put them off and away.

We can use the Word not only to see and understand when something is wrong in ourselves or when we hear conflicting thoughts or when we feel troubling emotions, but we can also use the Word as a spiritual weapon to cast them and Satan away.

As Paul said:

> The weapons we fight with are not the weapons of the world. On the contrary, they have divine power to demolish strongholds. We demolish arguments and every pretension that sets itself up against the knowledge of God, and we take captive every thought to make it obedient to Christ. Su*bmit* yourselves, then, to *God. Resist the devil, and he will flee from you.*[13]

As Christians we should be gladiators for Christ, wielding the Word of God as our sword against Satan. Just as Dr. S's umbrella metaphor provides us with a worldly application to shield us from the storm, God has provided us with His divine armor to shield us from Satan. Let me repeat what Paul said:

> For though we live in the world, we do not wage war as the world does. The weapons we fight with are not the weapons of the world. On the contrary, they have divine power to demolish strongholds. We demolish *arguments* and every pretension that sets itself up against the knowledge of God, and we take captive *every thought* to make it obedient to Christ.[14]

Reflection then is the exercise of discernment regarding the little thoughts and words inside our mind. They may arise with temptation. They may excite during a confrontation. They may tell you that you have been wronged or hurt and you deserve better. Reflection is the discernment process you engage in that allows you to analyze the situation before you simply react. It not only allows you to stop and think, but helps you reflect and understand what is happening to you. Discernment asks questions. Reflecting upon the situation and asking questions will allow you to exercise discernment and consider whether the voice leading you to react is justified by faith.

"Trust in the LORD with all your heart and lean not on your own understanding; in all your ways submit to him, and he will make your paths straight" (Proverbs 3:5–6).

In exercising reflection and discernment, if the voice you hear will take you down a path that has not been directed by God, then it is to be avoided and put off (Proverbs 3:5–6).

When you stop and reflect, ask yourself the following questions:

> Why is this happening to me?
> Why is this happening now?
> Am I jumping to a conclusion?
> Am I being judgmental?

Am I making assumptions?
What is the message?
Is the voice leading me to or from the Holy Spirit?
Is the voice taking me down a path not supported by
biblical principles?

Dr. S. often counseled me to "stay in the moment." This
means to force yourself to focus only on what is immediately
happening to you in that moment. For example, if someone says
something that hurts your feelings or another driver cuts you
off, that little voice inside your head may urge you to react in
a negative manner. You may be prompted and encouraged to
react in a way you may regret later. You may be compelled to
react based on regret over past events or fear of future events. By
staying in the moment, you refuse to allow your mind to wander
to the blame and regret of the past or to the fear and anxiety of
the future in such a way that will influence your present.

The devil will try to deceive you into attaching improper
meaning to the present moment to effect a destructive result.
Satan will try to steal your joy and influence your behavior by
placing undue importance on and keeping you stuck in your
past. He will want you to perceive the present through the
lens of the past so you focus on fault, blame, loss, failure, and
mistakes. Alternatively, Satan will paralyze you from acting
because he will persuade you that what is happening in the
present somehow should make you fearful of the future. You
fear the future by being afraid you will repeat past mistakes.

By staying in the moment, your focus remains only on the
unfiltered present, experiencing it for what it offers without
the influence of past mistakes or future fears. By practicing
reflection and discernment, you can ask yourself where you will
go if you follow the voice you hear in your mind. If the result is
confusion, discouragement, and destruction, then you are being

deceived by the devil. If the result is love, joy, and peace, then you are being led by the Holy Spirit.

The practical works with the spiritual. Staying in the moment keeps you focused on the present instead of focused on past mistakes or future anxieties. However, staying in the moment also means prayerfully living each moment in Christ. It means focusing on the Word and using the Word to repel and cast out Satan, just as Christ did when He was tempted.[15]

Whether we like it or not, everything we say and do or what we fail to say and do, serves as our body of work and testimony. Our words and actions are evidence of who we are and what we represent. My favorite quote attributed to Francis of Assisi is "Preach the Gospel and, if necessary, use words." What he actually said was "Let all the brothers preach by their works."[16]

Whichever line you enjoy more, the message is the same—we either let people know Christ by our conduct, or we push people away from Christ by our conduct. Either way, our conduct and our words become our witness and our testimony for or against Christ. When I finally began trying to live each moment in Christ, and with Christ, I realized that discernment was much easier. I learned that I may still experience sadness, but that it will not spiral into depression. Reflection and discernment bring knowledge, then wisdom, and then understanding.

The book of Proverbs speaks of wisdom and understanding:

> Wisdom is the principal thing; therefore get wisdom: and with all thy getting get understanding. (Proverbs 4:7)

> The fear of the Lord is the beginning of wisdom, and knowledge of the Holy One is understanding. (Proverbs 9:10)

When we submit to depression or to Satan's temptations, our negative thoughts imprison us. We are no longer free to exercise our independent thoughts and minds but are enslaved to automatic negative thoughts. However, when we exercise the skill set of reflection and discernment, we recognize the automatic negative thoughts that accompany depression, and we discard them off and away. When we put on the full armor of God and stand firmly in the Word, we can exercise biblical discernment to recognize Satan's deceit and temptation. As it is written by the prophet Hosea: "Who is wise? He will realize these things. Who is discerning? He will understand them" (Hosea 14:9).

When we stand firmly in the Word (Jesus), we have authority over Satan (John 1:1, 14). The chains that once bound us are broken. The truth (Jesus) has set us free (John 14:6). We no longer are a slave to sin or a prisoner to depression. We are a new creation in Christ.

When we stand on the Word, we become gladiators for Christ and wield the sword of the Spirit. We not only use the full armor of God to defend against Satan's devices and tactics, but we also go on the offensive and on the attack against Satan and his schemes. We become gladiators and warriors for Christ and "demolish arguments and every pretension that sets itself up against the knowledge of God." We can exercise discernment and cast away Satan's negative meanings. "We take captive every thought to make it obedient to Christ" (2 Corinthians 10:5).

Retreat

> When I tried to understand all this, it was oppressive to
> me till I entered the sanctuary of God.
>
> —Psalm 73:16–17

Even when you recognize the triggers and the automatic negative thoughts, and even after you exercise discernment and reflect, you may still need to retreat from the intensity of the situation. When you suffer from depression, you are battling automatic negative thoughts. You are battling Satan who wants to control those thoughts. Just like in a military battle, you may find yourself in a situation where you have to retreat. Maybe you were blindsided and you simply aren't ready to engage in the battle. Maybe you are weary and exhausted and just don't have the energy to fight right now.

Even after you win a battle against Satan and he flees from you, he most assuredly will try again. Satan is relentless. If one of his tools or schemes doesn't work, he will try another. If you find yourself in this situation, the best thing to do is to retreat. You need to get out of harm's way. You need to back off so the situation doesn't escalate. In the heat of the moment, you may need to protect yourself and retreat to a safe sanctuary.

Psalm 23 is a favorite psalm:

> The LORD is my shepherd, I shall not want. He makes me lie down in green pastures, He leads me beside quiet waters, He restores my soul. He guides me in paths of righteousness for His name's sake. Even though I walk through the valley of the shadow of death, I will fear no evil, for You are with me; Your rod and Your staff, they comfort me. You prepare a table before me in the presence of my enemies. You anoint my head with oil; my cup overflows. Surely goodness and love will follow me all the days of my life, and I will dwell in the house of the LORD forever.[17]

For me, my favorite line in Psalm 23 is the one where David states, "He makes me lie down in green pastures." The word I focus on when I read this line is the word *makes*. God makes me lie down in green pastures. He knows what is best for me and forces me to stop. Sometimes when our lives get too hectic or out of control, God will intervene and make us stop what we're doing so we can reflect.

The skill set of retreat means just what it suggests—you need to stop, rest, and give yourself a time-out. When you find yourself entrenched in a situation and you recognize the triggers making you feel like reacting in a negative way, sometimes the best action you can take is just to back away. If you don't have time to reflect or if the situation is too confusing or volatile, the best behavior and course of action to take is to withdraw so you don't escalate the situation.

This is often easier said than done. In the heat of an exchange or in the suddenness of an unexpected event, old habits kick into autopilot. This is why you have to *train* your mind not to react in autopilot. You have to exercise discretion, but sometimes the only way to accomplish that is to step back and just stop. In the construction industry, there is a truism that says, "When you find yourself in a hole, stop digging."

The line "He makes me lie down in green pastures" resonates with me because it takes me back to my youth growing up on a farm. I would often lie on the lush green grass just to think.

You didn't have to grow up on a farm to know what I'm talking about. Whether it was in the park in your yard or on a ball field, lying on the grass made time run slower. If your life is too hectic or if you just need to take time out to be able to reflect, then listen to the Lord and allow Him to make you lie down. Notice that Psalm 23 says He makes us lie *in*, not *on*, green pastures. Not sitting *on* the grass. Not sitting *on* a park bench. Rather, get down on the ground and get *in* the grass. Smell the grass. Feel its texture as it surrounds and comforts you. Let your mind be still. Close your eyes and listen to the birds or to the laughter of children playing or even to the busyness of life clamoring on all around you—without you—while you are still and quiet.

As you lay in the green grass, lie on your back and look up at the sky. Whether you are looking at the trees, hills, mountains, clouds, sun, or sky during the day or whether you are looking at the moon, stars, constellations, planets, or galaxies during the night, you cannot help but wonder at God's creation. When God makes you lie down in green pastures, He is reminding you that you are small and He is the Almighty. God makes us lie down in green pastures to remind us we are not to lean on our own understanding. Instead, He wants us to lean on Him for guidance. Instead of trying to solve every problem ourselves, He wants us to turn to Him and to trust Him.

Part of verse three within Psalm 23 pertains to the skill set of reflection where it is written, "He guides me in paths of righteousness for his name's sake." Sometimes we need to stop what is happening to and around us and retreat so we can pause and give ourselves the opportunity for reflection and discernment. Perhaps the plan we have made and the path we have chosen hasn't been working out so well.

The skill set of retreat also lets us check our margins, that area in our lives where we allow for the unexpected, the setbacks, and the disappointments.

Dr. S explains it this way. Imagine a full glass of water. For all you optimists, the glass is not half full of water but is actually full of water, level with the top of the glass. Even though the glass is full of water, you can continue to add another drop of water. And another drop. And another drop. You can continue to add drops of water one at a time so the level of water actually crowns above the rim of the glass. In other words, the glass of water is more than full. It is over full.

This is the capacity we have with our minds and bodies. We seemingly can be superhuman at times and work more than one job, burn the midnight oil, take on another project, and otherwise just refuse to say no to anything. The result is that our lives become overscheduled and overbusy. They become over full. We all have done it. We even have done it to our children. We have overscheduled our children and vicariously ourselves, with all their classes, activities, sports, and even with the split custodial arrangements with their other parent. Our minds and bodies have the capacity to handle it, but they don't have the capacity to sustain it. Everyone talks about how they are so *busy* and exhausted. Nobody is that resilient.

Back to the glass full of water experiment. After you have continued to add additional drops of water to an already full glass, watch what happens. That's right. The water spills out on to the counter. But look closely to see what really happens. Before you added that last little drop of water, the glass was over full, and the amount of water had crowned out of the glass and over the level line represented by the rim of the glass. However, when you added the additional last little single drop of water that made the water spill, you might think that only one single drop of water should have become displaced and spilled out of the glass. However, that's not what happened. Rather, a lot of water spilled out of the glass and on to the counter. That seemingly harmless single drop of water displaced many times its mass.

This same phenomenon happens with our minds and with our lives. When we pack so many activities and so many thoughts into our minds and lives, they become filled beyond their normal capacity. When that next argument, disappointment, fight, event, or activity then gets added to our plate, our bodies, minds, and lives just can't handle the extra load. Just like the glass of water, we don't just react a little bit. We react a lot to the point where we overreact and maybe even explode. The result is that our lives have spilled out and over into our margin. We no longer have a margin.

This is why God makes us stop and lie down in green pastures. When we no longer have a margin, we risk having part of our lives spill out. When that happens, we become tempted to blame, get angry, and escalate the situation. I know this is true because this is what happened to me and led to my depression.

Of course, we all know how we can schedule and stuff our lives with too much of the present—work, school, kids, church, projects, and so on, until we no longer have a margin. Similarly, we also can schedule and stuff our lives with too much of our past. While technology is wonderful, it tends to make us turned on and tuned in all the time. Sometimes we need to unplug so that we can recharge. Schedule times during the day away from the technology.

By not dealing with things, emotions, and feelings, we never resolve them. As a result, we never get to experience closure and peace. By not letting go and by holding on to guilt, regret, blame, mistakes, and failure, we fill up our present lives with our past. We keep carrying it around, and it keeps getting in the way.

One of my favorite rides at the Disneyland Resort is the Haunted Mansion. The ride gives you a tour of the haunted mansion and lets you see the ghosts and goblins that haunt it. The ride also takes you through the haunted cemetery.

I was guilty of not dealing with and resolving my past. At the time, probably because I thought the emotions and feelings were just too painful, I buried them. Instead of talking about them, I buried them in what I call my cemetery of emotions. Pretty soon, there no longer was any available space left in my emotional cemetery. Because there wasn't any more room, my past emotions had nowhere to go but to live with me in the present. They were just like the ghosts in the Disneyland Haunted Mansion. Because I hadn't properly put them to rest, they continued to haunt me in the present.

For me, this actually became more than just a metaphor, but rather my reality. Sometimes I would have nightmares about past events that would reoccur. This happened with me in regards to 9-11. I also had night terrors about family issues. Because I had not dealt with my emotions and put them to rest properly so I could process and understand them, they were continuing to haunt my present. Believe me, you don't want that to happen. The only ghost you want in your present is the Holy Ghost.

Similarly, this happened with my work. Just like my past crept into my present so I didn't have any margins, my work also took all my margins. I thought the answer to many of my personal problems was to bury myself in my work. I was driven to succeed in one part of my life to compensate for what I considered failure in another part of my life. I became determined to be more than just the best law student or the best attorney I could be. For me, it wasn't enough that I did my best. The best had to be what I did.

As a result, I no longer had any margin or room for error. What had been a successful career then also suffered. There was no longer any balance. My glass didn't just spill over. It spilled way over, and it kept spilling over and over and over again because, even though water had spilled all over the place, I just kept on driving ahead, refilling the glass with more life and with more work until the glass would spill over yet again. So I just filled up the glass again. I never stopped. I never rested. I never retreated. The impact was that sadness became depression. Grief became despair. God finally stepped in and said, "John, stop. Wait. Don't hurry. Look's what happening. Lie down and rest. Reflect. Retreat."

We need margins in all aspects of our lives, not just to be able to handle the unexpected, but also to be receptive to God's calling. If we have no margin with our time, how can we answer God's call to serve or to do anything for Him? If we have no margin with our finances, how can we answer God's call to give when asked? If we have no margin with our thoughts, how can we listen to the Holy Spirit? The answer is that we can't. Instead, our lives become full of excuses for why we can't serve, why we can't give, why we can't minister, and why we can't listen.

The skill set Retreat is a verb. It is the means by which you pause and take inventory. Step back. Withdraw. Get out of harm's way. Give yourself some breathing room and space to evaluate the situation. Create margin.

However, the skill set Retreat can also be used as a noun. Used in this way, it becomes just that, namely, a retreat or a Hideaway—a Sanctuary. It is a safe place for both your mind and your body. When the storm is raging all around you or inside of you, you need to find that safe place. Go there and find *peace*. Our God is the God of peace. Let God be your sanctuary.

As David said in Psalm 23, "He leads me beside quiet waters." God wants us to be at peace with others, with our work, with our lives, and with ourselves.

I love the story about Jesus and the disciples in a boat on a lake in a storm. The storm was described as a furious squall where "the waves broke over the boat, so that it was nearly swamped."[18] Even though the disciples were afraid they might drown, Jesus was sound asleep, "sleeping on a cushion."[19]

Because the disciples were afraid they may drown, they woke Jesus and said to Him, "Teacher, don't you care if we drown?"[20]

Jesus awoke and performed a miracle: "He got up, rebuked the wind and said to the waves, "Quiet! Be still!" Then the wind died down and it was completely calm."[21]

Notwithstanding that the disciples had witnessed Jesus perform many miracles before the storm occurred, they said to one another, "Who is this? Even the wind and the waves obey him!"[22] The disciples wondered among themselves "Who is this?" that commands authority over everything—even the seas. When Jesus spoke, the seas bowed in submission at His feet.

David actually wrote the answer to the disciples' question about one thousand years earlier when he said in Psalm 107:

> Then they cried out to the Lord in their trouble, and He brought them out of their distress. He stilled the storm to a whisper; the waves of the sea were hushed.[23]

Jesus "stilled the storm to a whisper." To the seas He said, "This far you may come and no father; here is where your proud waves halt."[24] I find the story about the disciples with Jesus in a boat on a lake in a storm remarkable for several reasons. First, even though it was a raging storm described as "a furious squall" where "the waves broke over the boat so that it was nearly swamped," Jesus was sleeping. Even though the storm was so violent the disciples feared they may drown, Jesus was "sleeping on a cushion." What we think is fearful, even life threatening, is miniscule comparatively to Him. He hushed the raging storm by simply saying, "Quiet! Be still!"

The second reason this story is remarkable to me is because the disciples had Jesus with them in the boat. They knew He was the Son of God. They followed His calling to follow Him. They already had seen Him perform many miracles. Even with God's Son in the boat with them, they were afraid for their lives and feared they might drown. Why? What was their mind-set? Jesus could walk on water. Were they afraid for their own lives because He could walk on water and they could not? I don't think their thought process was that logical. Rather, they were just afraid and on negative autopilot, and they leaned on their own understanding and fears instead of leaning on Him and trusting in Him.

The third reason I find this story remarkable is because the disciples had to ask the question, "Who is this?" They had witnessed Him perform many miracles by healing the sick and curing many diseases.[25] They witnessed Him cure a man with leprosy.[26] They witnessed four men who brought a paralytic to Jesus to be healed, but because the crowd prevented them from reaching Jesus, they cut a hole in the roof above Jesus and lowered the paralytic and his mat down through the roof. When Jesus saw their faith, "He said to the paralytic, 'I tell you, get up, take your mat and go home.'"[27] The disciples witnessed Jesus perform all these miracles, but then when He stilled the storm, they asked, "Who is this?" Remarkable.

This is also how it is with us. Just like the disciples, as Christians, we have Christ with us. We have the Holy Spirit in us. Yet when the storm comes, we don't rely and trust on Him, even though He is with us in the boat in the storm. We keep charging and driving ahead, trying to control the events and people around us. Our mind-set is that we want to eliminate our problems and make them go away. We think if our problems were removed, our lives would be better or easier. I know because this is what I did.

Instead of that mind-set, we need a new mind-set. We need to trust in God. Even though the disciples questioned, "Who is this?" they still eventually got it right. They woke up Jesus and said, "Lord, save us! We're going to drown."[28] They looked to the Lord and trusted Him to save them.

Indeed, God is all-powerful and almighty. He not only has authority over rulers, nations, and the earthly realms, but He also has power "against the rulers, against the authorities, against the powers of this dark world and against the spiritual forces of evil in the heavenly realms."[29]

If you find yourself in a storm, you can find a safe haven and a retreat and a sanctuary in the protection of God's peace. When you find yourself in a storm, know that God is present with you in the storm. If you trust Him, believe in Him and call out to Him in prayer. He will still and quiet the storm raging in your life to a whisper. He will make you lie down in green pastures. He will lead you beside still waters. He will guide you in paths of righteousness. He will restore your soul.

Renewal

Create in me a pure heart, O God, and renew a steadfast
spirit within me.

—Psalm 51:10

Perhaps you find yourself seemingly repeating the same
mistakes, behaviors, habits, and failings, and eventually, they
become chronic. This is what happened with me. Nothing got
resolved. Sadness turned into depression.

When such a condition is allowed to percolate and fester for
so long, the little voices in your head begin to tell you what to
believe about what is happening around you. They begin to tell
you that you are a failure and a loser. They begin to tell you that
you have disappointed not only others but also yourself. Soon
you begin to believe the voices. Those negative meanings and
beliefs begin to define you. A feeling of despair shrouds you,
and doubt becomes your companion. Haunted by past mistakes,
you lose confidence in your ability in the present, and you
become fearful of the future. As a result, you become paralyzed.
You become just like the paralytic in the Bible who could not
get off his mat. When someone is chronically depressed, they
may not want to get off the couch or leave the house. They
eventually may not want to get out of bed. This happened to
me. Some days, I could not walk down the driveway and get the
mail out of the mailbox. Other days, when I found the strength
and courage to get the mail, I couldn't bring myself to open it.

When life has lost its purpose, desire becomes a forgotten
memory. This is particularly true if the person depressed is
alone or isolated and doesn't have a support group to provide
encouragement. If not arrested, those feelings become so
prevalent that life appears hopeless and depression begins
to choke you. Sometimes you feel like you can't breathe.

When depression's grip gets too strong, people lose hope and become suicidal.

If you are reading this and have felt this way or if you know someone who may feel this way, please immediately seek professional help. Get a correct diagnosis of your condition. Follow advice. If you need to take medication, get the prescription. If you need therapy, get someone knowledgeable in cognitive behavioral therapy like Dr. S. Don't let your situation become chronic.

If you think your life is not worth living, think about the comparison between Peter and Judas Iscariot. Both Peter and Judas betrayed Jesus the same night. When "Satan entered into him" (John 13:27), Judas betrayed Jesus and arranged for Jesus to be arrested.[30] Thereafter, Judas felt remorse. "'I have sinned,' he said, 'for I have betrayed innocent blood.'"[31] However, the chief priests and elders said to Judas, "'What is that to us?' they replied, 'That's your responsibility.'"[32] Judas "threw the money into the temple" and "went away and hanged himself."[33]

At about the same time this was happening, Peter also betrayed Jesus. He disowned Jesus three times and twice even said, "I don't know the man [Jesus]."[34] Peter also felt remorse. After the rooster crowed, signaling the end of that long night and confirming that Jesus's prediction had come true, "he [Peter] went outside and wept bitterly."[35]

However, Peter didn't commit suicide like Judas.

When the women returned from the tomb and told the apostles the tomb was empty, the disciples did not believe them—except Peter, who "got up and ran to the tomb."[36] When Jesus again appeared to the disciples after His resurrection while they were fishing at the Sea of Galilee, as soon as John told Peter it was Jesus standing on the shore, Peter immediately jumped out of the boat and joined Jesus on the shore.[37] After breakfast, Jesus then asked Peter three times, "Do you love me?" and Peter told Jesus three times, "You know that I love you."[38] Jesus asked and Peter answered, three times—once for each of the number of times Peter betrayed Christ and denied knowing Him.

Jesus not only predicted Peter's denial, but earlier, Jesus predicted Peter's test of faith. At the Last Supper, Jesus said "Simon, Simon, Satan has asked to sift you as wheat. But I have prayed for you, Simon, that your faith may not fail. And when you have turned back, strengthen your brothers."[39] Jesus emphasized, "And when you have turned back." Jesus not only told Peter he would deny Jesus three times, but Jesus also told Peter He had prayed that Peter's "faith may not fail."

I don't think what Jesus is talking about here is the test of Peter's faith just before Peter denied knowing Jesus three times. I think what Jesus is talking about when He said He prayed that Peter's faith would not fail is the test of faith Peter experienced after he betrayed Jesus. Jesus said to Peter, "And when you have turned back, strengthen your brothers." I think Jesus here is talking about how Peter relied on his faith and repented and turned back to Jesus after he betrayed Jesus and denied knowing Jesus three times.

Even though Peter betrayed Christ and denied him three times, Peter's faith facilitated his forgiveness. He didn't lose faith. Peter, just like Judas, betrayed Christ. But where Judas committed suicide, Peter turned back to Christ. Peter found redemption.

If you believe there is no hope, you're wrong. There is always hope. God will redeem you. God has a purpose for you. Just like with Peter, even after you make mistakes or life gets messed up, you can still turn back to God if you believe and have faith in Him. It is never too late. God can use your hurts and your past for His glory. As Paul said in the book of Romans 8:28, "We know that all things work together for good to those who love God."

It doesn't matter what mistakes you made. It doesn't matter how you failed or what you have done. There is nothing you possibly could have done that cannot be forgiven. Peter denied knowing Jesus. Three times! Yet he was forgiven when he turned back in faith to God. If God can forgive Peter, He can forgive you. If God can forgive me, He can forgive you.

Perhaps you feel you have lost hope, not for something you have done but because of something that has happened to you or has been done to you. Nothing is so bad or so lost or so unforgivable that it cannot be restored by God. All things are possible with God. He will restore your soul. You can be renewed. Don't give up. Don't give in. Be strong and courageous. Even if people have failed and disappointed you, God won't fail you. God is faithful. Get help. Reach out. Turn back. Take the first courageous step.

Once you seek help, then what? You've begun treatment and applied the skill sets of recognition, reflection, and retreat.

However, you still experience setbacks. To be able to push through the setbacks and the relapses, you need to be able to reprogram your mind and your thinking. You may even have to unlearn some things. If you continue to approach the problems and issues the way I did, in the same manner and mind-set as before, you will find you are susceptible to repeat the same mistakes. This is inevitable because your mind-set and your negative thoughts have become automatic. They have to be interrupted, unlearned, and reprogrammed.

Worse still, each time you experience a setback, you begin to question yourself and your recovery. Doubt creeps back. Before you can change your behavior, you have to change your mind. This skill set is called *renewal*.

The 2004 movie *50 First Dates* portrayed Drew Barrymore's character as suffering from a fictional condition similar to short-term memory loss that caused her to relive each day as if it were the same day, October 13, yet each day was unfamiliar and totally new. In the 1993 movie *Ground Hog Day,* all the characters, except Bill Murray's character, were in a time loop, forcing them to relive each new day as February 2, but again, each day was an unfamiliar and a totally new experience. In both movies, even though the characters were repeating each day, they were living each day as if they were experiencing each day for the very first time. The phenomenon of "staying in the moment" is to experience each moment something like the characters in those two movies.

When you stay in the moment, you focus on the present and only on the present. You refuse to allow memories of past mistakes, failures, or disappointments to enter your thought pattern. You also refuse to allow any anxieties about the future creep into your thoughts. As a result, you allow yourself to experience each moment of each day for what it is—a fresh, new, unfamiliar, and exciting experience.

Dr. S calls this technique having a "beginner's brain" or a "beginner's mind." With a beginner's mind, you are beginning each experience, each moment, as if you are experiencing it for the first time.

Having a beginner's mind allows you to experience and live in the present moment without any preconceived perceptions, assumptions, judgments, or influences either from the past or the future. If you are reminded of something that makes you sad, that's okay, but just let that feeling or emotion wash over you and move on. Don't let those feelings of sadness linger or disrupt your being able to experience fully the present. Don't hold onto them. Release them.

You may experience a rush of emotion that is incredibly intense and you may begin to feel pulled backward to past events and emotions. That's okay. As uncomfortable as it may make you feel, just let it wash over you. When it happens, you, at first, may want to fight it, thinking that if you don't you will be sucked back into those same old feelings of sadness or remorse. Often this happens with PTSD, where something will remind you of something from your painful past. This feeling or phenomenon may frighten you and cause you to fear you may be relapsing in your recovery.

Instead of resisting, get comfortable with the uncomfortable. Train your mind to understand you now have a new mind-set and a beginner's mind. Reassure yourself those feelings are from the past and belong in the past.

In practicing this skill set, you are training your mind into believing that whatever happened before needs to stay in the past instead of being able to influence the present. You are now living in and experiencing a new moment, and you don't have to relive the past experience again. You don't have to reexperience the past trauma or event. In doing so, you treat the past experience and emotion for what it is—a memory. The more you practice this technique and train your mind, the more distant your memory will become. With a "beginner's mind," you are unlearning the old, tired, automatic negative thoughts and looking at each event and situation from a fresh, new perspective. Even if you revisit or reexperience an event or situation, you should approach it with this new perspective. By staying in the moment and having a beginner's mind, you are looking at each event with a renewed mind.

Imagine yourself looking at a photo album. You see the photo or the trauma from the past, but you experience it or view it from a distance by separating yourself from the past vision, photo, or trauma. If you are about to encounter an event or a person with whom you have had difficulty in the past, try to change your mind-set to that of a beginner's mind and experience the new encounter with the person independently from the past encounter, without cluttering the new moment by bringing along the past as an uninvited guest. Train your mind and imagine you are meeting the person for the first time, because for that particular encounter, in that moment, you actually are.

In this way, you can achieve a beginner's mind—a renewed mind. You can look forward to each day as a new experience unburdened by the past. You can stop condemning yourself for past mistakes. You can stop defining yourself by past experiences.

One of the reasons we clutter the present with the past is that we become judgmental. We make value judgments all the time about our past. We're not content just to have a history.

Instead, we have to attach meaning to that history.

Have you ever read an obituary? It is a recitation of facts concerning a person's life. All the main facts are there, such as which relatives are remembered and what kind of activities and work the person performed. That's it—it's just the facts. The obituary author rarely adds any commentary about the facts. Even a eulogy spoken at a funeral service that includes such commentary will only have wonderful and glowing observations—never any negative meanings or judgments.

However, when we hear the voices inside our head about our past, the devil wants us to attach meaning and significance to all the facts about our past in a negative way. Satan wants us to be ashamed of our mistakes. He wants to use our mistakes against us to be able to steal our joy from our present. *Satan wants us to believe we are condemned for our mistakes.*

When people confront problems, I like to say there are two kinds of people. First, there are problem thinkers. These people focus on the problem. They live in the past where the problem arose. Their focus is on fault, blame, and guilt. Initially, the fault, blame, and guilt are for the existence of the problem. However, if an attempt to solve the problem failed, then their focus is to accuse and blame and to assign fault and guilt to the failed attempt to correct the problem. I believe problem thinkers or people who work for problem thinkers are more stressed in their work and live more stressful lives.

Second, there are solutions thinkers. These people don't focus on the problem. Instead, they focus on the solution. They live in the present, with a view toward the future instead of the past. Their focus is on possibility, experimentation, hope, creativity, and trust. They only visit the past to look at the problem as a tool to be used to create a solution. If an attempt to correct the problem wasn't successful, they don't view that attempt as a failure or as a mistake but, instead, view that attempt as important additional information and knowledge about the problem. They view the attempt to correct the problem as additional empirical, experimental, and experiential evidence. I believe solution thinkers or people who work for solution thinkers are less stressed, more creative, happier, and more involved in their work and lives.

It is the same way with a beginner's mind. By looking at an event or situation as if experiencing it for the first time, and by staying in the moment, you focus on the solution. You create hope, promise and faith. Past mistakes are only tools to be used to teach us what didn't work, and opportunities to create something even better. With a beginner's mind, with a new mind-set, we train our minds not to remember the mistakes in a negative way.

Such hope, trust, and faith are also created by a renewal in Christ that is permanent when we ask forgiveness for our sins. God not only promises He will forgive our sins, but God also promises He will not remember them. God gave us Jesus, His son, who died for our sins as a new covenant between God and us:

> This is the covenant I will make with them after that time, says the Lord.
>
> I will put my laws in their hearts, and I will write them on their minds. Their sins and lawless acts I will remember no more.[40]

When God forgives our sins, He doesn't forget them, but He will "remember them no more." David said it this way after he had committed adultery with Bathsheba, "For I know my transgressions, and my sin is always before me…Cleanse me with hyssop, and I will be clean; wash me, and I will be whiter than snow."[41]

The prophet Isaiah said God will "blot out" sins, "I, even I, am He who blots out your transgressions, for my own sake, and remembers your sins no more."[42] Apostle John said, "If we confess our sins, He is faithful and just and will forgive us our sins and purify us from all unrighteousness" (1 John 1:9). So in other words, all our sins and mistakes are blotted out so there no longer is a record of them. David said, "As far as the east is from the west, so far has He removed our transgressions from us."[43]

When people suffer from depression, they just can't seem to get past thoughts out of their mind. As David said, "For I know my transgressions, and my sin is always before me." If you ask someone suffering from depression, he will tell you those past mistakes are "always before me" and those negative, automatic thoughts are always in his mind. When I suffered from depression, I could not get out of my own way. I could not get past my past. I didn't know how. My negative thoughts about the past were "always before me."

You don't have to continue to live this way. You can overcome depression. You can use these skill sets to unlearn those negative thoughts and create a new mind-set. Stop experiencing new events through the lens of the past. Leave past sins and past regrets in the past. Instead of having your past mistakes and regrets always before you, develop a beginner's mind so you no longer remember them.

Some people have difficulty differentiating the concept of not remembering from forgetting. God does not forget our sins. Rather, He will "remember no more." So exactly how is this possible? How is it that God can remember no more when He does not forget? How then can we remember no more our past when we can't forget a hurt or a trauma or a tragedy?

The answer is that the act to remember no more is an intentional, conscious, and purposeful decision and action. Conversely, the act of forgetting is accidental. Whether it is because someone has amnesia or memory loss or whether it is because of the lapse of time, forgetting something is accidental and usually not intentional. Even memory loss or forgetfulness from trauma such as a concussion or shock is neurological and not intentional and purposeful. Not remembering, however, is a purposeful decision. It is making up our mind, with a beginner's mind, not to hold onto a past hurt and allow that past hurt to influence and affect our present. It is the conscious, determined decision we make when we forgive.

In this sense then, not remembering is not simply burying our emotions or hurt feelings. While burying your hurt feelings may be a deliberate decision, it is not letting go. When you bury your hurt feelings, you may be making an intentional decision not to think about them, but you are still holding on to them. They are still there, stored in your memory bank, subject to recall. You are not letting go.

Conversely, when you remember no more, you are not burying your hurt feelings but consciously letting go of them. You are making a conscious and deliberate decision to not remember them. You are erasing the memory bank and the record of them. You are blotting them out. As the Apostle Paul said in Ephesians, as Christians, "You were taught with regard to your former way of life, to put off your old self which is being corrupted by its deceitful desires; to be made new in the attitude of your minds; and to put on the new self" (Ephesians 4:22–23). In Romans, Paul described it as being "transformed by the renewing of your mind" (Romans 12:2). We are made new in the attitude of our minds by the renewing of our minds. It is a new mind-set. It is a renewed mind.

How then, as a Christian, can someone still be depressed? This was my conundrum. I knew by admitting my sins and repenting of my sins and asking for forgiveness and accepting Christ, all my sins were forgiven. As Paul says:

> Therefore, if anyone is in Christ, he is a new creation; the old has gone, the new has come! All this is from God, who reconciled us to Himself through Christ and gave us the ministry of reconciliation that God was reconciling the world to Himself in Christ, not counting men's sins against them.[44]

Even though I knew God would not remember my sins, I wouldn't allow myself that same luxury. I did not feel like a new creation. I kept remembering my past. Satan kept telling me I had failed, which meant I was a failure. Satan kept telling me that I had lost, which meant I was a loser. Satan kept telling me what negative meanings to attach to my thoughts.

Becoming saved and a Christian doesn't insulate us from the devil's trials, voices, lies, and deception. The Bible states that once saved, we can expect the battle to be waged against us even more intensely. That is why Paul said, "Be strong in the Lord and in His mighty power. Put on *the full armour of God* so that you can take your stand against the devil's schemes" (Ephesians 6:13). I had to create a new mind-set where I trusted God and the truth of His Word. I needed a renewed mind.

Even though I knew the Word, I was still trying to overcome depression with my old mind-set of thinking I should be able to overcome depression by my own intellect and intelligence. I was not willing to trust God. Not completely. Not entirely. Each trial with Satan was like another round in the courtroom. It was him against me, but this time, I was losing every trial.

To trust God completely meant I had to admit to myself I was suffering from a mental illness called depression. It meant I had to be completely vulnerable to all the emotional shame, indignity, humiliation, and embarrassment I felt and experienced. Satan convinced me I was weak and broken. He persuaded me to be prideful about my intellect, but now my mind was being defined as damaged goods—a mental illness.

On the one hand, God remembers our sins no more. On the other hand, Satan is the great accuser and continues to accuse us and remind us of our past so we live in guilt and shame. If you are reading this and have experienced feeling the same stigmatism, perhaps this resonates with you. I felt disgraced. I felt ashamed.

A stigmatism is just that—a blemish or a stain. Yet when God forgives sin, He wipes out the stain and stigmatism:

> Come now, let us reason together, says the Lord. Though
> your sins are like scarlet, they shall be as white as snow;
> though they are red as crimson, they shall be like wool.[45]

When we stand on the Word, we have a complete defense against the devil's schemes. This is God's promise. This promise not only spoke to my heart, it also spoke to my mind.

God begins the verse by asking me to reason with Him. He invites me to sit down with Him and think this through—pray this through. "Come now, let us reason together." God extends the same invitation to you. He wants you to reason with Him. This is how you begin to have a personal relationship with God.

God was telling me to exercise discernment. He was telling me to trust Him and His Word. He promises He will blot out my stain, my defect, my mental illness and see me "as white as snow." David, as only David can, described the effect as being even "whiter than snow."

In this verse, God is saying He doesn't see me or my past mistakes or my mind as an imperfection or a defect or a stain. He's saying we should not believe Satan or his lies. God is saying He already has forgiven our sins and that Jesus's death and resurrection have already won victory over Satan "because the prince of this world now stands condemned" (John 16:11). We just need to develop a new mind-set to accept and believe His promise. We need to let go and let God.

I finally realized that when God forgives our sins and remembers them no more, He isn't just blotting out and erasing the record of those sins, but He also is "not counting men's sins against them." Satan is the great accuser and does just the opposite. Satan deliberately uses and counts men's sins against them to the point we become prisoners to guilt and shame. Satan then uses our past mistakes to trick us into believing we should use our own past mistakes to condemn ourselves. When you create a new mind-set, when you reason with God, when you accept God's forgiveness, when you forgive others, and when you forgive yourself, you then overcome Satan.

God doesn't want or need us to be perfect. He accepts us just the way we are. Don't buy into the devil's lies and accusations. The devil uses guilt as one of his tools to make us believe we somehow are at fault for whatever may have happened to us. This happens in many cases of abuse, where the victims are made to believe or feel the abuse somehow was invited or deserved and they should believe they were at fault. The same principle applies to depression, where someone feels they are damaged or defective because they have what has been described as a mental illness.

Everything Satan says is a lie meant to enslave you and imprison your mind. Satan is the accuser. Conversely, Jesus is the truth, and the truth shall set you free.

> If you hold to my teaching, you are really my disciples. Then you will know the truth, and the truth will set you free.[46]

Jesus said, "I am the way and the truth and the life. No one comes to the Father except through me" (John 14:6). Jesus is the truth. His death and resurrection is what frees you from sin. You only need to accept that truth. You only need to accept Jesus.

If we accept the truth that God already has forgiven us, then why can't we forgive ourselves? Why do we continue to judge and condemn ourselves? "There is no condemnation for those who are in Christ Jesus" (Romans 8:1).

When I finally accepted God's invitation to reason together, I was able to trade my mind-set for the Lord's. I no longer leaned on my own understanding but accepted God's promise. As a Christian, I finally realized that "If anyone is in Christ, he is a new creation; the old has gone, the new has come!"

I no longer viewed my past with my old mind-set, capable of being influenced and distorted. I put on the full armor of God. I firmly stand on the Word, and I am equipped with the breastplate of righteousness, the shield of faith, the helmet of salvation, and the sword of the Spirit. As promised in Psalm 23, God had restored my soul. As Paul said in Romans, "What, then, shall we say in response to this? If God is for us, who can be against us?"[47]

Satan has no answer. He already has been defeated. Stop condemning yourself. Forgive yourself. Renew your mind. Develop a new mind-set. God has forgiven you, so you should forgive yourself.

Recovery

My Presence will go with you,
and I will give you rest.

—Exodus 33:14

The next skill set of recovery includes getting sufficient rest and relaxation, which are vital to any wellness program. Different people suffering from depression may exhibit different symptoms, sometimes simultaneously. Common symptoms associated with depression include:

- Feelings of hopelessness, helplessness, and sadness.
- Thoughts of death or suicide.
- Loss of interest in things that were once pleasurable.
- Concentration problems.
- Forgetfulness.
- Loss of libido.
- Changes in weight and appetite.
- Daytime sleepiness.
- Loss of energy.
- Anxiety.
- Low self-esteem.
- Insomnia.

If you recognize you are suffering from one or more of these symptoms, you should immediately consult a professional so you can obtain a proper diagnosis. In my situation, I experienced most of these symptoms at differing times.

Some think sleeplessness leads to depression and some think depression leads to sleeplessness, but there is a definite correlation between lack of sleep and depression. In one study, people suffering from insomnia were found to be more than seventeen times more likely to suffer from clinically significant depression than people not suffering from insomnia.[48]

Insomnia may take the form of sleep onset insomnia (SOI), which is the difficulty of falling asleep. It also may take the form of sleep maintenance insomnia (SMI), which is the difficulty of staying asleep. The study found that the risk of depression is highest among people suffering from both SOI and SMI. The study also found the risk of depression among patients with insomnia was higher among women than among men.

In another study, a direct association was found between sleep apnea and major depression.[49] A Stanford researcher found that people who have been diagnosed with depression were five times more likely to suffer from obstructive sleep apnea. The study compared a large sample of people diagnosed with a major depressive disorder with another large sample of people diagnosed with a DSM-IV breathing-related sleep disorder. The study found that in eighteen percent of the cases, people who had been diagnosed with a major depressive disorder also suffered from a sleep disorder, and people who had been diagnosed with a DSM-IV breathing-related sleep disorder also suffered from depression. The Stanford study concluded that because symptoms of depression overlap with symptoms of sleep disorders, a risk of improper diagnosis exists between the two types of patients.

As a result, it is extremely important for people who exhibit symptoms of depression to make sure they get a proper diagnosis. In my case, I suffered from insomnia and sleep apnea. My family doctor diagnosed me with sleep apnea, but he never questioned me about the possibility that I may have depression. My situation also was complicated because I experienced night terrors due to the PTSD. Until I was diagnosed with depression and PTSD, I was constantly exhausted. To counter being tired all the time, I would drink a couple of pots of coffee in the morning and an energy drink in the afternoon.

Once I was diagnosed with depression and PTSD, I was prescribed a minor dosage of Ambien to help me sleep. Because I had an active mind (meaning at night I couldn't relax and stop thinking about work or problems), I often couldn't go to sleep and instead would watch television or read. My PTSD also made me hypervigilant, and the heightened alertness and awareness made it more difficult to fall asleep or to stay asleep. I would then fall asleep for two or three hours, but then I would awake again. My REM sleep was constantly being interrupted, and I rarely slept through the night.

With Ambien, I was able to fall asleep and sleep through the night. However, the dosage left me groggy in the morning after I woke up, so the doctor gave me another prescription for a stimulant to make me alert. I felt like an idiot. I was taking a sleeping pill to fall asleep and stayed asleep through the night, but then I was taking a stimulant to help me wake up and stay alert.

Even though the medication was designed to help me, taking both medications made me anxious. I was worried I could become addicted to the sleeping pills or to the stimulants, so I just stopped taking them. I thought I was better without them. When I got really tired, I would take an Ambien at night to fall asleep, or I would take a stimulant during the day to stay alert. Otherwise, I wouldn't take either one. I was trying to manage the situation by myself.

Clearly, this was the wrong approach. After consulting with my doctor and his trial and error with the dosage amount, we found a combination that seemed to work. After a period of time, my doctor began to reduce the dosage, and finally, I was able to begin sleeping more regularly without the aid of

Ambien. Once I got the rest I needed, I no longer needed to take the stimulants. The cognitive therapy with Dr. S was working effectively, and I was beginning to apply the skill sets with good results. I no longer need to be on medication.

If you are suffering from a lack of sleep, interrupted sleep, or the inability to fall asleep, you may have sleep apnea, depression, or both. A number of symptoms of depression and sleep apnea are directly connected with each other. For example, concentration problems, forgetfulness, daytime sleepiness, and a feeling of loss of energy all are the result of lack of sleep. However, they are also symptoms of depression.

When you are suffering from these symptoms, it is important to discuss clearly with your doctor or therapist what you are experiencing so you can get the proper medication if needed. Often, the prescriptions are made on a trial basis and you have to work with your doctor to see what works best for your situation after trial and error and clear communication.

In addition to monitoring your sleep, it is also important to get some form of exercise. When you exercise, your brain releases neurotransmitters and endorphins that can ease depression. Exercising will inhibit weight gain, which often occurs with depression, and can improve personal confidence. Working out can help keep your mind off the negative thoughts and energy that fuel anxiety and depression, and it can change your scenery, which will brighten your mood.

Keep in mind that any kind of physical activity is helpful and productive. Don't get hung up on performing a particular exercise routine. It is important for people suffering from depression to be able to accomplish small goals. If you are suffering from depression and are unable to maintain or keep an exercise regimen or routine, it is easy to become discouraged and tell yourself you have failed at something seemingly simple. Believe me, it's not that simple.

If you are suffering from depression, you need to begin building a series of steps and habits that can serve as achievements to help build confidence. Think small and stay in the moment. Tell yourself you are going to stay in the moment and just concentrate and focus on only the next hour. Maybe you have to back off that goal and make your focus only the next half hour. Tell yourself you are going to set a certain goal to be accomplished during that period of time. Then block out all possible distractions and interruptions and accomplish that goal, however small it may seem at first. Once you achieve that goal, you can build upon it and move on to the next goal.

You can use this technique with exercise. Instead of telling yourself you are going to go to the gym so many days a week or according to such and such schedule, just use the next hour or half hour as your time frame for getting exercise. Start small. Walk the dog. Just do whatever you can do successfully for the next half hour.

If you are reading this and not personally suffering from depression, you may think this advice is trivial and perhaps even nonsensical. If you know someone suffering from depression, however, these symptoms are very real. The symptoms listed in this section seem fairly benign. Fatigue or low self esteem or loss of energy all seem generally nondescript. However, to someone suffering from depression, they mean and are interpreted as not being able to leave the house. They may mean not being able to get out of bed, or if someone can get out of bed, they may struggle just to take a shower and get dressed. By the time they manage that, the thought of getting out of the house and getting the mail or even going for a walk becomes exhausting and insurmountable.

For me, taking a walk worked wonders. When you take a walk, you change your scenery, get outside, and get some fresh air. You see other people, even if you don't talk to them.

You no longer are by yourself, even if you are alone. You are accomplishing something. It's a big deal. Get up and get out. Don't be paralyzed. Get up and get off your mat.

If you are able to get to the gym and participate in a yoga class or a group activity then so much the better, because you are performing a task in a group setting. Socializing with others is important. However, if you can't, just go for a walk or ride a bike or go to the park.

Dogs and cats are great for people with depression because they provide empathy and companionship. Dogs have proven to be effective in helping veterans overcome depression and PTSD. Later in this book, I devote a special section to a pioneer program using dogs to overcome depression and PTSD. When I take our dogs for a walk, they are just so happy to see me and so happy to be able to go for another walk. Their demonstration of unconditional love and affection is important. When I walk the dogs, I usually pray or sing a little song of praise. Our dogs must be the most prayed-over dogs in the world.

Other activities are equally beneficial. You can go to a museum, the theater, or walk along a farmers' market or a flea market.

Having a small support group is an extremely important part of your recovery program. Sometimes a spouse or parent can serve to be supportive. However, sometimes a person suffering from depression feels they can't talk to a spouse or parent about their condition because they view it as a problem and as a failing, which is not something they want to discuss and admit, especially to a spouse, parent, or family member. For this reason, group therapy often can be a tremendous help.

Part of recovery also is making sure you address your diet and nutrition. One of the symptoms of depression is overeating and weight gain. When we are depressed, we take solace in comfort food. Compatible with exercise is limiting your caloric intake and eating nutritious foods. Change your diet. Eat more fruits and vegetables. Consult with a dietician or someone who can help you begin a program of eating better. Begin with small steps. Don't get discouraged. Feel better by eating better.

Similarly, reduce your alcohol intake. Often people who are depressed try to avoid or numb the negative thoughts or emotions through alcohol or other substances. Doing so will only exacerbate the problem. Alcohol actually is a depressant and will not help your situation. If you want to overcome your depression you have to be willing to make some changes. By changing how you think about things and by changing how you see things, you can change your behavior. If you need to, get some help. Get a trainer or a coach. Get into therapy. Get and seek the support you need. Take small steps.

It is vital, particularly at the beginning of your recovery, that you get into therapy with a qualified psychologist, preferably one who is trained in cognitive behavior therapy. For me, I not only was able to meet individually with Dr. S, but I also participated in a weekly group session. Group therapy was helpful because it made me aware I was not on this journey alone. It helped me to hear from others who struggled with similar problems. Also, in a group setting, you start to interact with others, and you acquire a sense of belonging. The group provides a sense of encouragement, holds you accountable to your recovery program, and keeps you on track on your journey to recovery. This is invaluable when you experience setbacks.

Getting out is also important because it reminds you God created a beautiful world. If you live near the beach, walk along the beach and wonder at the waves. If you live near the mountains, admire their majesty. If you live in the plains or live near ranches or farms, contemplate the stillness. If you live in the city, get to a park where you can appreciate nature, the trees, and the grass. Or visit the zoo where you can be amazed at all God's creations. Enjoy a concert. Visit a museum or an art gallery. Watch a sunrise or a sunset. Any of these activities, as simple as they sound, will start you on a program of getting out and getting exercise. More importantly, you will appreciate the wonderful world God created.

God does not want us to be anxious or depressed. God comforts the depressed (2 Corinthians 7:6). He wants us to have peace. He wants us to put on the full armor of God. He wants us to be at peace. Jesus said,

> Come to me, all you who are weary and burdened, and I will give you rest. Take my yoke upon you and learn from me, for I am gentle and humble in heart, and you will find rest for your souls. For my yoke is easy and my burden is light.[50]

In addition to meditation, prayer can help you with your depression. As David said, "Search me, O God, and know my heart; try me, and know my anxieties."[51] "God is not the author of confusion, but of peace."[52] He said, "My presence will go with you and I will give you rest."[53]

The effective, fervent "prayer of a righteous man is powerful and effective."[54] Moses reassured us of God's promise that when we call on Him, He will hear our prayer:

> "Because he loves Me," says the Lord, "I will rescue him; I will protect him, for he acknowledges My name. He will call upon Me, and I will answer him; I will be with him in trouble, I will deliver him and honor him. With long life will I satisfy him and show him My salvation."[55]

We don't have to be held captive and a prisoner to guilt, shame, or depression. He will be with us in trouble if we call on Him. As foretold in Isaiah and confirmed in the Gospel of Luke, God sent Jesus to rescue us.

> The Spirit of the Lord is on me, because He has anointed me to proclaim good news to the poor. He has sent me to proclaim freedom for the prisoners and recovery of sight for the blind, to set the oppressed free.[56]

He heals the brokenhearted and binds up their wounds.[57] He restores my soul.

Let Him restore your soul. Let Him give you rest and peace.

Rejoice

> We rejoice in the hope of the glory of God. Not only so, but we also rejoice in our sufferings, because we know that suffering produces perseverance; perseverance, character; and character, hope.
>
> And hope does not disappoint us, because God has poured out his love into our hearts by the Holy Spirit, whom He has given us.
>
> —Romans 5:2–5

The skill set rejoice means to give thanks, count our blessings, and serve others. Often when we become sad or disappointed, it is because we have experienced some kind of loss. We stay sad because our focus stays on our loss.

The skill set of rejoicing is just the opposite. Its focus is not on what we have lost but on what we still *have*.

Satan would have us believe we can't possibly take pleasure in who we still are and in what blessings we still have because we are no longer complete. Satan tells us we have lost something and we will never get that hole in our heart or in our lives healed again. He would have us believe we are defined by that loss and we now are something less—less of a father, less of a mother, less of a son, less of a daughter, less of a person. Worse, Satan would have us believe we are at fault and responsible for the loss. He wants us to live the rest of our lives in regret, revenge, or remorse.

Satan is wrong, and Satan is a liar. The Greek word for *Satan* is *diabolos* (devil), which means "slanderer." The Hebrew word for *Satan* is *Ha-Satan* (Satan), which means "the accuser" or "the adversary." Don't buy into his lies, his deceits, or his accusations.

One way to defeat Satan's lies is to refuse to focus on the past and your loss. Instead, keep your focus in the moment and on the present. Focus on what you still have and on your blessings. Just because you experienced a loss, don't accept the meaning that Satan would have you apply to that loss. Don't let Satan rewrite your history.

Instead, turn your history over to God. Make your history His story. Attach your own meaning, or better yet, His meaning, to your history, your past, your story. Don't accept Satan's meaning. It only will take you to a place where you don't want to go. It will only take you to a place where you will get stuck. That place is not happy; in fact, that place is called hell. If Satan gets his way with you, he will have you stuck in a pit called hell.

If allowed, Satan will destroy. He will try to destroy relationships. He will try to destroy plans. He will try to destroy marriages and families. He will try to destroy hope and love. He will try to destroy goals, careers, and dreams. He will try to destroy lives. He will try to destroy your will to live.

The secret to understanding Satan is to remember that his *shtik* (Yiddish for "act, gimmick") is just that—an act, a gimmick, or a scheme. It is not real. When you hear his voice, he may try to trick you into thinking it is real. He may tell you half-truths or include just enough factual information or partial truths to make his lies seem believable. Or he may use someone else or something else to convey the message he wants you to hear to try to create credibility and to try to make you believe that negative meaning.

A good example of the use of this technique is the defense of a criminal case by a criminal defense attorney. Now I'm not saying attorneys are analogous to Satan, even though there are some who may possess this opinion. What I am saying is that when a criminal defense attorney defends someone accused of a crime, it is not the attorney's job to prove his client's innocence (unless the accused has been accused of committing a crime in Mexico).

When someone is accused of committing a crime, the burden of proof is that proof "beyond a reasonable doubt." So often the job of a criminal defense attorney is to create doubt in the minds of the jurors. This is particularly true when the evidence of the commission of a crime is circumstantial. Even if there is considerable evidence supporting an indictment or a criminal charge that someone committed a crime, the job of a criminal defense attorney is to create doubt about that evidence. The successful criminal defense attorney will create the existence of reasonable doubt in the minds of the jurors.

This is what Satan does. He creates doubt in our minds. He manufactures meaning, usually of a negative nature, and wants you to attach that malicious meaning to the facts or evidence before you in the present. He uses all the tools at his disposal to create doubt and confusion. His goal is division and separation. He wants to separate us from our spouse, our children, our parents, our dreams, our goals, ourselves, and our God.

In my example of the criminal defense attorney, a successful prosecutor will remind the jury that what the criminal defense attorney says is not evidence. The successful prosecutor will bring the jury's focus back to the empirical evidence and remind the jury it is only to apply the law to the actual evidence. The successful prosecutor will remind each of the members of the jury that each of them shall look at the evidence and reach his own conclusion concerning the search for the truth.

This is the exercise of discernment. We are to examine the evidence. That is our solemn responsibility. We are not to attach extraneous meaning to the events in our lives. We are to stand firmly on the Word and put on the full armor of God to resist Satan's temptations. We are to remember God is not the author of confusion. When we exercise this discernment and restraint, we can control our thoughts and our minds instead of relinquishing them to Satan's schemes.

By applying this skill set of rejoice to a loss, we remind ourselves we should look at the loss empirically as if reading a fact in an obituary. Yes, there was a loss. Yes, it hurt. Yes, it made you sad. You should hurt and feel sad. Whatever was lost mattered. You should grieve.

The loss should not be denied. Sadness and grief are normal and natural responses. But then let it go. Even if there clearly can be fault attributed or blame assigned to the loss, let it go. Even if someone terribly hurt you or even if you were abused or abandoned, release it. Even if some kind of traumatic event disrupted your life, forgive. "Remember it no more."

When God forgives, he blots out our sins and remembers them no more. This doesn't mean He forgets them. It means He will remember them no more, "not counting men's sins against them."[58] Similarly, even if there clearly can be fault attributed or blame assigned or even if you feel *justified* in holding onto your anger, rage, regret, or remorse, you still just have to let it go and forgive.

No one is suggesting you can deny or forget the loss or hurt. However, you are to let it go and remember it no more. The longer you hold on to the loss or blame or guilt, the longer that loss will be an impediment and stumbling block to your ability to move beyond it. You have to forgive the other person, the event, or yourself. Forgiveness is not a matter of fairness or right and wrong or something done only after someone else first apologizes for hurting you. Forgiveness is voluntary. It is mercy. It is a gift. It is freely given.

We often confuse forgiveness with justice. What is just and fair is subjective. What is just to one person often is unjust to another. Under the law, justice often is excused by certain defenses or extenuating circumstances. The defenses, the excuses, the justifications, and extenuating circumstances are the subject of debate and argument and may or may not be applied fairly or justly. All these terms are subjective, and depending on the application, may mean different things to different people.

Forgiveness doesn't involve fairness or justice, and it isn't conditional upon first receiving an apology. While forgiveness may be accompanied first with an apology, it is not an essential element or requirement or precondition of forgiveness. Forgiveness is mercy. It is a gift.

Most everyone is familiar with the story or parable Jesus told of the lost or prodigal son. (Luke 15:11–31) This is a good comparison and example between justice and compassion and between fairness and forgiveness.

In the story, the prodigal son demanded his inheritance and squandered it in another country. Upon realizing his mistake, he resolved to return to his father, repent, and ask for his father's forgiveness. However, while the son was still "a long way off, his father saw him and was filled with compassion for him; he ran to his son, threw his arms around him and kissed him" (Luke 15:20). His father showed compassion and mercy even before his son apologized, without first requiring an apology.

In this parable, the father extended mercy to his son instead of the justice the son deserved. The father's older son was indignant that the father held a party in honor of the prodigal son's return. The older son became angry, and his reaction reflects another kind of justice and fairness.

One kind of fairness and justice reflected in the behavior of the older son is the belief the prodigal son should have received the punishment he deserved for his bad behavior. This is in part why the older son is angry. However, the older son's anger also reflects another kind of fairness and justice. The older son reflects the belief that responsible behavior is the kind of behavior that should be rewarded. The older son was angry because he followed the rules and the celebration by the father did not reflect that set of values. The older son lived by a set of rules, morals, and values requiring works to determine and justify the rewards. Both sets of values exhibited by the older son demonstrate how one's sense of fairness and justice can interfere with and interrupt the ability to forgive.

I believe the parable of the prodigal son instructs even further. I believe the older son's value system based on fairness, justice, and works is representative of the old covenant represented by keeping the commandments in the Old Testament. The older son believed his righteousness came from his following the rules. God made it clear though that righteousness could not be earned or won by obeying the rules and commandments. The actions of the father toward his son who was lost and now was found demonstrate the mercy and love represented by the new covenant made possible with Christ's death and resurrection. The father's mercy demonstrates we are saved only by the grace of God through Christ's death and resurrection. It is not something that can be earned by obeying the commandments or by following the rules. It is not a reward to be earned by our good works.

To me, this is an important and integral principal in overcoming depression. We may not want to forgive because the other person hurt or offended us. We may not want to forgive because we believe the person who offended us is deserving of punishment instead of forgiveness. We also may not want to forgive because, in our minds, forgiving the other person would diminish or devalue our own efforts and works at following the rules, being responsible, and doing the right thing. Either way, we are attaching unjustified meanings and judgments to events and actions. Such meanings and judgments only serve to make us hold on to past hurts.

It may help you to think of forgiveness in terms that forgiveness doesn't mean that you are condoning or forgiving the behavior or wrongful act. The person who hurt you may have exhibited behavior that can still be wrong, very wrong. However, the act of forgiving that person for his behavior is the recognition that you are releasing and giving up that anger and hurt you feel as a result. Such resulting anger and hurt affects you—not the other person who wronged you.

Someone once said that not forgiving someone is like drinking poison with the expectation that the person who offended you will die. By not forgiving the other person you only hurt yourself.

By forgiving the other person, you instead release that anger and hurt that you are feeling so that you can heal. By not forgiving the other person, you allow that hurt or wrong to continue to hurt and affect you, long after the event. It is the realization that it is your thoughts and feelings of anger and hurt that affect you—not the other person. Whether those thoughts and feelings of anger and hurt get released is not up to the other person or within the other person's control—that is up to you. That is within your control. Release them and let them go.

Another way of viewing forgiveness is that you are forgiving the person, not the wrongful act. Some people say, "Hate the sin, not the sinner." Applied to forgiveness, the expression becomes, "Forgive the sinner, not the sin." When you do this, you are not being *judgmental*. On the practical side, you are recognizing that by forgiving and releasing the anger and hurt, you are not allowing the other person or wrongful act to continue to affect and hurt you. On the spiritual side, you are recognizing that it is not your place to judge. I often say that it is God's place to judge, and I'm not Him. Even on the cross, Christ said, "Father, forgive them, for they do not know what they are doing" (Luke 23:34). Christ gave us the greatest example of forgiveness: forgive the person and not the behavior.

By not forgiving and by attaching such negative meanings such as anger and hurt, and by being judgmental, we become easy prey to Satan's tricks and deceits. Satan deceives us into finding justification for not forgiving. Satan tricks us into judging others. In the Gospel of John, Jesus said we are not to judge and that even He didn't come to judge: "As for the person who hears my words but does not keep them, I do not judge him. For I did not come to judge the world, but to save it" (John 12:47). Don't judge, but forgive so you can release the past hurts and losses and let them go. Perhaps we not only need to forgive others, but perhaps we also need to forgive ourselves.

I love the story where Peter asked Jesus how many times we are to forgive:

> Then Peter came to Jesus and asked, "Lord, how many times shall I forgive my brother when he sins against me? Up to seven times? Jesus answered, "I tell you, not seven times, But seventy-seven times."[59]

Among all the disciples who could have asked this question, it's interesting that Peter was the one disciple who asked Jesus the question on forgiveness. Christ answered Peter, knowing Peter later would betray Him and deny even knowing Him not only once, but three times.

After commanding us to forgive seventy-seven times, Jesus then proceeded to tell the disciples a parable about forgiveness. He told about a king, also called a master, who had a servant who owed the king a debt of ten thousand talents. The king extended compassion to his servant and forgave and cancelled the debt. The servant, however, later refused to cancel a debt another person owed to the servant in the amount of only one hundred denarii.

A denarius was a silver Roman coin containing four grams of silver. A talent also was a unit of currency and weighed about seventy-five pounds (www.convertunits.com/from/pounds/to/talent+[Hebrew]). Because a talent could be either gold or silver, for comparison purposes, let's assume the talents referenced in the parable were silver, so the silver content in the talents could be compared easily to the silver content in the denarii.

The comparison between the value of the one debt in the amount of ten thousand talents and the value of the other debt in the amount of one hundred denarii is absolutely remarkable (http://coinapps.com/silver/pound/calculator/):

1 gram	=	.03 troy ounce	=	$0.70
31.1 grams	=	1 troy ounce	=	$21.88
14.583 troy ounces	=	1 pound	=	$319.08
1 denarius	=	4 grams	=	$2.80
1 talent	=	75 pounds	=	$23,931.00
100 denarii	=	400 grams	=	$280.00
10,000 talents	=	750,000 pounds	=	$239,310,000.00

Let's put this into perspective. In Jesus's parable, the servant owed the king ten thousand talents. In today's value, the debt the king forgave (10,000 talents) was more than $239 million dollars compared to the value of the debt the servant refused to forgive (100 denarii) of only $280 dollars.

Jesus's example was not just an exaggeration or comparison unimaginable to Peter and the other disciples. Even though Peter was an uneducated fisherman, he and the other disciples undoubtedly understood Jesus's point. They probably knew it was written in the Old Testament in 1 Chronicles that King David had set aside ten thousand talents (3,000 gold talents and 7,000 silver talents) from his personal treasure not to be used to build the temple, but to be used just to decorate it "for the overlaying of the walls of the buildings, for the gold work and the silver work, and for all the work to be done by the craftsmen."[60] So the disciples could compare the amount of the debt forgiven by the king (10,000 talents) to be equivalent to the value or the amount King David set aside from his personal wealth to decorate the temple.

Jesus's parable is referred to as the "unmerciful servant," and in the parable, the king said to the servant, "Shouldn't you have had mercy on your fellow servant just as I had on you?"[61]

The question the king asked his servant was the same principle Jesus taught his disciples when he taught them how to pray.

> Our Father in heaven, hallowed be your name. Your kingdom come, Your will be done, on earth as it is in heaven. Give us today our daily bread. Forgive us our debts, as we also have forgiven our debtors. And lead us not into temptation, but deliver us from the evil one.[62]

Jesus referred to sins as debts. In fact, when Peter asked Jesus the question about how many times we are to forgive, Peter said, "Lord, how many times shall I forgive my brother when he sins against me?" Peter didn't frame the question he asked Jesus in terms about a debt. Rather, Peter asked Jesus about the forgiveness of sins. Yet Jesus answered Peter's question with a parable about debts, and when teaching the disciples how to pray, He said we should pray to God and ask that He "forgive us our debts, as we also have forgiven our debtors."

This is why the unmerciful servant parable is so poignant. The servant wanted forgiveness (mercy) for his debt, but he was not willing to extend the same forgiveness (mercy) to one indebted to him for only a fraction of the amount for which the servant wanted forgiveness. When Jesus commanded Peter and the disciples that we are to forgive seventy-seven times, Jesus was instructing that we should continue to forgive sins and debts and trespasses just as God forgives—so we will remember them no more.

In the parable of the unmerciful servant, before the king forgave the debt, the king ordered the servant, his family, and his possessions all be sold to repay the debt: "Since he was not able to pay, the master ordered that he and his wife and his children and all that he had be sold to repay the debt."[63] Although the servant then "fell on his knees" and begged for mercy, the servant actually didn't ask the king to forgive the debt. Rather, the servant said, "Be patient with me," he begged, "and I will pay back everything." The king then "took pity on him, cancelled the debt and let him go." The king gave the servant even more mercy than the servant requested.

Although Peter was just a fisherman, and although he and the other disciples may not have been able to comprehend the magnitude of the precise amount of money represented by the equivalent of ten thousand talents, I believe they grasped Jesus's point. Jesus said the parable of the unmerciful servant was like the kingdom of heaven.[64] When the king in the parable heard how the servant refused to forgive the one hundred denarii debt, "In anger his master turned him over to the jailers to be tortured, until he should pay back all he owed."[65] Jesus ended the parable by saying, "This is how my heavenly Father will treat each of you unless you forgive your brother from your heart."[66]

As a result, Jesus commanded us to forgive "seventy-seven times." Each time we forgive, the sin or debt is blotted out. It is cancelled. Consequently, even if someone has hurt us in the past, we are to continue to forgive. We are "not to remember" the offense so we are "not counting men's sins against them." By the same principle, we also are to forgive ourselves. Forgiveness is mercy.

Jesus commands us to forgive. This is not something we need to pray about. We are not just to forgive, but we are to forgive seventy-seven times. Even though that seems impossible, it is nothing compared to the debt Jesus paid for us when He died on the cross. This is probably why, in the parable, Jesus had the king forgive a debt more than 850,000 times greater than the amount the servant had been asked to forgive. We are to be Christlike and forgive others, just as we are forgiven. In fact, how we forgive others shall determine how we will be forgiven.

This is the significance of the parable of the unmerciful servant. Even though the disciples might not have comprehended the exact amount of the debt the king forgave in the parable, they could certainly comprehend the magnitude of the debt represented by all the collective world's sins Jesus would forgive with His death and resurrection. They also surely could comprehend the admonition in the Lord's Prayer that we ourselves will establish the measure or extent by which we will be forgiven. The manner or measure in which we will be forgiven will be to the same extent "as we also have forgiven our debtors."

Satan knows Christ already has claimed victory over him. In fact, the Bible illustrates that Satan needed God's permission before he could tempt Job and Peter. Satan knows that he really has no power over us. "But the Lord is faithful, who will establish you and guard you from the evil one" (2 Thessalonians 3:3). To claim that victory, we need only confess and repent our sins and believe in the sanctification of Jesus's death and resurrection. We then become children of God. When we stand firm in the Word and put on and use the full armor of God, Satan will flee. "His truth will be your shield" (Psalm 91:4). "The peace of God, which surpasses all understanding, will guard your hearts and minds through Christ Jesus" (Philippians 4:7). God promises that "The God of peace will soon crush Satan under your feet."[67]

When we apply this skill set, we can rejoice in several ways. The first way is to rejoice in all the blessings we have received.

Rather than focusing on our loss, we should instead focus on our blessings. When we focus on our blessings, we should praise God and give Him thanks. We should engage in an exercise that requires us to take an inventory of our blessings so we can be thankful for what we still have in our lives.

Once we have done this, we can even train our mind to be thankful for experiencing our loss. What I mean by this is that our loss can still serve a purpose. Instead of attaching the meaning Satan wants us to attach to our loss, we instead choose to attach a powerful and positive meaning to the loss. Even the worst kind of a loss, the death of a loved one, in this way can be the catalyst for the start of something purposeful. You can begin or join a foundation or a cause to make a positive change. You can take back control of your own thoughts and mind and choose your own meaning to assign to your loss. In the same way, you can choose your own meaning to assign to your life.

Another way to rejoice is to volunteer to serve others. When we volunteer or help others, we take our minds off our own problems and troubles. Like Christ, we then serve other's needs. Not only does volunteering and serving others take our minds off our own problems and losses, but it also provides meaning and purpose in our lives. Part of severe depression is not having any motivation or desire to pursue activities. When you volunteer and serve others' needs, your life soon has a purpose and meaning greater than you and your loss.

When you volunteer and serve others, you discover that your loss may not be as great, or at least you are able to put it into perspective, because you are helping others who may not be as fortunate. Once again, let me use the extreme example of the loss of a loved one. There is absolutely nothing I can say to heal the hurt for that kind of a loss. Only God can heal that loss. However, there is something you can do to help you move past that loss and release it. Many people begin a foundation or create a scholarship in the memory of the lost loved one. Others create awareness to the issue that contributed to or related to the loss such as MADD (Mothers Against Drunk Driving). Others simply speak out to educate or enlighten others to a greater awareness.

The point is that each of these steps is a positive action you can and should take to help you overcome the loss. Satan wants you to do nothing. He wants you to lay on your mat, paralyzed. He wants you to suffer. He wants to defeat you. He wants to assign a negative meaning to your loss. Don't let him. He is already defeated. Create your own meaning. Create your own constructive, positive, and purposeful meaning for the loss you experienced so you can release it and let it go. You could not control or prevent the loss, but you can control how you react to the loss.

Finally, we can rejoice in knowing that Christ's death and resurrection has already won victory over Satan. The idea that "the God of peace will soon crush Satan under your feet" is a reference to an old custom after battle where the victor would step on the throat of his enemy, as referenced in the book of Joshua. After the Lord defeated the Amorites, Joshua had the defeated kings brought to him. Joshua said to his commanders, "Come here and put your feet on the necks of these kings."[68] The commanders then put their feet on the necks of each of the defeated kings. Just before Joshua killed the kings, he said, "This is what the Lord will do to all the enemies you are going to fight."[69] It is probably from this custom of stepping on the necks of the vanquished we obtain the phrase "Going for the jugular."

God told Joshua, "Be strong and courageous. Do not be terrified; do not be discouraged, for the Lord your God will be with you wherever you go."[70] Stand firm on God's Word and on His promises. Be strong and courageous. When tempted to judge and to demand retribution, instead show mercy. Forgive.

In the Lord's Prayer, we are to seek God's will ("Your will be done on earth as it is in heaven."). What is God's will? How do we accomplish God's will? Paul tells us in his letter to the Thessalonians God's will for us is to have us rejoice, pray and give thanks, "Rejoice always, pray continually, give thanks in all circumstances; for this is God's will for you in Christ Jesus."[71]

Therefore, we should rejoice. If we harbor resentment and are unforgiving, we can never fully rejoice and receive the full measure of grace and blessings that come with it. This is the next lesson learned from the parable of the prodigal son.

In the parable of the prodigal son, when the father saw his prodigal son returning home, he immediately knew his son had repented and turned back. The Greek word for *repent* is *metanoia*, which means a "change of mind." It literally means to "turn back." It is conversion. It is changing one's mind-set to turn back and make a complete change from one mind-set and way of life to another. It is more than just remorse or sorrow or regret. It is the purposeful act of conversion.

In the prior section of renewal, I discussed the difference between Peter and Judas Iscariot. They both were remorseful for having betrayed Jesus. However, only Peter turned back and repented. While repentance may include sorrow and remorse, the actual act of repentance is the *metanoia*. It is the turning back, the conversion, from one's self-trust and self-assertion and self-will to an obedient commitment and trust to God's will.

The same can be said for the practical and therapeutic application. By changing one's mind-set, there is a *metanoia* where one releases the loss or the hurt and experiences a similar conversion to a different way of thinking and acting to the development of a renewed mind.

In the parable of the prodigal son, the older brother could not bring himself to join in the celebration. While the father orchestrated a party to celebrate that his lost son was now found, the older brother was outside the party, outside the house. He was on the outside, looking in. In fact, he "refused to go in" (Luke 15:28). The older brother's selfish and stubborn mind-set, his self-righteous value system, his superior sense of right and wrong, and his proud sense of fairness and justice, all prevented him from being able to rejoice and join in the celebration.

I love the wisdom expressed by the father in explaining to the older brother the cause for celebration. The father said, "But we had to celebrate and be glad, because this brother of yours was dead and is alive again; he was lost and is found" (Luke 15:32). The father said, "We *had* to celebrate." We are to rejoice and give thanks.

The irony of the story of the prodigal son is that the prodigal son repented, but the older brother did not. While it is easy to comprehend the prodigal son's repentance and the need for repentance, it is more difficult to understand the older brother's need for repentance. The older brother's mind-set was prideful indignation. His prideful sense of fairness and justice provided him with a sense of entitlement and superiority that prevented him from understanding the true value of repentance and forgiveness. The older brother only wanted to see things from his way and point of view. He wanted to exercise his will instead of God's will.

I'm sure the older brother would not have been so stubborn and indignant had he been able to forgive his brother without forgiving or condoning what the brother, the prodigal son, had done. This is exactly what the father had done.

Often overlooked in the story of the prodigal son is how the father forgave the prodigal son. Clearly, by forgiving his son, the father had not condoned what his prodigal son had done. By demanding his inheritance, the prodigal son undoubtedly hurt and embarrassed the father. Yet the father forgave him. The father's forgiveness didn't condone what his son had done, but rather the father forgave *him*. By forgiving his son, the father was able to release that hurt and embarrassment occasioned by the prodigal son's actions. By not forgiving his brother, the older brother held on to the hurt and anger and could not heal.

This is the way it is with depression and PTSD. When we attach negative meanings, we get stuck in that mind-set. We have to develop a changed mind and a renewed mind. We have to undergo and experience a conversion, a *metanoia*. Often, that means we have to forgive someone. More often, it means we have to forgive ourselves. We have to forgive to be able to move on. If we fail to forgive, we are unable to release the hurt feelings and loss.

The same is true with the spiritual application. God commands us to forgive seventy-seven times. God knows what is best for us. Unless and until we forgive, we will not be able to rejoice. Satan wants us to hold on to those false meanings.

Satan wants us to lean on our own understanding, on our own value system, and on our own sense of fairness and justice because Satan knows we then will not be obedient to God. We cannot adhere to our own sense of values and continue to do what we want (our will) and, at the same time, pray the Lord's Prayer that God's will shall be done ("your will be done").

Moreover, we can't slide by and expect God or someone else to take responsibility for our forgiveness business. Like I said, the act of forgiveness is deliberate and intentional. It is not something we can delegate. It is our own individual personal responsibility, and it is the measure by which our own debts, sins and transgressions will be forgiven (Forgive us our debts, as we also have forgiven our debtors).

Pray continually and give thanks "in all circumstances." Give thanks and rejoice for our blessings, not only in the good times but also during the storms. Give thanks especially during the storms. Repent, forgive, and join the celebration. Don't be on the outside of the celebration, refusing to go in and refusing to join the party. Join the party. Celebrate your blessings. Rejoice and praise God.

Because of my depression and PTSD, I lost my way. You also may feel like you lost your way because you are suffering from depression or from some form of mental illness. That's okay. There is help, and there is hope. Satan wants you to stay lost. Satan doesn't want you to experience a conversion and a changed mind and heart. Satan will even deceive you as he deceived me into thinking you should be embarrassed and ashamed because you have suffered from depression, PTSD, or some other form of mental illness or substance use disorder. Satan knows that such shame, embarrassment or stigmatism can keep you from getting help.

Later in this book, I devote an entire chapter to overcoming the stigmatism and shame attached to mental illness, but now let me just say there is no shame in suffering from depression, PTSD, or some other form of mental illness. The only shame, the only tragedy, is when someone stays stuck in depression or mental illness and doesn't get the help he needs. My prayer is that this book will encourage and inspire you to seek help and treatment so you can use these skill sets during your own road to recovery. Experience the peace and joy that comes from conversion. Experience a changed mind and a changed heart. Rejoice, pray and give thanks—especially in the storm.

Reliance

I have fought the good fight. I have finished the race. I
have kept the faith.

—2 Timothy 4:7

The last skill set to utilize in overcoming depression is reliance.
This is the belief that your application of all the skills you
learned and the tools you acquired can be effectively employed
to resist and overcome depression. In this sense then, it is faith.

The biggest part of depression is the doubt and fear
accompanying the setbacks. Just when you think things are
getting better, something will happen. Someone will hurt you.
Something won't work out. You will get discouraged. You will
get sad. You will feel depressed again.

When this happens, the biggest fear is you are not getting
better. You desperately want to be better. You don't want to be
on medication. You want to be happy. You see other people
laughing and you can't understand why you can't laugh. You get
angry and irritable. You want to know why you can't get better.
You don't want sympathy or pity.

You just want to get better!

This is when you have to trust and have faith. You have to
know, understand, believe, and accept that setbacks are a normal
part of the recovery process. When you experience a setback,
don't get discouraged. You can't give up. You can't quit. You have
to trust the cognitive behavioral skills you have learned and
acquired. You just have to keep practicing them and trust you
will get better. Trust your stuff.

Accepting the fact that setbacks and relapses are part of the
normal recovery process is easier when you remind yourself
depression is an illness. Just like many other illnesses or diseases,
you may have a relapse and you may need additional treatment.
After remission, cancer can reoccur. You can get bronchitis or

pneumonia again. The skill sets have worked in the past, and they will work again. By not quitting and giving up and giving in, you can overcome and defeat depression.

In many respects, this is the hardest skill set. It is the one that allows you to develop the tenacity to trust and push through the pain.

When I was living in Kansas, I played basketball on Monday nights in pickup games in the church gym. It was great fun. Everybody who played in these pick-up games had played high school ball and a few had even played ball in college. I was in my comfort zone playing guard because I could just graze around the three-point line and shoot from the outside. More importantly, I didn't have to run the full length of the court. I only played between the three-point lines. However, on one occasion, I ventured into the paint among the tall timbers and went for the rim. When I came back down to earth my size 9 foot landed on top of a size 13. I tore the ligaments on both sides of my ankle. I remember the doctor telling me I was going to wish I had broken my ankle instead.

When I began therapy, I learned what the doctor meant. It was absolutely excruciatingly painful. I wanted to stop. He told me I might not be able to run again if I didn't power through the therapy. I remember receiving a lot of sympathy each time I went into court on crutches, but I would never want to endure that therapy again. My recovery and therapy following the meniscus surgeries I later had on each of my knees was comparatively easy.

Just like physical therapy following an accident or surgery, a patient suffering from depression needs to participate in therapy. It is painful. I have to admit there were some occasions where it was even more painful than my physical therapy after I blew out my ankle ligaments.

Reliance is the skill set and the process of trusting what you learned so you can fight through the pain. It is relying on the skills you learned so you can handle that next wave of emotion that washes over you without being fearful of drowning. You have to tell yourself you have been through it before and you can handle it again. Remind yourself to stay in the moment and practice your skill sets.

If you are going through depression, know it is not an easy fix. There is no happy pill you can take. There is no get-out-of-jail free card you can use to help you escape from your emotional prison. It is hard. The pain is real. But do you know what? Because the pain is real, you know you are alive. You know you still have feelings because you feel them getting crushed time and time again. Just know that the hurt feelings, the setbacks, and the emotional roller-coaster ride you are on are all part of the process. It is a process, and you have to give it time to allow yourself to be able to process your feelings and emotions. It is a recovery journey. It will get better.

When I was in group therapy, there were two occasions where I just had to get up and leave. On one occasion, it was just too painful to talk anymore. I just had to excuse myself and leave. Even though I was in a nonthreatening environment, I felt too threatened and vulnerable at that moment. By the next week, I was able to continue to talk about the issue.

On the other occasion, the group facilitator wanted to show a short film on PTSD to help those in the group better understand the illness. I didn't make it past the first two minutes of the film. When I saw the flashing lights and heard the sirens at the beginning, I was immediately transported back to 9-11.

Although I was sitting in a safe environment, without warning, I began to experience a flashback. I just started crying uncontrollably and ran out of the room. By running out of the room, I was trying to run away from the trauma. By the next week,

I was okay. The group thought the facilitator was brilliant using me as a prop and a visual device for the movie to demonstrate the effect of PTSD. It was as if I had run out of the room right on cue. Seriously, although there were many times in group therapy when I didn't want to attend and had to force myself to go, I honestly can say I never left a session without having felt better for having been there and for having participated.

I relate and share my experiences to be an encouragement to you. Group therapy was effective for me in that it allowed me to interact with others encountering similar difficulties and the group was helpful in providing support, accountability, and camaraderie. It provided me the safe setting I needed to be able to vocalize my feelings and emotions. It also provided me the opportunity to be supportive and encouraging to the other members of the group. Group therapy may be beneficial to you.

However, the most effective therapy in overcoming depression is cognitive behavioral therapy (CBT). Three principles involved in cognitive therapy definitely will help you in your battle with depression. First, your thoughts greatly influence your moods. Second, those thoughts are often automatic and usually negative. Third, there are certain techniques or tools you can implement that work effectively to change those thoughts to improve your moods.

CBT usually is a series of sessions where a psychologist trained in cognitive behavioral therapy will teach the patient how to recognize patterns of thought that affect behavior and mood. The therapist then will teach certain tools or techniques that will allow the patient to challenge and change those patterns of thoughts. These tools and skills are similar to the skill sets I have identified in this book.

The advantage of CBT is that it is transparent. This means the therapist engages with the patient in explaining what is happening and how the patient's thoughts are affecting his moods and causing the depression. The therapist then explains how the tools work in altering or changing those thought patterns. For me, this transparency not only was enlightening, but it also was empowering. Dr. S showed me I have the ability to change how I think and feel. I didn't have to be a victim to depression and PTSD. Part of being depressed is feeling you have no control over your thoughts or emotions. Learning that you alone control your thoughts and emotions is empowering.

I learned depression often is fueled by automatic thoughts and responses to situations. Usually, those automatic thoughts are of a negative nature, or at least of an irrational nature. What I mean by this is that the thoughts are not grounded in reality. They have untrue meaning attached to them. The events and situations are real, but the meaning being attached to those events and situations is not real. They are perceived or imagined. They are judgments about those events.

For example, if you tend to be a perfectionist or at least have perfectionist tendencies, when you experience even a small setback, disappointment, or failure, you may tend to blow it out of proportion or exaggerate its consequence. The same phenomenon applies if you tend to be a pessimist or tend to think negatively about events or situations. In either of these two examples, your thoughts are predisposed toward a particular outcome. Often, that outcome is in the form of an absolute, and with depression the absolutism is usually expressed in the negative. When making a mistake, even a small one, the perfectionist may think something like, "I'm the worst (fill in the blank)." Similarly the pessimist may think something like, "I always (fill in blank)." These absolutes and predispositions of a negative nature distort the reality of the moment.

This is particularly true with depression when someone's thoughts are distorted by views of the past. Predisposed thoughts, usually negative, use the past to distort the reality of the present and make us anxious about the future. They tell you that you should just give up because you are destined to repeat your past failures. They tell you everything is hopeless because you can't get past your past.

Cognitive behavioral therapy is not simply the power of positive thinking. It is not, "Don't worry; Be Happy." Rather, it is the recognition that your thoughts about a situation or event are not totally grounded in the reality of the moment because those thoughts are being automatically interpreted and distorted in a negative way. In this way, cognitive behavioral therapy is not positive thinking, but reality thinking. It is first recognizing that those automatic thoughts are irrational and then taking steps and applying learned techniques and skill sets to change those automatic negative and irrational thoughts and responses into new, real thoughts based on the reality of the present moment.

When we are depressed, we think or respond automatically to a situation or event in a way that keeps us depressed. When we assess a situation, we automatically filter and distort the new experience by our thoughts and feelings about past experiences. In this sense, we learned how to think automatically or negatively about things, and that negative thought process has become automatic or habitual. Simply because such thoughts are automatic, however, doesn't mean that you have no control over them, or that you can't control them. To be able to change those habitual, automatic thought processes, you have to unlearn them. You may have learned them from parents. You may have acquired them from prior experiences such as being bullied or abused. You may have had them seared into your mind from a traumatic event. However you acquired them, they have to be unlearned.

The tricky part is recognizing your thoughts are not grounded in reality. The reason it is tricky is because many of your thoughts may have partial elements of truth imbedded in them. This is where the devil comes in. He will deceive you with partial or half-truths to make your thoughts seem believable. This is why you have to exercise discernment.

Depending on the situation, most of cognitive behavioral therapy is short-term, usually between six and twenty sessions. Your therapist, depending upon your situation, will determine the frequency of the sessions. You will be taught certain skill sets you will have in your toolbox that you will utilize to alter your thoughts and affect your moods. They may be different from or similar to the skill sets I have related here. The reason the number of therapy sessions is relatively short is because the application of your learned skill sets have to be practiced and applied to your thoughts as you experience new situations. In this way, you will understand how your thoughts (cognitions) and behavior are connected with your emotions and moods. As needed, the therapist can intervene and assist you in applying and using the tools and skills differently or more effectively.

Through CBT, the patient and therapist work closely together to establish short-term goals of different behavioral results. The skill sets are employed in a step-by-step process and in a methodical way to change your thinking from an automatic negative response to one grounded in the reality of the present.

Patients learn to use their skill sets and tools to challenge their automatic thoughts and responses to situations and to distinguish thoughts from emotions. By using their new skills, patients unlearn past patterns of thinking. They learn to recognize when those automatic thoughts occur, to arrest and interrupt them, and then to eliminate them through discernment.

Cognitive behavioral therapy engages small changes in thinking and behavior over a period of time. It is not a quick fix or an instant remedy. Like I said before, there is no happy pill. It is hard work. Sometimes it is painful. Sometimes there will be setbacks. Sometimes you will seem like you are experiencing a relapse and not getting better. It is at these times that Satan will try to discourage you and make you quit. You can't quit. You can't give up. Just like God told Joshua, "Be strong and courageous."

In God's commands to Joshua before leading the Israelites into the promised land, God didn't tell Joshua just once to be "strong and courageous." He repeated it five times. Joshua had just been anointed to rule and lead the Israelites into the promised land. Moses, God's prophet and ambassador in leading the Israelites out of Egypt, had died.[72] Joshua was replacing Moses, and God wanted him to be courageous.

Just before Moses died, Moses told Joshua and the Israelites that Joshua, and not Moses, would lead them into the promised land. Moses told Joshua to be "strong and courageous" three times.[73] This was not accidental. This was purposeful and intentional. God then told Joshua to be strong and courageous another five times. We have to be encouraged. We have to be reminded to be strong. Satan is relentless. Even if you beat him in battle, he will keep coming after you. Satan (*diablos*) is diabolical. Nevertheless, don't get discouraged. Don't give up. Be strong and courageous.

It is the same kind of intentional, purposeful thinking you need to have as you progress through therapy on your journey to recovery. You have to exercise the last skill set of reliance. You have to rely on the skill sets and tools you learned. You have to trust. You have to have faith.

Through therapy, concentrate on making small changes in your thinking and in your behavior over a period of time. Don't allow your mind to focus on your setbacks. Instead, focus on your goals and the accomplishment of each small goal along the way. Each one is a milestone or signpost representing you are in fact getting better. Don't let Satan deceive you into thinking or believing you are stuck in depression and you always are going to be stuck in depression. It's not true. Satan is a liar. Don't buy into the negativity. He knows how to push your buttons. Don't let him do it. Use your skill sets to change your thoughts and defeat him. With depression, and with Satan, you are engaged in a battle over your thoughts and mind. He only has the limited power over you that you give him. He has no real power over you.

During the storm, the disciples were afraid they were going to drown. They woke Jesus and asked Him to save them. After Jesus calmed the storm, "He said to his disciples, 'Why are you so afraid? Do you still have no faith?'"[74] Jesus asked this of His disciples because they had already witnessed His miracles, but yet they were afraid because of their lack of trust.

The skill set of reliance is having faith in knowing the skills you learned and tools you acquired through therapy effectively work in defeating depression. You can have faith in that knowledge because you will learn to trust in those skills and tools that worked in the past. They have worked for me. They have worked for others. They will work for you.

The skill set of reliance is also having faith in God and in the knowledge that He already defeated Satan with Christ's death and resurrection. That faith is based on the knowledge, wisdom, and understanding that is in the Word, the Bible. It contains God's promises that He will give you the strength and courage you need to overcome Satan.

After fasting for forty days in the desert, Jesus was tempted by Satan three times. Each time, Jesus repelled Satan by invoking the power of the Word. On the third time, Satan tempted Jesus, Jesus ordered Satan to leave Him:

> Jesus said to him, "Away from me, Satan! For it is written: Worship the Lord your God, and serve Him only." Then the devil left him.[75]

As Christians, we have the same power over Satan because we have Christ in us. If we invoke the power of the Word, we also have the power to make Satan retreat and flee. As James said, "Resist the devil, and he will flee from you. Come near to God and He will come near to you" (James 4:7–8). Use the skill set of reliance to rely on God's promise that you actually have the power and authority in Christ in you to make the devil flee from you.

When I became discouraged during one of my relapses or setbacks, I was reminded of one of my favorite poems called "Footsteps."

> One night I dreamed a dream as I was walking along the beach with my Lord. Across the dark sky flashed scenes from my life. For each scene, I noticed two sets of footprints in the sand, one belonging to me and one to my Lord. After the last scene of my life flashed before me, I looked back at the footprints in the sand. I noticed that at many times along the path of my life, especially at the very lowest and saddest times, there was only one set of footprints. This really troubled me so I asked the Lord about it. "Lord, you said once I decided to follow you, You'd walk with me all the way. But I noticed that during the saddest and most troublesome times of my life, there was only one set of footprints. I don't understand why, when I needed You the most, You would leave me." He whispered, "My precious child, I love you and will never leave you. Never, ever, during your trials and testings. When you saw only one set of footprints, It was then that I carried you.[76]

I purchased a framed copy of this poem during college, and I have kept it with me on my desk all these years until I recently gave it to my son now that he is going to college. This poem reminds me God is always with us and is always there to help us if we only will ask Him. As the prophet Isaiah said, "He tends

His flock like a shepherd: He gathers the lambs in His arms and carries them close to His heart" (Isaiah 40:11).

He will carry us when we stumble, and He will not let us fall. As David said in Psalm 37:

> If the LORD delights in a man's way, He makes his steps firm; though he stumble, he will not fall, for the LORD upholds him with His hand.[77]

You can rely on God. He is faithful and will never leave you nor forsake you. Even if you stumble, even if you experience a setback, even if you encounter a relapse, the Lord will not let you fall. He will lift you up.

As Paul said in Ephesians, "Finally, be strong in the Lord and in his mighty power. Put on the full armor of God so that you can take your stand against the devil's schemes."[78] When you experience a setback and get disappointed, exercise this last skill set of reliance. Keep practicing the skills you learn.

These seven skill sets are effective tools in my battle with depression, and I want to encourage you and help you help yourself with your own battle with depression or PTSD or with any other illness, but I stress they are not a replacement for medical treatment and therapy. Each case is different and requires a different diagnosis and treatment plan.

In providing these skill sets, I have presented them both from the cognitive therapy practical perspective, as well as from the spiritual Christian perspective. I believe we need both. The absence of evil is not goodness. The absence of depression is not joy.

We need to implement and utilize the therapeutic and practical application of the skill sets with a treatment program that may include medication and cognitive behavioral therapy to be able to overcome and defeat depression or PTSD or another form of mental illness. However, we also need to incorporate into our recovery program the spiritual and Christian application of the Word to be able experience the joy and peace God intends for us.

Happiness is fleeting and dependent upon circumstances. When those circumstances change, so does our degree of happiness. Joy, however, is deep and comforting and sustains us when life's circumstances change. That is the wellspring of peace and assurance upon which we rely and depend during storms.

Eliminating depression and overcoming PTSD or any other form of mental illness is only half of the battle. The other half is the addition of hope, joy, peace, and love. These are not elusive platitudes, but are real and transforming. Just as you need a psychological conversion and change of mind, you also need to experience a spiritual conversion and a renewed mind. You need to let go of your own mind-set and lean not on your own understanding. You need to substitute God's will for your will.

I strongly encourage you to get professional help so you can be successful in overcoming your own battles with depression, PTSD, or other form of mental illness. I also strongly encourage you to accept Christ and develop a personal relationship with Him that will sustain you on your journey to recovery. Trust in His Word. Secure your hope in His promises. Even if you stumble along your journey, He will carry you. Be strong and courageous. He will not let you fall. He will lift you up.

- Recognition
  * Recognize the triggers and automatic negative thoughts.
  † Extend mercy and grace—to others and to yourself.

- Reflection
  * Exercise discernment to eliminate negative thoughts.
  † Exercise discernment. Put on the full armor of God.

- Retreat
  * Retreat from negative thoughts and situations.
  † Retreat to the God of peace. God is your sanctuary.

- Renewal
  * Stay in the moment with a renewed beginner's mind.
  † When we repent, we are completely forgiven and renewed.

- Recovery
  * Get rest; exercise; relax your mind.
  † Rest on the Word. God will give you rest and peace.

- Rejoice
  * Focus on your blessings instead of on your loss.
  † Forgive others, forgive yourself, give thanks.

- Reliance
  * Rely on learned skills; trust your skill sets.
  † Have faith in God. Trust in God.

7

Overcoming the Stigmatism

Do not judge, and you will not be judged. Do not
condemn, and you will not be condemned.

—Luke 6:37

Almost two thousand years ago, the Greek philosopher Epictetus said, "Men are disturbed, not by things, but by the principles and notions which they form concerning things."[1] Now almost two thousand years later, society still struggles with "the principles and notions, which [people] form concerning things"—the melancholy malady known as depression.

I've described how someone depressed will attach negative thoughts and meaning to events and situations and how the use of learned skill sets and tools will help disregard those negative thoughts. It is my hope that someone suffering from depression could benefit from reading about my experience. Although I have done my best in writing this story, my efforts here are woefully inadequate and a poor substitute for effective professional treatment and therapy. While these self-help skill sets and techniques should be helpful and beneficial, if you are suffering from depression, please do not hesitate to seek professional help.

I also wish to caution that my discourse here in no way is intended to convey the impression that overcoming depression is simply mind over matter. Unfortunately, society still has the impression that someone depressed simply has to think differently and he or she should just get over it. If my writing has oversimplified and led to the perpetuation of that perception, I sincerely apologize. That clearly was not my intent. Depression is complicated. Depression is a medical illness. Someone may as well say a cancer patient should just get over it.

Let me explain my point. Earlier, I referenced the Holmes-Rahe Life Stress Inventory (the Social Readjustment Rating Scale—SRRS). The SRRS assigns a stress value to each life event in an effort to determine whether the cumulative amount of stress a person experiences within a twelve-month period of time might forewarn of a physical injury or illness. The assumption is that the inventory is valid because the amount of value or points assigned to each of the life events in the SRRS is the same for each person tested.

However, each life event may not be equally stressful to every person tested. For example, the death of a parent or a divorce may be perceived to be greatly more stressful to one person than to another. In that case, the value or scale assigned to each life event would be different for each person.

For example, one person involved in the divorce may be blindsided and devastated by the divorce while the other person may have planned the divorce and be relieved that the marriage is ending. In this situation, each of the two people involved in the divorce would perceive the associated stress differently.

Consider how the effect or result of the Holmes-Rahe Life Stress Inventory would be changed if people were given the same inventory without any values assigned to each life event. In this example, consider what would happen if each person taking the test were instructed to assign the value to each life event. Those depressed probably would assign values markedly different from those not depressed. Now the SRRS, before considered a fairly straightforward and a "fun little test to take," gets complicated.

This phenomenon was investigated in a recent study conducted by French researchers on stress.[2] The researchers reviewed data from a previous British study of approximately 7300 London civil service employees conducted over approximately twenty years. The conclusion reached was that the perception of stress, more than the actual stress from each life event, had a greater impact on health.

In the study, people were asked to rate their perceived level of stress to the following question, "To what extent do you consider the stress or pressure that you have experienced in your life has an effect on your health?" They were asked this question during Phase 3 of the study (1991–1993). Then almost twenty years later, their respective responses to this question were compared to whether they each actually experienced an illness, disease, or death as the result of a heart attack.

Participants were asked to respond to the question by answering *not at all*, *a little*, *moderately*, *a lot*, or *extremely*. The result of the study was that the people who responded by answering *a lot* or *extremely* later suffered a heart attack more than twice as often as the others who responded *not at all*, *a little*, or *moderately*. Taking all variables into consideration (age, gender, alcohol intake, smoking, systolic and diastolic blood pressures, total cholesterol, triglycerides, diabetes, and body mass index [BMI]), the people who answered in 1993 that they considered the stress or pressure they experienced in their lives affected their health either *a lot* or *extremely* actually suffered a heart attack over the next twenty years at a rate of 2.12 times more often than those who answered *"not at all," "a little," or "moderately."*

Dr. Nabi, the lead author of the study, stated in the press release concerning the article:

> We found that the association we observed between an individual's perception of the impact of stress on their

health and their risk of a heart attack was independent of biological factors, unhealthy behaviors and other psychological factors. One of the important messages from our findings is that people's perceptions about the impact of stress on their health are likely to be correct.[3]

The study confirmed a situation that is perceived to be stressful for one person might not be perceived to be stressful to another. In commenting on this study, Dr. Gregg Fonarow, a UCLA professor of cardiology, said this 2013 study was only one of a few in existence that studied how an individual's perception of stress is associated with cardiovascular outcomes."[4]

What someone thinks about a life event can be more stressful and destructive than the life event itself. If someone views or perceives life events cause *a lot* of stress or create an *extremely* large amount of stress, then that person is more than twice as likely to have a heart attack than a person who views the same life events as *not at all* or only *a little* or only *moderately* causing stress or pressure.

This study demonstrated people perceive the amount of stress and pressure caused by life events differently. The same conclusion can be said for depression. Similarly, people have differing degrees of negative thoughts in different degrees. What does this mean in understanding depression? Let me explain by using the Holmes-Rahe Life Stress Inventory again.

The Holmes-Rahe Life Stress Inventory assumes the value or the SRRS assigned to each life event is the same for each person. In other words, the amount of stress or pressure assigned to each life event in the Holmes-Rahe Life Stress Inventory is assumed to be the same for everyone. Each life event is assumed to affect everybody in the same way and to the same degree. However, as the French study discussed above concluded, that's simply not true. Not everybody perceives the level of stress or pressure experienced either in the same amount or in the same way.

More importantly, the Holmes-Rahe Life Stress Inventory assumes the frequency in which the life events occur are random. In other words, it assumes each of the forty-three life events listed in the SRRS will happen to people randomly at about the same rate of probability. However, that assumption may also not be accurate. People who are depressed or have automatic negative thoughts concerning life events may experience life events that can create stress at a different frequency than people not depressed or who don't have automatic negative thoughts. So like I said, it's complicated. There is no quick fix or happy pill. Someone just can't get over it or snap out of it.

It has been said the first step to being rescued is wanting to be rescued. I disagree with this statement. Rather, with depression and other mental illness, the first step in the rescue process is the training and education of the rescue party, which has to be able and knowledgeable and willing to perform the rescue.

Unfortunately, there is a stigmatism associated with mental illness and substance use disorders that has to be overcome by the rescue party. One of the major obstacles to treating mental illness is that the rescue party neither is able nor knowledgeable to provide support or encouragement to those suffering from mental illness. When I refer to the rescue party, I am not referring to the professionals (i.e., the psychiatrists, the psychologists, and the therapists). Those professionals are knowledgeable, and their professional help is available to treat those suffering from mental illness.

Rather, when I refer to the rescue party, I am making reference to the rest of society, including those friends and family members closest to those suffering and who serve as the rescue party to recognize the symptoms, to get those suffering the professional treatment they need and to provide support and encouragement.

People suffering from depression don't want sympathy. They don't want to be stereotyped as victims. They simply want to feel better. As I have described, battling depression is extremely difficult. However, it is made even more difficult when one battling depression also has to battle the stigmatism that society, friends, and family attach to depression and mental illnesses. To be able to win the battle and overcome depression and other mental illnesses, society must overcome the stigmatism.

The origin of the stigmatism attached to mental illness emanates from the same lineage linked to any prejudice—fear and ignorance. Most people in society are ignorant about depression, mental illnesses, and substance use disorders. When people are ignorant about something, they often fear what they neither know nor understand. Many people believe those who are depressed only have themselves to blame, are lazy, and use depression as an excuse for quitting or failing. Because most people don't understand depression or mental illnesses, they think someone suffering from depression and mental illness is dangerous and is to be avoided. As a result, people ostracize and avoid those suffering from depression, mental illnesses, and substance use disorders.

When Jesus began teaching and preaching, his own family became surprised at His teachings. At first, they neither understood nor believed Jesus was the Son of God. "When His family heard about this, they went to take charge of Him, for they said, 'He is out of His mind'" (Mark 3:21). Because they didn't understand, they said Jesus was out of His mind. Similarly, after Jesus healed a demon-possessed man, the people in the community described the man as once again in his right mind. (Mark 5:15). As far back as Jesus's time, if society was ignorant or didn't understand someone, society described him as being out of his mind. Even Jesus's own family said that Jesus was out of His mind.

This is the kind of prejudice about depression and mental illness that has continued in society. This is the perception that has to change. Such stigmatism sends the message that one's family and friends are embarrassed. Such stigmatism produces the extreme sense of guilt and shame felt by someone suffering from depression or mental illness. As a result, the guilt and shame subsequently serve to discourage the one suffering from seeking help. If the one suffering cannot find comfort and support from his own family and friends, how could he be expected to think he could find help from strangers?

Patrick J. Kennedy, who is championing the cause for mental illness, best made this point. Patrick Kennedy served in Congress for sixteen years. Recently, he gave an interview detailing his frustration with members of Congress in trying to pass parity legislation requiring insurance companies to provide coverage and benefits for mental illnesses on the same parity as provided for medical, surgery, and hospitalization coverage and benefits. Patrick Kennedy was one of the sponsors of the 2008 Mental Health Parity and Addiction Equity Act.

While Kennedy was in rehab after a 2006 DWI, he received numerous well wishes from other members of Congress who told Kennedy they also had been personally affected when their own family members experienced mental illness or substance abuse or addiction. Upon Kennedy's return to Congress, he sponsored and championed the 2008 mental health legislation.

Patrick Kennedy provided an interview on July 31, 2013, discussing the hypocrisy he encountered in the passage of the 2008 legislation. Kennedy described how the stigmatism and prejudice his fellow members of Congress associated with mental illness prevented them from voting for the mental health parity legislation even though they experienced their own personal encounters with mental illness or substance abuse. The following is an excerpt of that interview:

> All of them told me about how a parent committed suicide, or their spouse tried to commit suicide, or a daughter had an eating disorder, or a son a substance abuse disorder," Kennedy recalls. But many of those same members, Kennedy says, were unwilling to vote for the Mental Health Parity and Addiction Equity Act that Kennedy sponsored in the House of Representatives in 2008 in an effort to improve insurance coverage guidelines for mental illness. I went up to them and said, "Hey, how was it that you couldn't vote for this" and they said…"It's personal, and I can't afford to have any of you folks from the media ask me why did I vote for something called mental health and addiction?"[5]

Even though the 2008 legislation sponsored by Patrick Kennedy closed loopholes and finally provided coverage and benefits for mental illnesses and abuse disorders on parity with medical, surgery, and hospitalization coverage and benefits, Patrick Kennedy's recent interview illustrates the prejudice he encountered, a prejudice which still exists today.

If our leaders in Congress can't get past their prejudice and stigmatism toward mental illness and substance abuse disorders, how can society? If our leaders won't lead, then we have to find the courage to take up the cause ourselves.

Patrick Kennedy said that members of Congress, in spite of having members of their own families suffer from a mental illness, suicide, or an addiction, told him they couldn't afford to risk having their name or vote attached to or associated with legislation that would improve mental health. What can they not afford? Is it their own reputation or standing with an interest group, such as an insurance company?

While they worry about what they personally can't afford, how much more does society have to afford? How much more suffering and pain must a person or family afford? Mental illnesses and addictions indiscriminately attack regardless of gender, lifestyle, political affiliation, income, wealth, or social standing. While some members of Congress worry about what they can afford to their reputation, what is the cost to society in general from lost time at work, lost jobs and careers, lost marriages, lost parents, lost children, lost lives, lost hope, and lost dreams?

In a February 2013 article in Forbes magazine, writer Melanie Haiken relied on the latest available statistics from the Department of Veteran Affairs to report that, on average, there is one suicide every day among active duty military personnel and there is almost one suicide every hour among veterans![6] Haiken reported the rate of one suicide per day among active duty military troops is higher than the rate of troops killed in combat by the enemy.[7] We are losing more of our troops to suicide and to the deceiver, Satan, than we are to the enemy.

These statistics are underreported as only about half of the states participated in the reporting of suicides and the statistics didn't even include California and Texas. If these statistics weren't bad enough, consider the countless cases of PTSD and depression among our veterans, many (if not most) of which go unreported. Incredibly, Haiken reports the combined number of suicides of both military and nonmilitary people in the United States has risen thirty-one percent just over the last two decades between 1999 and 2013![8]

Just like those representatives had a problem with the terms mental illness and addiction, society in general has a problem with these terms. In an attempt to assuage that bias, at least as it pertains to veterans and active duty military personnel, the Americans with Disabilities Act classifies PTSD as a disability, and federal law makes it illegal for an employer to refuse to hire a veteran because he has PTSD. Struggling to find an appropriate and acceptable way to describe these mental illnesses as they pertain to veterans, many in the media have adopted the term *mentally wounded* to refer to those mental illnesses of depression and PTSD suffered by our active duty military and veterans. Such classification, however, may be a disservice to veterans and may further the stigmatism. One reason many employers may refuse to hire veterans who they suspect may have PTSD is because they consider the veterans to be emotionally damaged or dangerous.

Isn't it ironic that a Purple Heart is awarded for physical injuries incurred during combat, yet no similar medal exists for the mental injuries and wounds our active duty military personnel and veterans suffer? A similar phenomenon occurs outside of the military. When a friend or loved one suffers from a physical injury or disability or undergoes surgery or is hospitalized for a medical condition or illness, friends and family send "get well" cards and flowers to show support and to express empathy. Friends and family also visit them in the hospital or at home while they recuperate. However, those suffering from depression or mental illnesses are not similarly treated by friends and family. They don't send flowers.

This is a major reason why I wrote this book. When Patrick Kennedy asked his fellow members of Congress why they wouldn't support the mental health legislation he sponsored, even after they personally experienced depression, suicide, mental illness, and substance abuse in their own lives or families, they each said, "It's personal and I can't afford to have any of you folks from the media ask me why did I vote for something called mental health and addiction."

Incredible. Absolutely unbelievable.

Of course, it's *personal*. That's what depression or mental illness or substance abuse is. It is personal. Let me ask this question: How can society expect someone suffering from depression or mental illness or substance abuse to have the courage to overcome the pain and stigmatism when we have elected officials in Congress who don't have the courage to have their name or vote associated with legislation that will improve mental health just because the legislation contains the names or labels of mental illness or addiction?

How can we ask people suffering from depression or from some other mental illness or who are suicidal to dig deep and somehow find the courage to keep fighting and not quit when our own members of Congress act so cowardly? Is it any wonder the stigmatism toward mental illness has perpetuated? Who will fight for and speak for the millions who continue to suffer?

This is why I chose to be obedient and answer the call to write this book, even though it meant I would be completely vulnerable and expose my own painful past and even though writing this book has been terribly painful. If I can help one person recover from depression or PTSD or any other mental illness or if I can help one person find the hope and courage to fight on and not commit suicide, then the effort will have been worthwhile. If I can help family and friends become educated about depression and mental illness, if I can help family and friends learn how to recognize the symptoms associated with these illnesses, and if I can help family and friends acquire the empathy, understanding, and patience necessary to provide love and support, then I will have succeeded in this cause. It is with this purpose then that I hope that my message here can speak for all those silent sufferers and be a voice for needed change.

Perhaps people's perception and attitude toward depression and mental illnesses would be more accepting and tolerant if they could identify with others who suffered from depression and mental illness. Perhaps people could overcome their prejudice and stigmatism toward mental illness if they were more familiar with and knew of other people who suffered from depression or mental illness. Each of the following leaders, entertainers, film stars, writers, poets, painters, sculptors, composers, television personalities, scientists, mathematicians, celebrities, athletes, and musicians suffered from depression or other mental illness:

Leaders/Politicians

John Adams	Second president of the United States
John Quincy Adams	Sixth president of the United States
Menachem Begin	Prime minister of Israel
	Nobel Peace Prize Recipient
Kjell Magne Bondevik	Prime minister of Norway
Winston Churchill	Prime minister of Great Britain
Calvin Coolidge	Thirtieth president of the United States
Abraham Lincoln	Sixteenth president of the United States
James Madison	Fourth president of the United States
Teddy Roosevelt	Twenty-sixth president of the United States
William Howard Taft	Twenty-seventh president of the United States
Boris Yeltsin	President of Russia

◇◇◇

Entertainers / Film Stars

Woody Allen	Best Director Oscar
	Best Original Screenplay Oscar (3)
	Best Picture Oscar
	Writers Guild of America Award (5)
Marlon Brando	Best Actor Oscar (2)
Francis Ford Coppola	Best Director Oscar
	Best Picture Oscar
	Best Screenplay Oscar (3)
	Director's Guild Lifetime Achievement
	Irving G. Thalberg Memorial Award
Patty Duke	Best Supporting Actress Oscar

Judy Garland	Best Actress Oscar
Mel Gibson	Best Picture Oscar (producer)
	Best Director Oscar
Anne Hathaway	Best Supporting Actress Oscar
Audrey Hepburn	Best Actress Oscar
Sir Anthony Hopkins	Best Actor Oscar
Jessica Lange	Best Actress Oscar
	Best Supporting Actress Oscar
	Emmy Award (3)
Heath Ledger	Best Supporting Actor Oscar
Vivian Leigh	Best Actress Award (2)
Frank Sinatra	Best Supporting Actor Oscar
Rod Steiger	Best Actor Oscar
Emma Thompson	Best Actress Oscar
	Best Screenplay Oscar
Catherine Zeta Jones	Best Supporting Actress Oscar

◇◇

Authors / Writers

Agatha Christie	
William Faulkner	Nobel Prize for Literature
	Pulitzer Prize
F. Scott Fitzgerald	
Ernest Hemingway	Nobel Prize in Literature
	Pulitzer Prize
Henry James	
John Keats	
Jack London	
Herman Melville	
Eugene O'Neill	Nobel Prize in Literature
	Pulitzer Prize (4)
Sylvia Plath	Pulitzer Prize

Edgar Allan Poe

J. K. Rowling   Hans Christian Andersen Lit Award

                                          Hugo Award

                                          Locus Award

                                          Bram Stoker Award

                                          Blue Peter Badge Gold Award

                                          British Academy Film Award

                                          Freedom of the City of London Award

                                          Knight de la Legion d'Honneur

J. D. Salinger

Mark Twain

Walt Whitman

Tennessee Williams   Pulitzer Prize (2)

Painters / Sculptors

Edgar Degas

Paul Gauguin

Francisco de Goya

Ernst Ludwig Kirshner

Henri Matisse

Michelangelo

Jackson Pollock

Vincent van Gogh

Mark Rothko

Nicolas de Stael

Composers

Sir Malcolm Arnold   Best Musical Score Oscar

Irving Berlin   Best Original Song Oscar

                                          Presidential Medal of Freedom

                                          Congressional Gold Medal

	Army Medal of Merit
	Grammy Lifetime Achievement Award
	Songwriter Hall of Fame
Leonard Bernstein	Grammy Award (16)
Bob Dylan	Best Original Song Oscar
	Grammy Award (10)
	Rock and Roll Hall of Fame
	Grammy Hall of Fame
	Presidential Medal of Freedom
Sir Edward Elgar	Regia Accademia di Santa Cecilia
	Accademia del Reale Isituto Musicale
	Academie des Beaux Arts
	American Academy of Arts
Gustav Mahler	Director of Vienna court opera
	Director of Metropolitan opera
	Director New York philharmonic
Wolfgang Amadeus Mozart	Composed over six hundred works (symphony, concertos, operas, mass, chamber)
Cole Porter	Composed over nine hundred songs; musicals
	Tony Award (2)
	Lawrence Olivier Theater Award
	London Critics Circle Award (2)
	Songwriters Hall of Fame
Sergei Rachmaninoff	Concert pianist and composer
Hans Rott	Symphony composer
Robert Schumann	Pianist and composer
Pyotr Ilyich Tchaikovsky	Composer of symphonies, concertos, operas, ballets, chamber music, choral

◇◇◇◇◇◇◇◇◇◇◇◇◇◇◇◇◇◇◇◇◇◇◇◇◇◇◇◇◇◇◇◇◇◇◇◇

Television Personalities

Johnny Carson

Peabody Award

Television Academy Hall of Fame

Presidential Medal of Freedom

Kennedy Center Honoree

Dick CavettEmmy Award (3)

Dick Clark

Peabody Award

Emmy Lifetime Achievement Award

Rock and Roll Hall of Fame

National Radio Hall of Fame

Television Academy Hall of Fame

Jane Pauley

Broadcasting and Cable Hall of Fame

Edward R. Murrow Award

Walter Cronkite Award

Mike Wallace

Peabody Award (3)

21 Emmy Awards

Emmy Lifetime Achievement Award

Du Pont Columbia Univ. Award (3)

Oprah Winfrey

Peabody Award

Kennedy Center Honoree

Emmy Lifetime Achievement Award

Spingam Medal

Jean Hersholt Humanitarian Award

Bob Hope Humanitarian Award

◇◇

Scientists / Mathematicians

David Bohm

Theoretical physicist

Franklin Laureate Cresson Award

Ludwig Boltzman

Physicist and mathematician

Founder of statistical mechanics

Georg Cantor

Mathematician

Founder of set theory

Sir Julian Huxley	Biologist
	Kalinger Prize
	Darwin Medal
Salvador Luria	Microbiologist
	Nobel Prize in Physiology or Medicine
	Louisa Gross Horwitz Prize
	National Medal of Science
	National Book Award for Sciences
John Nash	Mathematician
	Nobel Prize in Economics
	John von Neumann Theory Prize
	Leroy P. Steele Prize
	Double Helix Medal
Sir Isaac Newton	Physicist and mathematician
	Created laws of motion
	Defined law of gravity
	Invented calculus
J. Robert Oppenheimer	Theoretical physicist
	Created atomic bomb
	Medal for Merit
	Enrico Fermi Award
Emil Post	Mathematician
Gabriele Rabel	Physicist and botanist
Lewis Wolpert	Developmental biologist
	Victor Hamburger Prize

◇◇

Celebrities / Famous

Buzz Aldrin	First person to walk on the moon
Barbara Bush	First lady
	Second lady
	Jefferson Award for Public Service
Sir Paul Getty	British philanthropist

Tipper Gore	Second lady
	Erasing the Stigma honoree
Stephen Hawking	Presidential Medal of Freedom
	Albert Einstein Award
	Wolf Prize in Physics
	Adams Prize
	Hughes Medal
	Royal Astronomical Soc. Gold Medal
	Fonseca Prize
	Eddington Medal
	Dannie Heineman Prize
	Dirac Medal
	Prince of Asturias Award
Yves Saint Laurent	Fashion designer
	Grand Officer de la Legion d'Honneur
	Commander de la Legion d'Honneur
George S. Patton	US general
	Silver star
	Bronze star
	Purple Heart
	Distinguished Service Cross
	Legion of Merit
	Distinguished Service Medal
T. Boone Pickens, Jr.	American oil tycoon and philanthropist
	Albert Schweitzer Leadership Award
	Bower Award
John D. Rockefeller	American industrialist and philanthropist
Lady Diana Spencer	Princess of Wales
Ted Turner	American businessman and media
Frank Lloyd Wright	American modernist architect

Athletes

Amanda Beard	Olympic Gold Medal Winner (2)
	Olympic Silver Medal Winner (4)
	Olympic Bronze Medal Winner (1)
Terry Bradshaw	Super Bowl Champion (4)
	Pro Football Hall of Fame
	College Football Hall of Fame
Earl Campbell	Heisman trophy winner
	Pro Football Hall of Fame
	College Football Hall of Fame
Ty Cobb	Batting Triple Crown Award
	Most Valuable Player
	Batting Title (12)
	Major League Baseball Hall of Fame
John Daly	PGA Championship
	British Open Champion
Dwight Gooden	World Series Champion (3)
	Cy Young Award
	Pitching Triple Crown Award
	Silver Slugger Award
	Rookie of the Year Award
Pat Lafontaine	Dodge/NHL Performer of the Year
	NHL Bill Masterton Memorial Trophy
	Distinguished Achievement Award
	Patriot Award
	International Hockey Hall of Fame
	USA Hockey Hall of Fame
Greg Louganis	Olympic Gold Medal (4)
	Olympic Silver Medal
Mickey Mantle	World Series Champion (7)
	Batting Triple Crown Award
	Most Valuable Player (3)
	Major League Baseball Hall of Fame

Ilie Nastase	French Open Singles Champion
	French Open Doubles Champion
	Wimbledon Doubles Champion
	Wimbledon Mixed Doubles Champion
	US Open Singles Champion
	US Open Doubles Champion
Jeret Peterson	Olympic Silver Medal Winner
Monica Seles	Olympic Bronze Medal
	Australian Open Singles Champion (4)
	French Open Singles Champion (3)
	US Open Singles Champion (2)
Ian Thorpe	Olympic Gold Medal (5)
	Olympic Silver Medal (3)
	Olympic Bronze Medal
	Australia Human Rights Award
Mike Tyson	Heavyweight Boxing Champion
Joey Votto	Most Valuable Player
	Hank Aaron Award
Jerry West	NBA Champion (1 player; 7 executive)
	NBA Executive of the Year (2)
	Olympic Gold Medal
	NBA Hall of Fame
	NBA Logo
Ricky Williams	Heisman Trophy Winner

◇◇◇◇◇◇◇◇◇◇◇◇◇◇◇◇◇◇◇◇◇◇◇◇◇◇◇◇◇◇◇◇◇◇◇◇◇

Musicians

Ray Charles	Songwriters Hall of Fame
	Rock and Roll Hall of Fame
	Grammy Lifetime Achievement Award
	Georgia State Music Hall of Fame
	National Medal of Arts

	George and Ira Gershwin Award
	Polar Music Prize
Eric Clapton	Grammy Lifetime Achievement Award
	Rock and Roll Hall of Fame (3)
	Grammy Award (17)
Natalie Cole	Grammy Award (9)
	NAACP Image Award (2)
	American Music Award (3)
	Songwriters Hall of Fame
	George and Ira Gershwin Award
Sheryl Crow	Grammy Award (9)
Peter Gabriel	Grammy Award (6)
	Brit Award (3)
	MTV Video Music Award (13)
	Pioneer Award
	Man of Peace Award (2)
	Ivor Novello Award
	Polar Music Prize
	Rock and Roll Hall of Fame
Janet Jackson	American Music Award (12)
	Billboard Award (33)
	Emmy Award
	Golden Globe Award
	Grammy Award (6)
	Hollywood Walk of Fame
	MTV Video Music Award (16)
	Soul Train Music Award (12)
Billy Joel	Grammy Award (6)
	Songwriters Hall of Fame
	Rock and Roll Hall of Fame
Sir Elton John	Best Original Song Oscar (3)
	Grammy Award (11)
	Golden Globe Award (4)

	Rock and Roll Hall of Fame
	Songwriters Hall of Fame
	Hollywood Walk of Fame
Alanis Morissette	Juno Award (12)
	Grammy Award (7)
	MTV Video Music Award (3)
	American Music Award (2)
Dolly Parton	Academy of Country Music Award (7)
	American Music Award (3)
	CMT Award (2)
	Country Music Association Award (9)
	Grammy Award (7)
	Nashville Songwriters Hall of Fame
	Country Music Hall of Fame
Paul Simon	Grammy Lifetime Achievement Award
	Grammy Award (12)
	Grammy Hall of Fame
	Rock and Roll Hall of Fame (2)
	Library of Congress Gershwin Prize
	Polar Music Prize
Gordon Sumner (Sting)	American Music Award (25)
	Grammy Award (16)
	Brit Award (3)
	Golden Globe Award
	Emmy Award
	Rock & Roll Hall of Fame
	Songwriters Hall of Fame
James Taylor	Grammy Award (5)
	Rock & Roll Hall of Fame
	Songwriters Hall of Fame
	George and Ira Gershwin Award
	North Carolina Music Hall of Fame
Brian Wilson	Grammy Award (2)

	Rock & Roll Hall of Fame
	Songwriters Hall of Fame
	George and Ira Gershwin Award
	UK Music Hall of Fame
Tammy Wynette	Grammy Hall of Fame
	Country Music Hall of Fame
	American Music Lifetime Award
	Alabama Music Hall of Fame
	Music City News Living Legend Award
	Grammy Award (2)
	Academy of Country Music Pioneer Award
	Nashville Songwriters Hall of Fame

Clearly, this is only a partial list, but anyone can identify with such luminaries. They include presidents, poets, and prime ministers. They are composers, painters, artists, writers, singers, musicians, and athletes. They have won Nobel Prizes and Pulitzer Prizes. They have won Academy Awards, Grammy Awards, and Emmy Awards. They have had awards named in their honor, and their images have been reproduced on coins and postage stamps. They have won Olympic medals, World Series, Super Bowls, and Heisman trophies. One even walked on the moon.

Depression, PTSD, bipolar disorder, substance use disorder, or any other mental illness is just that—it is a mental illness and a disease. Addiction to alcohol or drugs is a disorder, an illness, a disease. Unless we as a society finally come to terms—these terms, definitions, and labels—and recognize these illnesses and diseases exactly for what they are, then we will never get past the stigmatism associated with these diseases and illnesses. Unless we change our attitude and behavior toward mental illness, we will continue to suffer the pain and the agony associated with a suicide, depression, addiction, PTSD, or other mental illnesses.

The Patient Protection and Affordable Care Act (Obamacare) continues to receive criticism. Nevertheless, the Affordable Care Act provides many benefits. One major benefit is that the Affordable Care Act now requires insurance companies to provide insurance coverage and benefits for mental illnesses and addiction disorders, and those benefits for mental illnesses and substance use disorders have to be on parity with surgical and hospitalization benefits provided for physical illnesses.

No longer can insurance companies deny coverage for a mental illness or substance use disorder. No longer can insurance companies deny coverage for a mental illness or substance use disorder because of a loophole. No longer can insurance companies deny coverage for a mental illness or substance use disorder because of a preexisting condition. No longer can insurance companies deny coverage for a mental illness or substance use disorder because of arbitrary annual or lifetime caps or limits.

The first step we must take to change the stigmatism and prejudice is to become educated about depression, PTSD, and other mental illnesses. We need to learn how to help those friends and loved ones who need treatment. To be supportive, we need to acquire an understanding and knowledge of the symptoms of depression, PTSD, and other mental illnesses.

You or someone you know may be suffering from depression if you experience or observe any of the following symptoms:

- low energy
- feelings of sadness
- changes in weight gain or appetite
- feelings of helplessness
- feelings of hopelessness
- thoughts of suicide
- daytime sleepiness

- insomnia
- loss of interest in activities
- lack of concentration
- forgetfulness
- irritability
- anxiety
- low self-esteem

You need to be able to recognize these symptoms of depression so you can provide positive support and encouragement and, if necessary, obtain professional treatment.

You or someone you know may be suffering from PTSD if you experience or observe any of the following symptoms:

- reexperiencing the traumatic event
- attempts to numb or de-sensitize feelings
- avoidance or withdrawal from others or activities
- hypervigilance
- distrust
- intrusive memories
- feelings of vulnerability
- loneliness
- abandonment
- feelings of being out of control
- anxiety
- anger
- nightmares
- night sweats
- night terrors

Similarly, you need to be able to recognize these symptoms of PTSD so you can provide positive support and encouragement and, if necessary, obtain professional treatment.

At first, the person suffering from depression or PTSD will be confused about not knowing or comprehending what is happening or why it is happening. He will be irritable and frustrated. He will be cranky and exhausted. He will be despondent and discouraged. You will have to be patient and understanding. You will have to be patient and compassionate. You will have to be patient and supportive.

When he receives treatment and begins therapy, you will have to be patient and encouraging. When he suffers setbacks, you will have to be patient and loving. He will need your help. He will need to know that you will not abandon him. He will need to know that you will be there for him until he "gets over it" and "snaps out of it." Of course, I use the phrases "get over it" and "snap out of it" facetiously. These are some of the worst things you can say to someone suffering from depression or PTSD because they send the message that you don't understand his condition. While his PTSD may seem to switch on automatically when triggered by an event or sensation that forces him to reexperience the trauma, his ability to control his reaction or emotions is not like a switch that can be turned on or off. He will need your acceptance.

While I give all the credit for my recovery from depression and PTSD to Dr. S, who I think is a genius, I never would have been able to overcome depression and PTSD without the love and support from my wife and best friend, Janice. After my experience with my dad, two failed marriages, and a failed business relationship, I had serious abandonment and trust issues. Janice accepted me for who I am without any reservation or judgment. She figuratively and literally adopted my children as her own and became a wonderful stepmom and role model for them. She continued to support and encourage me unconditionally with her loyalty, faith, warmth, and love. She understood I didn't want to rush into another marriage, and she waited by my side for more than five years before we finally married in Christmas 2005.

I included the list of luminaries who suffered from depression and mental illnesses so that you may better identify with the subject matter and those individuals who were and are brilliant and creative thinkers, artists, athletes, writers, musicians, and leaders. Yet they each suffered from some form of mental illness.

I also included the suicide statistics of active duty military personnel and veterans so you may better identify with the subject matter and our troops who are the warriors who protect us and our freedoms. They don't want to be treated like victims. They don't want sympathy or a handout. Yet because they suffered from some form of mental illness such as depression and PTSD, they became despondent and committed suicide, and continue to commit suicide, at such an alarming rate. A single suicide is one too many. They served us and country, but we abandoned them because of our ignorance and fear.

What are the statistics? The American Foundation for Suicide Prevention website states that psychological autopsy studies and in-depth investigations revealed more than ninety percent of suicide victims suffered from some form of mental illness or disorder, with depression being the most common illness. In 2010, suicides were the tenth leading cause of death in America, with one occurring every 13.7 minutes. The economic cost associated with suicides is thirty-four billion dollars, with another eight billion dollars associated with attempted suicides. An even greater cost, incapable of being measured, is the loss of our loved ones to suicide.

Education is the key to overcoming the stigmatism associated with mental illness. As a society, we must become educated and knowledgeable about depression and mental illness before we can provide compassion and support. The website for the American Foundation for Suicide Prevention confirms this by stating, "One of the most important conclusions from this research is the importance of teaching lay people to recognize the symptoms of mental disorders in those they are close to so that they can support them to get help" (http://www.afsp.org / understanding-suicide/key-research-findings).

Rick Yount, the executive director of Warrior Canine Connection, has performed pioneering work in using dogs to help treat veterans with PTSD. More than three hundred thousand veterans of the wars in Iraq and Afghanistan have been diagnosed with PTSD, but countless more suffering from depression and PTSD have gone undiagnosed.[9]

Mr. Yount was the founder and director of the Paws for Purple Hearts program (PPH). As a licensed social worker and certified service dog instructor, Mr. Yount created the PPH program to provide meaningful therapeutic activities based on the continued mission of caring for the needs of a fellow veteran. The pilot program began in 2008 at the Palo Alto VA Trauma Recovery Program at Menlo Park, California, and it has expanded to other Department Of Defense medical facilities including the Walter Reed Army Medical Center in 2009 and the National Intrepid Center of Excellence for Psychological Health and Traumatic Brain Injury in 2010.

On August 26, 2013, Mr. Yount testified before a Congressional subcommittee considering House Resolution 198, a proposed law named the Veterans Dog Training Therapy Act and House Resolution 1154, a proposed law named the Veterans Equal Treatment for Service Dogs Act. Both proposed laws are based on the success of Mr. Yount's pioneer program at Menlo Park. H.R. 198 would allow veterans suffering from PTSD to train dogs to be used by other veterans with physical injuries, and H.R. 1154 would allow veterans with mental illnesses the same access to assist dogs as provided to veterans with physical injuries under the Americans with Disabilities Act. Mr. Yount graciously gave me permission to include here the following summary and excerpts of his testimony before Congress. It is my hope that sharing his testimony will improve the knowledge, education and understanding of PTSD and depression to help eliminate the associated stigmatism.[10]

In his testimony before Congress, Yount referenced a 2009 study published in *The American Journal of Public Health* found that close to forty percent of Iraq and Afghanistan veterans treated at American health centers during the previous six years were diagnosed with PTSD, depression, or other mental health issues. Yount testified his program was instrumental in helping veterans overcome the three main problems encountered by people diagnosed with PTSD:

1. Reexperiencing the trauma.

2. Avoidance/numbing.

3. Heightened vigilance.

Someone suffering from PTSD often reexperiences trauma when an image, sound, or similar stimulus associated with the original traumatic event serves as a trigger to transport his mind back to the original traumatic event, forcing him to reexperience that original traumatic event again. As a result, he often reacts by avoiding people or by avoiding interacting in society for fear of encountering such a triggering event. Someone suffering from PTSD also seeks devices, such as isolation or alcohol, in an attempt to numb or desensitize such an emotional response. Someone suffering from PTSD also has a continual heightened vigilance, causing his mind to be overactive, always on alert, and guarded against any perceived danger. It is for this reason people suffering from PTSD have such difficulty sleeping.

Yount's program does more than merely provide someone suffering from PTSD or depression with a comforting canine companion. In Yount's program, the veteran suffering from PTSD actually becomes involved in training the dog. Once the dog's training is complete, the dog is provided to another veteran who needs assistance with physical injuries and disabilities.

Regarding reexperiencing the trauma, Yount testified that the procedures used in training PPH service dogs require the patient/trainer to focus on the dog's "here and now" point of view to recognize the teachable moments when the instruction will be most effectively processed and retained. The presence of the dog during a stressful situation or encounter changes the context of the arousal event and anchors the patient/trainer in the present, reminding him that he is no longer in a dangerous circumstance. If the patient/trainee experiences a trigger for symptoms, the presence of the dog then can serve to lower his anxiety levels.

Regarding avoidance and numbing, the act of training a service dog requires it to be exposed carefully to a wide range of experiences in the community. This creates a need for the patient/trainee to challenge the impulse to isolate and avoid those same environments that the dogs must learn to tolerate. Yount describes dogs as natural social lubricants. It is nearly impossible for the patient/trainer to isolate from other people during this part of the training. Interacting with others in the company of the dogs is reported to be less threatening since the focus of the interaction is on the dog and the training.

The PTSD patient/trainer must overcome his instinctive defense mechanism to numb his emotional response. He has to engage actively in order to heighten his tone of voice, bodily movements, and capacity for patience to be able to deliver his commands with positive, assertive clarity of intention, and confidence. In doing this, the patient/trainer soon discovers he can earn his dog's attention and best guide it to the correct response. Because the dog's success must then be rewarded with emotionally based praise, the PPH training technique allows the patient/trainer to experience rewarding positive emotional stimulation and social feedback. The basic daily needs of a service dog involve structured activities that also bring the patient/trainer and dog into the kind of close nurturing contact that further creates a behavioral and psychological antidote to social avoidance.

Regarding heightened vigilance, Yount said each PPH service dog is bred to be responsive to human emotions and needs. The dog's sensitivity to and reflection of the emotional state of the patient/trainer provides immediate and accurate measures of the patient/trainer's projected emotion. This also challenges the patient/trainer to overcome his tendency for startle reactions in order to relay a sense of security and positive feedback when his young dog is faced with environmental challenges such as hearing a loud siren or seeing a stranger.

Yount said that each PPH service dog is also bred to be affectionate and have a low hypervigilance temperament that puts its patient/trainer at ease. With the dog at his side, a PPH patient/trainer perceives greater safety and social competence. He is able to shift out of his hypervigilant, defensive mode that accompanies PTSD. Because he is less guarded, he is less irritable and more socially compliant. He then is able to ease into a relaxed state that enables him to be able to connect socially with others. By losing his hypervigilance, he is able to sleep without interruption by nightmares and night terrors.

Yount testified that clinical observations and participant testimonials show the PPH program facilitated improvement in PTSD symptoms in the following ways:

- Increased patience, impulse control, and emotional regulation.
- Improved ability to display affect.
- Decreased emotional numbness.
- Improved sleep.
- Decreased depression.
- Increased positive sense of purpose.
- Decreased startle responses.
- Decreased pain medications.
- Increased sense of belongingness/acceptance.
- Increased assertiveness skills.
- Improved parenting skills and family dynamics.
- Decreased war stories and more in the moment thinking.
- Lowered stress levels and increased sense of calm.

In his testimony before Congress, Yount also presented six case studies to emphasize the effectiveness of the PPH program. All the people involved in these accounts gave consent to share their stories. I include them here because the actual accounts and statements by the participants provide a profound impact in improving the information and education about PTSD. Just as it is easier to understand and accept depression and mental illness by identifying with the luminaries who suffered, we are able to understand mental illness better through the veterans' own personal accounts of their improvement.

The following six case studies involve marines and other military veterans who faced fear and danger during their tours of duty. Yet these brave and courageous warriors suffered from depression and PTSD. What historically has been described as battle fatigue now more accurately has been defined as the mental illnesses of depression and PTSD. These are not individuals who want our pity and sympathy. These are not individuals who want a handout or who are afraid of challenges. They want to be understood. They want to understand their illness. They want to understand why they now behave and think differently than they did before they were injured. Just as many veterans sustained physical injuries, many veterans also sustained mental injuries. They were mentally wounded. Those who sustained mental injuries are also wounded warriors.

- *Case 1*: A Marine had been hit by several separate IED explosions during his multiple tours in Operation Iraqi Freedom (OIF), Operation Enduring Freedom (OEF), and the war in Afghanistan. He was in the PTSD treatment program for several weeks but was not participating in treatment despite a myriad of behavioral and pharmacological interventions. He sat in the corner with his sunglasses on, occasionally twitching his head from side to side in a tic-like manner. His peers were hesitant to interact with him due to his body language and lack of motivation to respond to their attempts to connect with him.

  His interest in the dogs prompted him to participate in the PPH program. Within two days of working in the PPH program, he began to smile and bond with the dog. His involvement led to his first positive interactions with staff and fellow veterans. Instead of leaving the PTSD program without successfully completing it, he was able to finish the entire program and process his trauma through the support of his dog, peers, and the treatment team.

- *Case 2*: A PPH participant with PTSD who served in Iraq as a National Guard Reservist and was struggling with family issues gave this testimony:

  "My family has noticed a difference in the way I interact with them as a result of working with my service-dog in training. I am patient with my children when they are around, I haven't yelled at them in several months and they aren't afraid of me when I'm around. I think that is a direct result of working with my dog. I have also benefited from the association with my service-dog in training as we spend time on bonding every day. I feel loved by him and I feel comforted when he is around. It's been nearly 4 years since I have felt comforted. When the dog is with me people that I pass come up and talk to me and I have social interaction that I wouldn't have had without the dog. I'm grateful the VA started this program and I got to be part of it. I wish more veterans got the opportunity I've been given to work with these amazing animals. Please consider this program on a larger scale so more veterans can benefit from training or receiving a service-dog."

- *Case 3:* A young soldier who recently returned from Iraq arrived in the PTSD program. He recently attempted to take his own life. His struggle with hopelessness continued to inhibit his affect and stifle his ability to engage in treatment. One of the dogs interacted with him while he was waiting for the next group to begin. He smiled as he pat the dog on his head. He began training the next day, taking the training tasks very seriously. His psychiatrist told the Director of the Service-dog Program that the dog had accomplished what the doctor had been unable to do in six months. After his discharge from the program, the soldier was partnered with a service-dog to continue helping with his PTSD symptoms.

- *Case 4:* A Marine serving as a "Devil Dog" (term used to refer to a Marine) for nineteen years was treated for PTSD in 2005. He returned for treatment in 2006 when he was unable to control his anger. He asked to join the newly instituted PPH program. He voluntarily provided this account of his experience with PPH:

  "I would have never imagined by working with these dogs my life would change forever. After over a year with severe sleep, depression and anger issues I found myself able to sleep for longer periods of time during the night and found myself calm during times where I would have exploded in anger. After analyzing this major change in my behavior the doctors quickly discovered that the common denominator was a service-dog trainee named Verde. Please understand that my story is not a rare one. I have seen remarkable changes in not only myself but in the other residents that have participated in the training of these animals. For years doctors have thrown medication at my issues with minimal results but Verde has caused my life that would have been surely shortened by my issues to be full again. I know that I will always suffer with PTSD issues but having my new friend by my side like a fellow Marine will ensure that my quality of life will improve."

- *Case 5*: An Army veteran who had returned from Iraq showing many of the signs of PTSD found that over the next four years his depression deepened, he lost his job and he was divorced. He tried many different medications and finally was enrolled in the PTSD program. He volunteered this testimony about PPH:

"While in the program I learned a lot about PTSD and gained many tools to help me cope with the disorder, but there was one part of the program that stood apart; Paws for Purple Hearts. Soon after signing up to train the dogs I found myself sleeping better and was in a surprisingly good mood; before I knew it I was not hiding in my room anymore. I started laughing again and I began to feel good. I felt good about myself and what I was doing; helping to train this dog for a fellow veteran. Going out and not isolating was a huge leap forward for me. When you are with one of these dogs everyone wants to stop you and talk to you. This is not the most comfortable thing for someone with PTSD. After a while I was having conversation with complete strangers. They come with such a positive attitude that it reinforces that not all people in the world are bad and it begins to rebuild trust, which is one of the many things that one with PTSD struggles with. Another struggle is self-restraint and patience and working with a dog will test your patience. If at any time I feel uneasy or start to have a little anxiety all I have to do is reach down and pet my dog or maybe even bend down and give him a hug, and it seems that everything is going to be just fine."

"As my time for being part of this program came near an end, I discovered I wanted and needed to continue being part of this program. So I enrolled in The Bergin University of Canine Studies, to further expand my education in the service-dog field. In May of 2010 I completed the AS program. The PPH program has not only helped me in learning to cope with PTSD, but it has also helped me find what it is that I want to do in life. I know without this I could easily slip back into a lot of the old patterns that I had. My hope is to share with other Veterans the wonder of working with these dogs and help them get the same help I got through this program."

- *Case 6:* The following is a personal account of how a PPH bred and veteran-trained service dog has affected the life of a veteran with PTSD who also uses a wheelchair as a result of his spinal cord injury. He suffered a spinal cord injury while serving in the Army during the Vietnam War. He received his service-dog in December 2009. His dog helps by pulling his wheelchair, retrieving dropped objects, bracing for transfers and opening doors. The impact his dog has had on his PTSD symptoms are expressed in his reflections:

> "Since being paired with my dog I have realized many benefits. Some nights I couldn't turn my brain off. I would be on hyper vigilance unable to sleep at all. I was given Trazadone (PRN). I hated the way I would feel the next day from Trazadone. Since receiving my dog, my sleep has improved 100 percent and I no longer use it. Over the years I've been prescribed many meds for pain (300 mg. TDI) Gabapentin for burning pain nerve, Morphine, and Oxycontin. I now take no pain meds and have learned to live with my constant pain which flairs with activity or weather. I have also taken several prescription drugs to treat depression including Prozac and Welbutron. I feel no need to take depression medication anymore either."

The veteran also reported significant improvement in his emotional control, positive social interaction and parenting skills and family dynamics.

Mr. Yount's testimony about the success of his pioneering program is illuminating. His program not only educates people about the symptoms and challenges associated with PTSD, but it also instructs people how support and compassion can be uplifting and life changing to those suffering from PTSD and depression. In supporting and encouraging someone suffering from PTSD and depression, we should at least be as comforting and nonjudgmental toward mental illnesses as a loyal canine companion.

Both the Canadian Mental Health Association and the National Alliance on Mental Illness in the United States launched an anti-stigma campaign during the 1990s in an effort to change the stigmatism and prejudice toward mental illness, and they sought to effect such a change by characterizing mental illness as a brain disorder and a biological medical disease. However, a Canadian study released in 2012 reported that this effort in describing and categorizing mental illness as a biological medical disease actually produced the opposite unintended effect. The unintended consequence of the anti-stigma campaign actually caused the stigmatism associated with mental illness to become worse after the campaign, and actually increased the stigmatism and intolerance.[11] A German study reached the same conclusion.[12]

What exactly is the stigmatism and intolerance toward mental illnesses? How is the stigmatism manifested? What is the prejudicial attitude that needs to be changed? A 2008 Canadian survey provided insight to these questions. Among those surveyed, the stigmatism and prejudice was described in the following personal terms, demonstrating just how the stigmatism is manifested within society:

> 42% would no longer socialize with a friend diagnosed with mental illness.
>
> 55% wouldn't marry someone who suffered from mental illness.
>
> 25% were afraid of being around someone who suffers from mental illness.
>
> 50% would not tell friends or coworkers a family member was suffering from mental illness.[13]

Is it any wonder that those suffering from depression, PTSD, or another form of mental illness would have such a difficult time overcoming their illness when their own family and friends hold these attitudes? This compares with the legislators encountered by Patrick Kennedy in trying to pass the mental health parity legislation.

The study concluded that the single most important component in eliminating the stigmatism and intolerance associated with mental illness is the need for educating the public with the recognition and understanding that people suffering from mental illness can and do recover. When people understand that depression or PTSD or bipolar disorder or any other mental illness can be overcome like any other physical illness or disease, then people can become more accepting and tolerant.

Other historical examples of societal stigmatism and intolerance involve prejudicial attitudes and bigotry concerning race, gender, and sexual orientation. However, all of these obvious examples remain completely controversial and distorted by political, religious, and economic attitudes and beliefs. For these reasons, I have chosen not to involve them in this discussion for comparison purposes. The effort to eliminate the stigmatism and prejudice toward mental illness should not be distorted by political, religious, or economic issues, attitudes, or beliefs. Mental illness indiscriminately attacks and affects people regardless of political views, religious beliefs, or economic status. Consequently, I instead have chosen another example for comparison purposes that is more universally suited to this discussion—leprosy.

The World Health Organization (WHO) says leprosy has existed throughout the world since the ancient civilizations of China, Egypt, and India, and one written mention of leprosy is dated 600 BC.[14] The Bible says Moses's sister Miriam was stricken with leprosy,[15] which would have occurred between 1350 and 1300 BC. Leprosy is also recorded in the Bible during prophet Elisha's time, which would have been about 850 BC.[16] Leprosy is also known as Hansen's disease, named after Norwegian scientist G. H. Armauer Hansen who, in 1873, identified the bacteria that causes leprosy.[17]

The drug dapsone was developed in 1940 to combat leprosy, and during the 1960s, the drugs—rifampicin and clofazimine— were also developed to provide a multidrug therapy using all three drugs in combination that cured the disease when administered.[18] In just over the past twenty years, more than fourteen million leprosy cases have been cured. Leprosy has been eliminated from 119 of the 122 countries where the disease had been considered a public health problem, and fewer than 200,000 leprosy cases still exist today.[19] Yet in spite of these scientific advances, people's knowledge of the disease is limited to the references in the Gospels of Matthew and Luke where Jesus cured people suffering from leprosy.[20]

A publication by the US Department of Health and Human Services states that "Hansen's disease (leprosy) remains the most misunderstood human infectious disease. The stigma long associated with the disease still exists in most of the world, and the psychological and social effects may be more difficult to deal with than the actual physical illness."[21]

Throughout history, people infected with leprosy have been ostracized and relegated to leper colonies. Their families and communities avoided them and treated them as outcasts from society. In many cases, simply because they contracted this disease, they even were denied basic human rights. The story of Kazuko To illustrates this point.

Kazuko To was born in 1930 in the Ehime Prefecture (Province) of Japan, and she was diagnosed with leprosy when she was only twelve years old.[22] Her diagnosis came only two years after the development of the vaccine dapsone, which would have cured her had she been vaccinated. Instead, her diagnosis of leprosy in Japan meant a life sentence of suffering, ridicule, and shame under a 1931 Japanese law requiring lepers to be isolated and quarantined.

On their way home from the hospital at Fukuoka following her diagnosis, her father said he was tempted to jump off the boat with his daughter in his arms so they could die together.[23] Kazuko lived the rest of her life in a sanitarium on an island in the Seto Inland Sea as a prisoner to leprosy, which in Japan was called *tenkeibyo,* the "disease of divine punishment."[24]

While living at the sanitarium, Kazuko wrote more than one thousand poems describing her isolation. Her poetry collection was later published in nineteen volumes, and in 1999, she was awarded the Takami Jun Prize.[25]

Kazuko's collection of poems described what she called her "proof of life":

> Because I was in a desert, I Understand the preciousness of a Drop of water.
>
> Because I was adrift in the ocean, I Understand the value of a piece of Driftwood.

Another poem titled "Kumo," which means "cloud," begins with the following words that define what it meant to be ostracized and treated as an outcast:

> A shape born without volition
> The pain of having to be that shape
> So long as the shape exists.

Another poem titled "Mune No Izumi Ni," which means "In the Fountain of my Heart," ends with this sorrowful refrain:

> Ah, even if there are hundreds of Millions of people
> They are all strangers.

> They would not drop even one Withered leaf
> In the fountain of my heart.

Kazuko passed away at age eighty-three on August 28, 2013.[26] When we stigmatize and ostracize people because of fear, ignorance, and prejudice, we as a society do so because we only selfishly think of ourselves and of how we are affected by those other people. We never stop to consider the plight of the other people. We only frame the issue out of consideration for our own concerns. This is how it is with all prejudices—we dehumanize what we do not understand because of our own insecurity, fear, and ignorance.

In the Old Testament, there was a clear connection symbolically between leprosy and sin. Left untreated, leprosy deforms and ruins the nerves sensitive to pain. As a result, over time a leper cannot feel or sense the pain in fingers and toes and may eventually lose them. The connection to sin was clear. Left unchecked, sin would spread and destroy, just like leprosy. When untreated, leprosy destroyed not only limbs but also destroyed relationships in families because the lepers were required to be banished to isolation. Lepers had to live outside the camp (Leviticus 13:45–46) and could not live in their own community (Numbers 5:2). Lepers were considered unclean, both physically and spiritually.

In the New Testament and under the new covenant, Christ came to save and to heal. Although lepers were banished to leper colonies so no one could come into physical contact with them, Jesus cured and healed the lepers by reaching out and actually physically touching them. Jesus extended compassion and love to the lepers he cured notwithstanding the stigmatism imposed upon them by society.[27]

The compassionate act by Jesus of physically touching the leper was contrary to society's stigmatism and prejudice toward lepers. The stigmatism of banishing the lepers actually served to prevent the lepers from seeking treatment. Today, the stigmatism toward mental illness serves to make it more difficult for people who suffer from mental illnesses to take that courageous first step to seek help and treatment. The stigmatism fuels the associated shame.

Society's stigmatism and prejudice toward mental illness is similar to that stigmatism and prejudice toward leprosy. Just like Kazuko To was relegated to a sanitarium on an island, many in our society would feel better or more comfortable if those with mental illnesses simply were relegated and confined to sanitariums—out of sight and out of mind. They don't want to be inconvenienced "in my neighborhood."

Cynthia Hubert reported a literal example of this stigmatism in her story about how the State of Nevada and the Rawson-Neal Psychiatric Hospital of Las Vegas bused five hundred mentally ill patients to various cities in California, and another thousand more patients to other states between July 2008 and March 2013. Hubert reported the City of San Francisco filed a class action lawsuit against Nevada and Rawson-Neal to recover the cost of caring for the twenty-four patients sent to San Francisco.

(www.sacbee.com/2013/09/10/5723995/san-francisco-files-class-action.html)

Hubert reported that the patient *dumping* coincided with funding cuts that reduced Nevada's mental health budget by twenty-eight percent between 2009 and 2012. San Francisco city attorney Daniel Herrera stated, "What the defendants have been doing for years is horribly wrong on two levels. It cruelly victimizes a defenseless population and punishes jurisdictions for providing health and human services that others won't provide." The lawsuit alleges the patients were given one-way tickets to

California without escorts, food, water, and medication, and that many "ended up on the streets of their destination cities without funds or means of support, shelter, or medication."

When our civic leaders exhibit this kind of shameful behavior, is it any wonder that the stigmatism is perpetuated in society? Nevada state law requires it to care for its poor and indigent residents. Such indifference and disdain for human rights is allegedly unconstitutional and violates civil rights.

These attitudes and prejudices are prevalent regardless of racial, gender, ethnic, economic, religious, sexual orientation, political affiliation, or social class or standing among people. The stigmatism affects everyone in society. Until it changes, people suffering will be, in the words of Kazuko To:

> A shape born without volition
> The pain of having to be that shape
> So long as the shape exists.

Even though the poetry of Kazuko To describes the stigmatism as it applied to leprosy, her words are equally applicable to the stigmatism associated with mental illness. To illustrate this point, what if we applied Kazuko To's poetry to mental illness? Her beautifully haunting lines could just as easily read like this:

> A mind changed without volition
> The pain of having a mind be in this shape
> So long as the shape exist.

Her lines now equally describe what it is like to suffer from depression, PTSD or any other mental illness. Worse still, we don't even have to change the lines in her poem entitled "Mune No Izumi Ni" to describe the effect of the stigmatism and prejudice of mental illnesses. Her words equally sting and hurt, whether they are applied to leprosy or mental illnesses, in describing society's stigmatism and prejudice:

> Ah, even if there are hundreds of Millions of people
> They are all strangers.
> They would not drop even one Withered leaf
> In the fountain of my heart.

It is my sincere hope that this book will contribute to educate and change society's stigmatism toward mental illness. Even if my message expressed here only represents a small pebble dropped into the sea, it is my hope that this message will reverberate and create a ripple effect to increase awareness toward the need to eradicate society's stigmatism toward mental illness.

Patrick Kennedy's Forum on mental health and his tireless efforts to champion mental health already have created a tide of change crashing against the stubborn shores of resistance. His tireless efforts already have raised awareness and have produced real and significant change.

Also, Rick Yount's pioneering program in using canines to help veterans suffering from depression and PTSD overcome their illnesses has begun a groundswell of support and provided yet another effective therapeutic tool not only to help individuals overcome these mental illnesses, but also to help society overcome the stigmatism and prejudice associated with them. Mr. Yount's work has produced the undeniable empirical data necessary to overcome even those most reluctant to change.

If we all work together, we can make that change. If we focus our energy and become resolute in our determination to increase education and understanding, we can overcome the stigmatism. We can change the world—one mind at a time.

8

Stepping Out in Faith

Yet he did not waver through unbelief regarding the
promise of God, being fully persuaded that God had
power to do what He had promised.

—Romans 4:20–21

I learned it is not enough just to have faith. You have to act
on that faith. Jesus said, "I tell you the truth, if you have faith
and do not doubt…you can say to this mountain, 'Go, throw
yourself into the sea,' and it will be done. If you believe, you will
receive whatever you ask for in prayer."[1]

Yet, faith alone is not enough. Paul said, "If I have a faith
that can move mountains, but have not love, I am nothing."[2]
Similarly, James said, "As the body without the spirit is dead,
so faith without deeds is dead."[3] These truths presented a
perplexing paradox that tested my faith when I was called to
complete an abandoned real estate development project.

By the end of 2009, I completed my group therapy and
my individual cognitive therapy with Dr. S. I was no longer
taking any medication. I graduated from the alternative
discipline program with the state bar. I finally completed more
than twenty years of custody litigation in family court. I had
overcome my battle with depression and PTSD. If I became
discouraged or sad, I would apply the skill sets I learned in my
therapy with Dr. S and move past and beyond that situation or
event. Nevertheless, my faith was about to be tested.

Four years earlier, I worked myself out of a job with Orval's company. After defending his product liability cases for seventeen years, he told me he now had insurance and attorneys hired by the insurance company could handle his caseload. Since we had won every case we tried across the country over seventeen years, he rarely was sued and now only had two pending cases. He thanked me for helping him, but told me he had to let me go. It was November, so he said he would pay me for one more month until the end of the year. Janice and I were getting married after Christmas. All the children were going to be part of the wedding, and we decided to make our honeymoon a family vacation and take the children with us to Hawaii. But after our wedding, I would no longer receive any further income from Orval's company.

A few weeks before Christmas, a friend of mine said he wanted me to accompany him to look at a car he was considering buying. While my friend was looking at the car, I began talking to one of the owners about their construction business, and he told me they were looking for an attorney to work for them. Just like Orval, he said they were looking for someone who could work for them inside their company. I interviewed the next week, and they hired me to begin work as soon as I would return from my honeymoon. This was not a coincidence. It was as if God had this job waiting for me.

I worked for the construction company for almost a year when they entered into a purchase agreement to buy property for a real estate development project in Arizona. Within an hour after receiving a call learning the property was for sale, the company I worked for signed a purchase agreement to buy the property. As our team proceeded to develop the project, we sought the funding we needed. Much more work needed to be done with the civil engineers and the architects. Many more meetings were needed with the city officials. However, the largest concern was to find funding.

As 2007 passed, the economy robustly rolled along, but as the end of the year approached, ominous signs began appearing in the economic forecast. Cracks in the economy began to develop. We had obtained some funding from private investors and a commitment from Wachovia Bank to provide the construction funding. However, Wachovia Bank failed in 2008, and during the following year, the economy worsened.

The construction industry was hit hard by the recession, which many said teetered on a depression. More banks failed. The financial sector of our economy looked like it was on the verge of collapsing. Major corporations threatened to go under. During that financial climate, no one was willing to fund this construction project. The construction company struggled, and by the end of 2009, it went out of business. Not only was I out of work, but the real estate development project also appeared to be finished.

I considered my options. I could have gone to work for another firm. I also considered teaching again. During the two years before attending law school, I taught college English while pursuing my master's degree in English. After graduating law school, I also taught at a local college one night a week while I worked for my first law firm.

However, I was being led in a different direction, away from those obvious options. I was being called to continue to work on the real estate development project—the one that was abandoned, finished, dead.

When I first felt pulled in that direction, it was easy to dismiss the idea. At the construction company, we had an entire team of professionals who worked together on the project. What could I possibly accomplish on my own? But no matter what other options I considered, I was being drawn back to the development project. I didn't know why or how. It just didn't make any sense. I had no money. During the last six months the construction company was in business, I agreed to work for a significantly reduced salary while we tried to keep the company afloat. As a result, by the time the company folded, I no longer had any money because we used our savings for living expenses. Since the car I drove was a company car, I no longer had a car. How would I be able to work on this project? Again, I dismissed the idea.

Then one night, I woke up in the middle of the night. At first, I wondered if I just couldn't sleep again. I had been anxious about the economy and my employer going out of business without paying me. I had two children attending a private Christian high school, and I worried I wouldn't be able to continue to afford the cost of their education.

However, the reason I couldn't sleep had nothing to do with the economy or with our lack of money or resources or with the mounting bills. Rather, the small, quiet, familiar voice I had heard before was again waking me up and calling me. It was calling me to complete this development project. It was telling me I was *supposed* to complete this development project. I hadn't thought about the project for some time, but now I was being called to it again. I felt pursued.

Once more, I protested. I wasn't qualified. I had no money. I had no credit. I had already lost the company car, and I had lost our house. We had overdue bills to pay, and the project had no funding. The economy was in a serious recession, and in grave danger of slipping into a depression. It didn't seem likely anyone would be interested in providing the needed funding. All of the reasons why I should not work on the project came fast and furious. Yet I was being called to the project. It wasn't like I was being asked. I was being directed.

I prayed about this decision. I talked with Janice about pursuing the project without receiving any income. I prayed about this decision and exercised discernment. I wanted to make sure the voice I was hearing was from the Holy Spirit.

I finally agreed to answer the call to pursue the project. I believed in my heart the Lord wanted me to obey His calling to complete this project. Although I answered the call to continue working on this project, my focus and priorities were misdirected.

I answered God's call to continue to work on this project, but my response was as if God were just another client seeking my services and hiring me for my talents and skills. I even fell into the prideful temptation of believing God was calling me because I believed I was the only one in the world who could pick up the pieces of this project, put it back together, and complete it by getting it funded. Wow, I was so wrong.

When I agreed to continue to work on this project, I accepted this as another challenge. I had faith God wanted me to complete the project, but my faith really was in my own abilities. I thought God was going to push me in the right direction and then get out of the way and let me go to work. I was all about what I had accomplished, what I could do, and what I was going to do. I don't even think I stopped to ask God to tell me His plan. Instead, I was working on my plan. I felt so prideful and important.

Imagine my mind-set. I just landed the biggest client of all. God Himself had called me to work on this project! I was such an idiot. I was so wrong. Imagine my thinking that God needed me. Sure, I wanted to serve God and accomplish this project for God, but my mind-set was that it was all about what I could do and about what I would be able to accomplish.

I had to get out of my own way. I had to surrender my pride and my vanity and my confidence in my own abilities. Instead of trusting in my own skills and abilities, I had to trust completely in God's providence. I had to surrender my will for God's will.

To be able to do this, I had to ask God for His forgiveness and mercy. I had to repent and lose everything. I had lost our house, our car, and our savings. Now I had to lose my selfish pride and humble myself.

I had no money and no income. The only income we had was the modest income from Janice's work. She worked only three days each week while the children were in school. Now she worked full time and, often, more than full time. I no longer could afford to have the children attend their Christian high school. I no longer could practice law. I was getting evicted from the house we rented, so I had no idea how I was going to be able to rent another house. We now had three children in high school.

Seizing the opportunity, Carmen told our daughter that she would pay her tuition for her last year of high school if she would move out of our residence and live with Carmen during her senior year of high school. Although both children had lived exclusively with me for the prior two and a half years, they now would be separated and living apart.

While our daughter continued to attend the Christian high school, our son was not able to continue to attend there. Since he didn't want to live with Carmen, she refused to pay his tuition. Since I couldn't afford to pay his tuition at the Christian high school, he had to leave his friends at the Christian high school and transfer to the local public high school.

Carmen couldn't persuade both children to live with her full time, so she resorted to using the tactic of paying our daughter's tuition during her last year of high school to get our daughter to live with her full time, even if it would be at the expense of splitting up our children. I again was reminded of the story of the two mothers and King Solomon, except that I didn't have

King Solomon as my family court judge. Satan was telling me that I was a loser and a failure, and that I had failed my children.

To say I was being tested is an understatement. A couple of years earlier, I purchased a used car for our daughter to drive when she received her driver's license. It was a ten-year-old car, but it was a cute convertible with really low miles, so I thought it would be a good car for her to drive during high school. It was relatively inexpensive when I bought it, so I paid cash for it back when the economy was still strong and my job with the construction company was still secure.

When our daughter decided to live with Carmen full time Carmen provided her with another car to drive, so our son drove the convertible to his school. When we later needed money just to pay bills, I took out a small loan against the title on the car. However, after awhile I couldn't keep making the payments and it was repossessed. Carmen used this opportunity to tell the children that I had failed them. Once again Satan told me that I was a failure.

That's when God revealed to me that it's not all about me or about the works I can perform. He let me understand it was not enough that I believed and had faith. He wanted me to step out in faith and act on my faith. He didn't want me to lean on my own understanding, but instead, He wanted me to lean on Him.

When Jesus said, "I tell you the truth, if you have faith and do not doubt…you can say to this mountain, 'Go, throw yourself into the sea,' and it will be done. If you believe, you will receive whatever you ask for in prayer."[4]

I believed I was called to work on this project, and I had faith that God would help me complete it, but I was struggling. No one was paying me to work on the project, and without income I couldn't pay for all of the things my children needed. I tried harder and harder, but still with no success.

It was at this moment that I realized that my approach was entirely wrong. My mind-set was still about me and about my abilities and my confidence in myself, and about my taking credit for my achievements and accomplishments. As I said, in my mind, it was as if God was another client. I was doing my thing.

What I had to understand is that God didn't need my ability. He needed my availability. He didn't want me to stand on my curriculum vitae, my resume, my body of work, and my achievements. He wanted me to stand on His Word. He didn't want me to complete the project and then take the credit and boast. He wanted me to work on a project so massive, so complex, and so huge that there would be no question or doubt whatsoever when it is completed that God Himself did it alone by divine grace and intervention, and that its success would not be because of anything I might have done. He wanted me to trust Him.

This is what Paul meant when he said, "If I have a faith that can move mountains, but have not love, I am nothing."[5] Even though I had faith, it wasn't enough. This is also what James meant when he said, "As the body without the spirit is dead, so faith without deeds is dead."[6] Faith without works is dead. What I had to learn and understand is that this means it is not enough just to know the Word and to believe in the Word. I had to stand on the Word and act on the Word. It is not enough to have faith. I had to step out in faith.

In this sense, Paul is saying our faith must be evidenced by our acts of love. James is saying we must have workable faith, and our faith must be evidenced by our acts and by our work and deeds. However, the work we are to perform in this regard is not our own work, but God's work. We are not supposed to work hard and then say, "Hey, God, look at what I did. Look at what I accomplished. Aren't I great?" Rather, we are to seek God and listen to God and answer God's calling to do whatever it is He places on our hearts to do. We are to respond in obedience. We are to let our faith be manifest in our actions and in our works and in our deeds that we perform in service of and for Him. Then we are to praise God and give Him thanks, saying, "God, you are great!" In this way, we can lead others to God.

The Bible contains many stories where people had to do more than just have faith. They had to act on that faith. Their faith and obedience to God was tested. Abraham had to build an altar and prepare Isaac to be sacrificed. Noah had to build an ark. The priests carrying the arc of the covenant had to step out and into the Jordan River before the waters flowing downstream at flood stage could be cut off and stand up in a heap.[7] They all obeyed and stepped out in faith. They all trusted God. Once they stepped out in faith, God worked in their lives.

The story of Elijah in 1 Kings 18 is my favorite. To turn the Israelites back to the Lord, Elijah challenged the prophets of Baal to a high-stakes duel. Elijah was determined to demonstrate that Baal was a false god. Elijah and the Baal prophets agreed they each would build an altar for a sacrifice, but neither would set the wood on fire. They agreed that the God who provided the fire for the sacrifice would be recognized as the one and only true God. Elijah was all in, winner take all.

The Baal prophets could not summon fire from their god. Elijah had so much faith, that he even taunted the Baal prophets during their efforts. Elijah suggested the Baal prophets should yell louder to Baal, their god, hinting that Baal couldn't hear them. He facetiously feigned concern, suggesting Baal was perhaps preoccupied and deep in thought. He also rhetorically reasoned that Baal wasn't answering them because perhaps he was busy. Elijah mocked them with additional excuses that Baal was absent because he was traveling or sleeping![8] It must have been an awesome sight to watch Elijah exercise such incredible faith. That's what I call Old Testament trash-talking! I'm sure God must have enjoyed the moment, watching Elijah's confidence in his faith in God and in God's faithfulness.

When it was Elijah's turn, he had servants pour water over the wood. Then he told them to do it again. And then he told them to do it again. More trash talk. I can only imagine the shocked look on the faces of each of the 450 Baal prophets when this was happening. The altar and the wood around it had been doused with so much water that the water not only soaked all the wood, but it also even filled the trench surrounding the altar.[9]

Elijah then prayed to the Lord to send fire for the sacrifice. God not only honored Elijah and answered his prayer, He exceeded it. In answer to Elijah's prayer, "Then the fire of the LORD fell and burned up the sacrifice, the wood, the stones and the soil, and also licked up the water in the trench."[10] God was so convincing even the stones and the soil and the water itself were on fire! When you step out in faith, God not only will answer your prayer, but He will exceed your expectations.

Elijah stepped out in faith. He built the altar so God could work through him. However, Elijah was so confident in his faith in God and in God's faithfulness that Elijah taunted the Baal prophets and their god. Elijah wanted everyone to know that God, and only God, could perform that miracle and take all the glory and credit.

Elijah may have showboated a little bit, but I like to think he was just acting confidently and boldly in knowing his God would deliver in spades. This is what I learned. I learned I had to step out in faith and trust God to provide what I needed—not just for the project, but also for everything in my life. While God has blessed me with certain skills, He let me know none of them would be adequate to complete this real estate construction project. He made me understand God didn't need my skill or ability. I wasn't qualified for the job.

My pride had to be broken. I had to lose everything to realize I am nothing without Him. As Paul wrote:

> But He said to me, "My grace is sufficient for you, for My power is made perfect in weakness." Therefore, I will boast all the more gladly about my weaknesses, so that Christ's power may rest on me. That is why, for Christ's sake, I delight in weaknesses, in insults, in hardships, in persecutions, in difficulties. For when I am weak, then I am strong.[11]

God said, "My grace is sufficient for you, for my power is made perfect in weakness" (2 Corinthians 12:9). When I am weak and broken, He is strong. When I applied this to my depression, I realized that my mistakes and failures, the very things Satan used to bring me down, are the very things God uses to lift me up.

When I litigated cases in court, a technique I often used to win the case was to take my adversary's best argument and make it my best argument. Whenever I employed that strategy my adversary had nothing left to argue.

In my situation, this is what God did with Satan. The best argument or tool Satan used in his battle with me was my mistakes and failures. Satan told me I was a failure and a loser. Carmen told me I was a failure and a loser. They told our children I was a failure and a loser. When I became depressed with my negative thoughts on autopilot, I began to believe them. Then God intervened. He took Satan's best argument and made it His best argument.

God took my weaknesses, my mistakes, my faults, and my failings, and He showed me those very weaknesses are what allows me to trust Him. God showed me that "when I am weak then I am strong." God then stepped in and provided me with what I needed to defeat Satan. God provided me with the discernment, the strength, the perseverance, the courage, the ability, the tenacity, the power, and the valor to kick Satan straight back to hell!

God is awesome! We serve an awesome God!

When we are bruised, we can be used. Either we can be used by Satan for his evil purposes, or we can be used by God for His glory. The choice is ours. God gave us the free will to exercise and to choose. However, we have to be vigilant and exercise discernment to avoid allowing our thoughts to switch to automatic, negative thoughts. Being a Christian does not give you immunity from Satan's temptations and threats. We have to use Biblical discernment and continue to pray for guidance. God will hear your prayer, and He will honor your prayer and guide your steps. He will direct your path. If you will honor God, He will honor you (1 Samuel 2:30).

As I conclude my story, the project has still not funded. The construction funding has been arranged, but we still need some additional funding to facilitate and activate the construction funding. However, that is not up to me. That's up to God. I simply work now as if the success of the project funding depends on me, but I pray knowing the outcome depends on God, which it does.[12]

This is an expression I learned from Pastor Mark Batterson, the lead pastor of National Community Church in Washington DC, when I read his book *In a Pit with a Lion on a Snowy Day.*[13] After I had been working on the real estate construction project for three years, I was beginning to get discouraged. His book encouraged me and led me to another book he wrote called *The Circle Maker,*[14] which also provided encouragement. I recommend both of them wholeheartedly.

Jesus said the greatest commandment is to "Love the Lord your God with all your heart and with all your soul and with all your mind."[15] Our heart is the compassion of our love. Our soul is the strength of our faith. Our mind is the courage and conviction of our trust in Him to allow us to step out in faith.

When Jesus predicted Peter would deny Him three times, Peter protested, saying that he would even die for Christ: "But Peter declared, 'Even if I have to die with you, I will never disown you.' And all the other disciples said the same."[16]

We all understand Peter and the other disciples exclaiming that they all, without exception, would be willing to die for Christ. Years later, after Christ's death and resurrection, most of them in fact did die for Christ. They chose death rather than deny Christ. Peter may have denied knowing Christ three times the night before Christ was crucified, but years later, he was killed for testifying for Christ and for spreading the Gospel—the Good News.

Today, we all like to think we would do the same—that we would be willing to die for Christ. As Christians though, the difficult question we need to ask ourselves is not whether we would be willing to die for Christ. Instead, the difficult question we need to ask ourselves is, "Are we willing to live for Christ?" For many of us, that's the more difficult question and choice. To be able to live for Christ, we have to be willing to give up our selves and our will and follow Him.

I obediently answered the call to write this book, and I sincerely presented my story in the hope that it would be encouraging. I obediently answered the call to work on the project, and I wait expectantly for Him to provide the funding. Until He removes that opportunity and sends me in a different direction, I will continue to work diligently and obediently. I will continue to wait on the Lord. My goal is not the funding.

My goal is being obedient to work on the project until it funds or until God sends me in a different direction.

I don't know if the project will fund, but I believe and hope it will. "Since we have such a hope, we are very bold."[17] I boldly believe He wants me to develop and build a Christian resort. I believe He wants me to build a Christian resort that will stand in stark contrast against the vortexes, the crystals, and the New Age mysticism prevalent in the community where the project will be built. I believe this Christian resort will host retreats and sabbaticals for pastors. I believe this Christian resort will host summer camps for churches and Christian schools. I believe this Christian resort will host conferences and workshops that will repair and restore broken marriages and families. I believe this Christian resort will have a church that not only will provide a setting for weddings, but that also will serve guests with a place to worship while away from home at a conference or on a vacation.

I boldly say I believe God will provide the funding for the project, and that God will use this project to be this kind of a resort because I have acted, because I am acting, and because I will continue to act in faith. I believe we are to be bold, audacious Christians without apology.

When I used to get up in the morning, I used to start each day by asking God or by telling God what I wanted Him to do for me that day. Now I begin each day with a conversation with God where I say a prayer of thanks and then I ask Him, "Lord, what do you want me to do for You today?" I then pray and listen for His response. He answers me by giving me direction and guidance.

Just as I believe God called me to write this book and work on this project, I also believe that God has a plan and a purpose for you. If you let Him, He will direct your path. He will be a lamp at your feet and send you out on the right path. Paul said that as ministers of the new covenant, "In Christ we speak before God with sincerity, like men sent from God."[18] "We are therefore Christ's ambassadors, as though God were making His appeal through us."[19]

The Greek word for *apostle* is *apóstolos* meaning "one sent," "messenger," or "envoy." An English definition might be *ambassador*. Paul said that as Christians "We are therefore Christ's ambassadors, as though God were making His appeal through us."[20] I believe God placed it on my heart to write this book to convey the message that the expression of real faith is more than just knowing or believing. It is not sufficient that we know God, but rather that "we are known by God."[21]

Some people will never believe unless they see miraculous signs and wonders.[22] "Blessed are those who have not seen and yet have believed."[23] Our faith is in that which is unseen. With this kind of faith the emphasis is transferred from me to God. It is not my faith, but my belief in God's faithfulness, in God's character, and in God's promises.

My message is that having faith is more than just believing. A true expression of faith is acting on that belief and faith without first seeing or receiving that for which you have prayed. It is stepping out in faith, knowing that "God will meet all your needs according to His glorious riches in Christ Jesus."[24] It is in this sense I want to be an ambassador of Christ. I want to be a man sent from God to be obedient to Him and to serve Him as though God were making His appeal through me. This is my goal, my mission, and my purpose.

In this construction project, God is my Architect. Christ is the Master Builder and Lead Carpenter. The Holy Spirit is the Director of Planning and Consulting. With a development team such as this, how can we fail? When God is for us, who can be against us?[25]

As I finish writing this story, the seller of the property has cancelled our purchase contract. However, I'm not worried or afraid. I believe God has His hands on this property and on this project and that He's watching over it until we can secure the rest of the funding we need. It is as if I have been running a marathon, and I can see the finish line about a hundred yards away. We have the construction funding arranged for the project and now only need to find the administrative costs to facilitate and activate the construction funding.

God is not just my architect for this project, but He also is the architect for my life. The past five years have been incredibly difficult and financially challenging. I now have worked more than five years on this project without receiving any income. There have been times when I could not provide for our children's needs. There have been times when Janice's modest income wasn't enough to pay all the bills when they had to be paid. However, I continued to listen and trust God to provide for our needs.

When I had to go to court because we were being evicted from the house we were renting, the owner of the house wasn't represented by an attorney. Not being an attorney herself, she was struggling to make her case in court, and she didn't have all her documents in order. I easily could have defeated her case. Although she later could have come back to court again, perhaps the next time with an attorney, by beating her in court, I could have extended the time by which we would have been able to continue to live in the house before we would have been required to move. Nevertheless, I felt God was telling me to humble myself, remove all my available defenses to the court, become totally vulnerable, and actually help my landlord evict me. Trusting God, I humbly made her case in court.

The judge appeared like he wanted to give me a break. I sensed he had seen many cases like this in his courtroom during the horrible economy over the past several years. The judge was questioning my landlord, and it looked like he was getting ready to dismiss her case. My landlord was getting flustered and frustrated. I interrupted the judge's questions, gave my landlord a reassuring look, and quietly said to her, "Let me handle this." In humility I admitted to the judge all the facts that were needed to prove my landlord's case against me so the judge could enter the eviction order.

When I left court, I didn't know where we were going to live. I knew the eviction order would become effective within the next two weeks. I knew I probably wouldn't be able to rent another house with an eviction on my credit report. I knew that if we had to move out of our school district the children would have to change schools again. However, as I was driving home, I wasn't worried. I was at peace because I had done what I believed I had been asked to do. I trusted God. Instead of being afraid, I said a little prayer of thanks.

As I drove the half-hour drive home from court, I prayed the Lord would again direct my path. After I entered our neighborhood and came closer to our house, I saw a sign directing me to a house only a few blocks away with a "For Lease" sign in the yard. The leasing agent was one of my old friends from the tennis club. The lease was approved, and we moved into the house. Only God could do that.

About a year later, we needed $150,000 to keep the real estate development project going. My former landlord, the one who evicted me, was the one who provided the money. Only God could make that happen by putting it in place and setting it in motion more than a year earlier. Only God.

The Lord continues to provide for us. Our children's fourth-grade teacher let us use their eighteen-year-old car that was her and her husband's second car. It had almost 140,000 miles, the seats and headliner were ripped and torn, the maroon paint was badly oxidized, the tires were bald, and it loudly squeaked when it passed over any bump or rut in the road. It had an electrical short somewhere that occasionally drained the battery, so we carried jumper cables in the car. We bought a new battery, but it sometimes failed as the short continued to drain the battery. We affectionately called it the Beast. However, it ran, and we were thankful to have been able to drive it. Each time I started the engine and saw the "check engine" light, I checked in with God and counted my blessings and thanked Him for the use of the Beast.

When we needed a second car for our son to drive, I unexpectedly received a call from the company that had repossessed the little convertible we had purchased for our daughter. The person on the phone said the company still had the car, and it had not sold the car at auction. Over six months had passed, but the company still had the car. The person on the phone said that if we would agree to pay $450 toward the outstanding balance owed, he would cancel our remaining debt and return the car to us. The only problem was we didn't have the $450 we needed to pay to get back the car.

When Janice came home from work that day, I said, "You're not going to believe what happened today." Before I could tell her about the phone call and the car, Janice said, "The most incredible thing happened to me today—a client gave me a five-hundred-dollar tip." It was absolutely amazing. I was speechless. I just smiled. Most of the time, Janice would receive a ten-or twenty-dollar tip and is blessed at Christmas to receive larger tips of fifty dollars. But a five-hundred dollar tip? Just like that, out of the blue? Only God could make that happen. Only God.

God continues to provide for our needs. Even though our funds are limited, Janice continues to tithe. I am happy (pun intended) to say I have overcome depression. Don't misunderstand my message, I still get sad sometimes. I still struggle at not being able to provide for my family. I still struggle with the past. Writing this book has been incredibly difficult, and there were times when writing about past events made me cry every day, having to relive those events.

However, I practiced my skill sets so that the sadness would not last. I prayed and trusted. Even though writing about these past events has been so very painful, I felt God wanted me to share my story, so I obediently kept writing. I continued to practice my skill sets. I continued to trust and pray. I continued to write through the tears. I would let the sadness wash over me and then move on again. To help keep it all in perspective, I continued to stay humble, get out of my own way, let go and let God.

However, the Lord must think I still need lessons in humility from time to time. I often am reminded to stay humble. Driving the Beast certainly has been an exercise in humility. It was those times when the Beast wouldn't start because the battery was dead that provided the additional humility lessons and reminders. I take solace in the verse, "He who humbles himself will be exalted" (Luke 14:11; 18:14). When I pray for patience, the Lord answers my prayer by giving me additional opportunities to practice patience.

The Lord also keeps me humble with His sense of humor. Last year when we had our tax return prepared, I asked the person who prepared our return why he didn't deduct the expenses I had incurred working on the project. He told me IRS regulations wouldn't allow him to use those expenses as deductions because he said if someone works for three or more consecutive years without making any money, the IRS considers that endeavor not to be work but to be a hobby. I'm glad I can make God laugh.

A frequently quoted statement by Jesus is, "From everyone who has been given much, much will be demanded" (Luke

12:48). It often is used in terms of giving back or in terms of making charitable or philanthropic contributions or donations. People who have been blessed with money and wealth often recite this verse upon providing their donation or gift. That may be a proper application of the verse, but to me, Jesus's words don't mean that at all. I believe Jesus is talking about His command that we are to spread the Gospel, the Good News.

The entire verse, the rest of Jesus's statement, is that, "From everyone who has been given much, much will be demanded; and from the one who has been entrusted with much, much more will be asked." To me, Jesus' statement doesn't refer to wealth, riches or stuff. Rather, I believe Jesus was talking about our responsibility to live our lives like Christ, to step out in faith and to spread the Gospel. Jesus' statement actually was part of His response to Peter's question, "Lord, are you telling this parable to us, or to everyone?" (Luke 12:41) Jesus answered Peter's question by saying, "From everyone who has been given much, much will be demanded; and from the one who has been entrusted with much, much more will be asked."

This same message appears in the parable of the talents where a master entrusted his property to three servants. In the parable of the talents, a master gave five talents to the first servant, two talents to the second servant, and one talent to the third servant. Upon his return, the master rewarded the first two servants for investing the talents given to them and for obtaining a return on their investment. However, when the master learned the third servant had buried the talent given to him, the master ordered it be taken from the third servant and given instead to the first servant. Although the parable of the talents speaks in terms of money, I don't believe Jesus was talking about money at all. I believe Jesus was talking about spreading the Gospel.

I believe the use of the term *talent* that the master gave to each of his servants symbolically refers to the knowledge, wisdom, and understanding of the Word of God. I believe the master in the parable of the talents refers to God, and the references to each of the servants symbolize all of us.

The third servant, who had buried and hid the talent he was given, said he had done so because he was afraid. "Master, he said, I knew you are a hard man, harvesting where you have not sown and gathering where you have not scattered seed. So I was afraid and went out and hid your talent in the ground" (Matthew 25:24–25). How could the master, who the servant described as "a hard man, harvesting where you have not sown and gathering where you have not scattered seed" be a reference to God? How could it be that God harvests where He has not sown and gathers where He has not planted seed?

Let me explain.

I believe the master in the parable of the talents symbolically refers to God. At the time of judgment, there will be what Jesus described as a harvest. The servant said he knew his master was "a hard man, harvesting where you have not sown and gathering where you have not scattered seed." I believe this reference refers to the harvest when God will come in judgment.

The parable of the weeds explains the symbolism in the parable of the talents. In the parable of the weeds, Jesus said:

> The kingdom of heaven is like a man who sowed good seed in his field. But while everyone was sleeping, his enemy came and sowed weeds among the wheat, and went away. When the wheat sprouted and formed heads, then the weeds also appeared.
>
> The owner's servants came to him and said, "Sir, didn't you sow good seed in your field? Where then did the weeds come from?" "An enemy did this," he replied. The servants asked him, "Do you want us to go and pull them up?" "No," he answered, "because while you are pulling the weeds, you may root up the wheat with them. Let both grow together

until the harvest. At that time I will tell the harvesters: first collect the weeds and tie them in bundles to be burned; then gather the wheat and bring it into my barn." (Matthew 13:24–30)

Jesus Himself explained the symbolism expressed in the parable of the weeds:

Then He left the crowd and went into the house. His disciples came to Him and said, "Explain to us the parable of the weeds in the field." He answered, "The one who sowed the good seed is the Son of Man. The field is the world, and the good seed stands for the sons of the kingdom. The weeds are the sons of the evil one, and the enemy who sows them is the devil. The harvest is the end of the age, and the harvesters are angels. As the weeds are pulled up and burned in the fire, so it will be at the end of the age. The Son of Man will send out his angels, and they will weed out of His kingdom everything that causes sin and all who do evil. They will throw them into the fiery furnace, where there will be weeping and gnashing of teeth. Then the righteous will shine like the sun in the kingdom of their Father. He who has ears, let him hear." (Matthew 13:36–43)

The parable of the weeds explains that the weeds were sown by the enemy, Satan. Even though Satan sowed the weeds, God will harvest and gather the weeds along with the wheat at the harvest at the time of judgment. It is for this reason the master in the parable of the talents is referred to as "a hard man, harvesting where you have not sown and gathering where you have not scattered seed" (Matthew 25:24). God did not sow the weeds. Satan did. However, God will harvest the weeds along with the wheat. The weeds will be thrown "into the fiery furnace, where there will be weeping and gnashing of teeth" (Matthew 13:42).

In the parable of the talents, the master referred to the third servant as a "wicked, lazy servant" (Matthew 25:26), and the master gave the order to "throw that worthless servant outside, into the darkness, where there will be weeping and gnashing of teeth" (Matthew 25:30). The same reference of throwing the weeds "into the fiery furnace, where there will be weeping and gnashing of teeth" used in the parable of the weeds is used in the parable of the talents to describe how the wicked, lazy servant will be thrown "into the darkness, where there will be weeping and gnashing of teeth."

When the parable of the talents is read in the context of the parable of the weeds, I believe each of the talents in the parable symbolically represents the knowledge, wisdom, and understanding of the Word of God made available and given to each of us to hear. As Jesus said, "He who has ears, let him hear." We can choose to accept Christ or not. God gave each of us that free will to choose. However, if we don't accept Christ, we in fact make the choice to reject Christ.

In the parable of the sower, Jesus explained that the servant in the parable of the talents who hid and buried his talent is like the person who hears the Word, but who does not cultivate it and care for it and grow it:

> The seed is the word of God. Those along the path are the ones who hear, and then the devil comes and takes away the word from their hearts, so that they may not believe and be saved. Those on the rock are the ones who receive the word with joy when they hear it, but they have no root. They believe for a while, but in the time of testing they fall away. The seed that fell among thorns stands for those who hear, but as they go on their way they are choked by life's worries, riches and pleasures, and they do not mature. But the seed on good soil stands for those with a noble and good heart,

who hear the word, retain it, and by persevering produce a
crop. (Luke 8:11–15)

All of us have heard the Word of God or have had the
opportunity to hear the Word. We must not be like "that servant
who knows his master's will and does not get ready or does not
do what his master wants" (Luke 12:47). Some of us have been
given more. "From everyone who has been given much, much
will be demanded; and from the one who has been entrusted
with much, much more will be asked" (Luke 12:48).

It is not enough to hear the Word. We must believe. We must
have faith. It is not enough to know the Word of God. We must
accept the Word of God. We must accept Christ. Then we must
spread the Gospel with our deeds and with our actions and with
our love. We must act on our faith, and we must step out in
faith. In that way, we can demonstrate that our faith is evidence
of what is not seen. In that way, we can spread the Gospel—the
Good News of Christ. We can be like "those with a noble and
good heart, who hear the word, retain it, and by persevering
produce a crop." The people we lead to Christ represent the crop
we will produce.

It is for this reason Jesus said, "Therefore, consider carefully
how you listen. Whoever has will be given more; whoever does
not have, even what he thinks he has will be taken from him"
(Luke 8:18). There is only one way to salvation.

I have gained wisdom and understanding by having endured
all my challenges and trials. God taught me to lean on Him and
on His Word instead of on my own understanding. Jesus said,
"I am the vine; you are the branches. If a man remains in Me
and I in him, he will bear much fruit; apart from Me you can do
nothing" (John 15:5). Again, the fruit we produce is the crop of
new believers we lead to Christ.

To most people, losing everything and suffering from chronic
depression and PTSD would not be considered a blessing.

However, for me, it has been the best learning laboratory and the best teacher and the best blessing. Through this process, this storm, God has refined and distilled me and opened my eyes. Through my troubles and hardships, I turned back to Him. I became closer to Him. He now has called me to write this book and share the Good News so my story may encourage you and inspire you and lead you to Christ. In writing this book, I am serving Him. This book is not the result of my efforts or works, but was inspired by the Holy Spirit within me. God is using me and working through me to reach others through this book. If the message in this book reaches out and touches someone, helps someone and rescues someone, all the glory and honor belong to God. "I will praise you, O Lord, with my whole heart, I will tell of all Your marvelous works" (Psalm 9:1).

I hope this book will help people overcome their depression and PTSD as "weeping may remain for a night, but rejoicing comes in the morning" (Psalm 30:5). Each of the seven skill sets can be used practically to defeat and overcome depression and PTSD. However, each of the seven skill sets also can be used spiritually to defeat and overcome Satan and to produce lasting joy and peace. I hope this book will help you find, know, and accept Christ.

Conclusion

Those who hope in the LORD will renew their strength.
They will soar on wings like eagles; they will run and not
grow weary, they will walk and not be faint.

—Isaiah 40:31

God said, "Those who honor me I will honor."[1] It is my prayer that I have honored God in being obedient to answer God's call to write this book. It is my prayer that I have honored God in being obedient to answer God's call to pursue the completion of the real estate project. It is my hope and prayer that reading this book has provided some enlightenment on depression and PTSD specifically, and on mental health issues generally, to help overcome the associated stigmatism. I did not write this book to endear empathy or to seek sympathy. People who are depressed don't want sympathy. They want compassionate understanding, they want encouraging support, and they want to get well.

If you are reading this and you have experienced any of the symptoms of depression or PTSD I have described or if you have been (or are) depressed or sad or discouraged or angry, I hope you have learned something from having read this book and that you have benefited from the seven skill sets, both from the practical cognitive behavioral therapy application and from the spiritual Christian application. Depression occurs when the normal period of time for grief or sadness is prolonged or perpetuated. Depression also occurs when we automatically apply negative meaning to life's events. Depression also occurs when the grief or sadness returns, either by a flashback to an event in the past or by a new event or situation. I hope you will be able to benefit by applying the seven skill sets.

As I conclude this story, I can tell you I still get sad. In fact, I became extremely sad writing this book. Writing about the past circumstances and situations reminded me of those past events and made me sad all over again. I also get sad sometimes from my present circumstances. For example, as I have been working on the real estate development project for over five years with no income, I have not been able to provide for my family as much as I would like, as much as they have been accustomed to, and certainly not as much as they would like. You can imagine just how difficult this has been with three teenagers in high school and now college. However, when I apply my skill sets, I can overcome the sadness and find contentment and peace even in this set of circumstances.

Part of the reason for my sadness is that when I haven't been able to provide for my family, particularly my children, they have been thinking or were being told I am not a good father and a good provider. Carmen has told them that. Satan has told them I am a failure and a loser and not a good provider or father. Satan has told me I am a failure and a loser and not a good provider or father. When this happens, I begin to think I am not a good provider or father. However, when this happens, I immediately apply and practice my seven skill sets, and I overcome being sad.

Let me explain how I utilize the seven skill sets by using the example of our son becoming angry with me when I have to tell him I can't purchase something he wants or I can't pay for something he needs. Satan will tell us both that I am a failure and a loser and a bad father. When our son hears this, he becomes angry. Satan will attach negative meaning for him and tell him he deserves better, that he deserves to have something, and I have failed him by not providing it for him. Similarly, Satan will attach negative meaning for me and tell me I deserve better and our son is spoiled, entitled, and disrespectful toward me. Instead of focusing on his behavior, I am tempted to overreact in anger and inflict labels directed at him personally.

However, none of those negative meanings are real. None of those meanings are truthful. Nevertheless, Satan will have both our son and me believe those hurtful and negative meanings. The reality of the situation simply is that, at the present time, we can't afford to purchase what he wants or needs. That's it. Nothing more. Satan wants us to attach those negative meanings because he wants to create division, distrust, and separation between us. Nevertheless, when I exercise my practical and spiritual skill sets, I can overcome Satan's deceitful voices. Let me illustrate.

I first exercise *recognition*. I recognize the trigger and the automatic negative thoughts. I see the negative meaning being attached and attributed to the action. If, for example, our son is angry with me because I have to tell him I can't pay for something he wants or needs, I recognize the trigger, and I refuse to allow Satan to push my buttons. By recognizing what is happening, I can avoid escalating the situation. I can avoid reacting or overacting in anger. I can avoid becoming defensive, justifying my anger. I also then practice the spiritual skill set of recognition. Instead of becoming angry with our son, I extend mercy toward him. I try to express words that communicate to him that I understand his message and his frustration in not being able to get what he wants or needs.

I next practice *reflection*. When I reflect on the situation and search the meaning for our son's reaction or outburst, I use my discernment to seize those negative thoughts and cast them off and away. When I exercise biblical discernment, I realize those negative thoughts can't possibly originate from God because they only can lead to separation and division in my relationship with our son. I then put on the full armor of God and go back to the Word to lean on God's promises and summon the strength and courage from Him that I am going to need.

I then *retreat*. If the particular exchange with our son is intense and heated, I will retreat by calling a time-out. I remain calm so I don't escalate the situation and get angry myself. I remember to be the thermostat instead of the thermometer. I tell our son we'll talk about it later and try together to arrive at an acceptable solution. I also find a retreat or sanctuary in God's Word and in His peace in the Word. I am reminded of His promise in Jeremiah where He says, "I will refresh the weary and satisfy the faint" (Jeremiah 31:25).

Now that I have put up my umbrella and the storm has passed, I can proceed toward *renewal*. I can remind myself Satan is a deceiver and a liar. I stay in the moment and do not dwell on the hurtful past and the meanings Satan is assigning to the past and present events. I remind myself I am a great dad and I use the next opportunity to talk with our son about the reality of the financial situation and turn the situation into a teaching moment. I create a beginner's mind, a renewed mind, and allow the present experience to be accepted in the real moment and in the reality that it is without the negative meanings and connection to the past. I don't resent our son, and I don't allow the confrontation to interfere with the present or the future.

Applying the spiritual side of this skill set, I forgive myself for not being able to provide for my family right now, and I remind myself that all things come from God and that He will provide for our needs. I also forgive our son and stay mindful that he is receiving the same negative messages from Satan. In this way, I am able to remember this no more and let it pass by extending fatherly love to our son, even in a difficult moment. In this way, I am renewed, and I have a renewed mind:

> Those who hope in the LORD will renew their strength.
> They will soar on wings like eagles; they will run and not
> grow weary, they will walk and not be faint. (Isaiah 40:31)

Once I am renewed, then I can proceed to *recovery*. I make
sure I get plenty of rest and exercise. Instead of leaning on my
own understanding, I let God speak to me. Whenever I feel
the need to hear God's voice, all I have to do is open my Bible
and read the Word of God. What God thinks and what God
has to say about something—His assurances and promises—are
there in the Word. I am reminded that sometimes I just need to
hear God say to me, "Be still, and know that I am God" (Psalm
46:10). I find solace in the Psalms:

> Search me, O God, and know my heart; Test me and know
> my anxious thoughts. (Psalm 139:23)
>
> O LORD, hear my prayer, listen to my cry for mercy; In Your
> faithfulness and righteousness Come to my relief. (Psalm
> 143:1)
>
> Show me the way I should go, For to you I lift up my soul.
> (Psalm 143:8)
>
> The LORD is near to all who call on Him, To all who call on
> Him in truth. (Psalm 145:18)
>
> He fulfills the desires of those who fear Him; He hears
> their cry and saves them. (Psalm 145:19)
>
> The LORD watches over all who love Him. (Psalm 145:20)
>
> The LORD who remains faithful forever. (Psalm 146:6)

I then *rejoice*. Instead of focusing on the present situation
and my financial predicament, I focus on the many blessings
I have in my life right now. I also help our son focus on the
blessings he has in his life and help him focus on the solution
instead of the problem. Applying the spiritual application, I
remember to "be joyful always; pray continually; give thanks in

all circumstances, for this is God's will for you in Christ Jesus"
(1 Thessalonians 5:17–18). By staying in the moment spiritually,
I thank God for this opportunity to serve Him and be a living
testimony and model of my demonstrable faith. By staying in
the moment spiritually, I can be content in my present situation,
even in financial difficulty and financial stress, by remembering
that "this is the day the Lord has made; let us rejoice and be
glad in it" (Psalm 118:24).

Finally, I demonstrate *reliance* through my faith. I trust in
the practical skill sets and know they have worked for me in
overcoming the negative thoughts and depression. I remind
myself it is okay to be sad, but I let it just wash over me and
not let the sadness or grief linger. Practicing the spiritual side, I
remind myself that "God is faithful, who will not allow you to
be tempted beyond what you are able" (1 Corinthians 10:13). I
remind myself that "He will thrust out the enemy from before
you" (Deuteronomy 33:27) and that "the Lord is faithful,
and He will strengthen and protect you from the evil one" (2
Thessalonians 3:3). By having faith in God and by trusting in
Him, I then can demonstrate God's love even in the midst of
the storm.

"Blessed is he …whose hope is in the LORD his God" (Psalm
146:5).

This is only one example as to how I have applied the seven
skill sets in my life in a single situation. Try to apply them in
your own life examples and different situations. When you
apply them, you will be renewed. Your faith, trust, and hope will
be renewed. Your soul will be restored.

When we become Christians, the Bible tells us we are to love.
Christ said the greatest commandment is to love the Lord our
God, and the second commandment is to love our neighbors
as ourselves (Mark 12:29–31). The Bible also tells us we are to
forgive. Christ said we will be forgiven based on how we forgive

others. The Bible also tells us we are to pray. Christ taught us how to pray by providing us with the Lord's Prayer.

When I read the Bible, I believed. When I studied the Bible and participated in Bible studies, I learned how to strengthen my faith. However, for me, I didn't really know *how* to practice or use my faith in my battles with Satan. Even when I "put on the full armor of God," I didn't really know how to use that armor. When the storms came, I still believed and I still prayed and I still had faith, but that belief, prayer and faith didn't seem to be able to overcome the storms. Maybe that has happened with you.

When people accept Christ and become new Christians, they are equipped with the full armor of God, but they're not really prepared to use it against Satan. Although the full armor of God is all they need to fight Satan, they don't yet know how to use God's full armor. When it seems Satan keeps winning the battles, it is easy to get frustrated. You begin to doubt and question your faith. You begin to think you maybe aren't praying hard enough or the right way. This was how it was with me. Loving more, believing more, and praying more didn't seem to work. I was wearing all the armor, but I didn't know how to use it against all of Satan's tools.

I make the comparison between a new Christian in this regard and a high school football player. The football player loves football. He has watched, studied, and practiced football. He has been outfitted with his uniform—his armor. He has put on his football helmet with the protective padding inside and the sturdy face guard outside. He has put on his protective padding over his shoulders, chest, hips, and legs. He has put on his compression shorts, his shirt, and his sleeves. He has taped his ankles. He has put on his uniform. He has put on his football cleats and special socks. He literally has put on his armor and is ready to compete in a football game. Although he may be ready to play in a high school football game against another high school football team, he's not prepared to play a football game against a National Football League team.

Imagine such an absurd proposition. Imagine telling the high school football player all he has to do to win the battle is to get into the end zone while, at the same time, prevent the other team from getting into its end zone. Imagine telling him he is prepared simply because he wears his uniform—his armor. Imagine telling him he is ready simply because he knows the game and loves the game and has faith that he will win the game. Imagine then giving him a pat on the back, providing him with an inspirational and motivational message and then sending him out onto the football field to face his opponent for the upcoming battle—the NFL Detroit Lions.

In my humble opinion, this is what we do as Christians. We read and study the Bible to strengthen our faith. We also attend church where we read and study the Bible to encourage and deepen our faith. As a result, we spend most of our time reading and studying the Bible toward learning and believing God's Word, but we spend very little time learning how to apply and practice that faith and use God's Word to help us in our battles with Satan. Do we apply that faith daily in our lives, or do we only reflect on Sunday or in time of need? My example of the high school football player being sent to fight the NFL Detroit Lions is like when the early Christians were sent into the Coliseum to fight the lions.

I believe the skill sets I presented in this book will help you in your battles against Satan. This is why I presented not only the cognitive behavioral application but also the spiritual Christian application. They can be used not only in the fight against depression and despair but also in the fight against Satan as he battles for control of your mind.

In this sense, the skill sets are not a substitute for prayer but a supplement to prayer. They are intended to make prayer effective. They are not designed to have you lean on your own understanding, but rather, they are designed to help you lean on God's Word more effectively. Begin by recognizing Satan's attack. If you feel your faith is being challenged, recognize that those negative meanings and doubts are coming from Satan. Then reflect on why this is happening and on how you can use biblical discernment and God's Word to overcome the attack and reject Satan's meanings. Retreat to God's sanctuary to pray, to restore your soul, and to find peace. Enter recovery by turning back to God, by renewing your mind, and by living in each moment for God. Then rejoice in God's blessings and protections. Finally, rely on God's faithfulness and promises to strengthen and deepen your faith.

Applying these skill sets helped me not only overcome depression and PTSD, but they also helped me fight and resist Satan's accusations, temptations and lies. They helped me be able to use God's Word in a practical way. In this sense, these skill sets are being offered not only to encourage you, but also to let you learn and apply them in your own life so you can be an encouragement and an inspiration to others.

You now know my story. I lost my way when I became sick and suffered from the effects of depression and PTSD. At the time, I didn't know what was wrong with me or what was happening to me. Perhaps you feel the same way. Perhaps you can relate to the symptoms I have described in this book. Perhaps, like me, you felt confused because you no longer felt you were in control of your life, of the people and events in your life, or worst of all, of your own thoughts and mind.

Depression is like being lost in a labyrinth. It is an enigma inside a conundrum. You know something is wrong, but you don't know what is wrong. Because you don't know what is wrong, you can't communicate or describe the problem. When you fail to follow the course of treatment, any explanation has escaped understanding. As a result, you become ashamed and embarrassed by the associated stigmatism. You withdraw, become paralyzed, and shut down.

However, the paradox of depression is also the secret to its cure. The ability to heal your mind and take control over your thoughts actually lies within your mind. By applying the seven skill sets with the cognitive behavioral application, you can exercise discernment, reject the negative thoughts, and overcome depression.

Similarly, the secret to defeating Satan is resting on the knowledge and promise that Satan already has been defeated by Christ's death and the victory represented by His resurrection. By applying the seven skill sets with the spiritual Christian application and the full armor of God, you can exercise biblical discernment, rely on the Word and God's promise that He will guard you from Satan. You can defeat Satan with a renewed mind.

For me, 9-11 was not the only contributing cause of my depression and PTSD. The trauma associated with repeated abandonment issues in my relationships and, with repeated custody litigation issues in family court, caused me to reexperience those traumatic events over several decades. Sadly, the laws and procedures surrounding family law encourage the manipulation of the system for monetary gain and selfish interests overcome any reprisal from any sense of shame.

In his book *Telling Lies: Clues to Deceit in the Marketplace, Politics, and Marriage*, Paul Ekman said that "the humiliation of shame requires disapproval or ridicule by others."[2]

Without any fear of retribution or sanction or shame, such behavior is not deterred. In a letter published on his website on July 24, 2012, Billy Graham said, "Self-centered indulgence, pride, and a lack of shame over sin are now emblems of the American lifestyle."[3]

In my view, the genesis of despair, depression, and PTSD is disillusionment and unmet expectations. What began as a given, a foundation, or a belief system ceased to be dependable, reliable, or trustworthy. A trust was betrayed. A relationship was abandoned. A commitment was dishonored. An expectation was not met. A dream was destroyed. A marriage vow was not kept. A loved one was lost. Disaster was experienced.

Often such disillusionment for Christians is exacerbated when they seek help from their church. The effect of mental illness among Christians was studied by Dr. Matthew Stanford of Baylor University. His research results are illuminating. He found that the frequency of mental illness among church members (27%) is the same as the frequency among non-Christians. Christians, however, are more likely to seek help for mental health symptoms from their clergy rather than from mental health professionals. Unfortunately, most pastors do not recognize mental health symptoms, and they are neither prepared nor equipped to provide the professional psychological or psychiatric care that people with mental illness require. As a result, most Christians who seek mental health care from pastors fail thereafter to seek treatment from mental health professionals. Frustrated, Christians suffering from depression or mental illness believe they are not praying hard enough or the right way. They conclude that they are to blame and that their depression is their fault. Their faith becomes weakened or lost altogether as result of church interaction.[4]

If this has happened to you, don't let Satan use your depression to compromise your faith. Instead, apply the skill set of recognition to understand that pastors and clergy simply are not trained or equipped to treat mental health issues. Your depression is not a faith issue. It is a mental health issue. If you are suffering from depression or PTSD it is not because you are not praying enough, or the right way. It is not because your faith is weak. Depression cannot be prayed away.

Rather, depression and PTSD are medical conditions that require professional psychological and/or psychiatric treatment. As I have described in this book, you certainly should incorporate the Christian biblical principals and skill sets in your recovery plan to secure joy and lasting peace. However, your condition requires a professional diagnosis and the benefit of cognitive behavioral therapy principles and treatment.

You don't have to stay depressed or traumatized. Practice the skill sets, the cognitive behavioral techniques, the spiritual Christian applications, and get professional help.

You can overcome your depression, PTSD, or other mental illness. You can get better. You can defeat Satan.

The purpose of this book is not to provide a happy ending by telling you the project has funded. As I have shared, the project funding still hasn't materialized, and I still struggle with providing for my family. But I am confident, and I boldly exclaim in faith that I believe God will provide the funding, and at that time, I then will write a sequel to this book and give the glory to God.

Rather, the purpose and goal of this book is the same purpose and goal I now have for my life. The funding, or whatever exists for which I pray to receive, is not itself the goal. The goal and what I pray for, is to do God's will and to serve Him. The goal is not what I want. The goal is the service of God and the performance of God's will along the journey. The goal is the demonstration of faith in the act of serving God, in being a servant of God, and in finding joy and contentment while completing the journey. The goal is allowing others to see God's will being done through my obedience and service in answering each of God's calls during the journey. If God funds the project then I will continue to serve Him in that endeavor until he leads me in another direction. If God does not fund the project, then I am confident that He will lead me and guide me in another way and direction.

Even though the project has not yet funded, I find it interesting that the land upon which the project will be built is still available. It has not sold. Even though more than five years has passed, the land is still available and that door remains open.

In the meantime, God provides for all of our needs. At the end of each month, the bills somehow get paid even though the math doesn't add up. Our sons have been able to receive the necessary financial aid to continue to attend college. When the Beast stopped running, we somehow were able to get a loan to purchase another car. When our son also needed a car we received a $1000 check in the mail in connection with a class-action settlement, even though we didn't even know we were part of the class-action lawsuit. During the recession Janice continued to receive new clients and steady business. In one particularly slow week she received clients without referrals who happened to be traveling from Las Vegas and Oregon.

I believe that Christians should expect miracles and, as Christians we should recognize those miracles, both small and large, that occur in our daily lives. We build on our faith by recognizing those miracles and then by giving God praise. We honor God by sharing and acknowledging with others those miracles and answered prayers in our lives.

Yet another example of God caring for us and protecting us involved the little convertible—the same one that was repossessed and that was returned to us. After our daughter drove it during high school, our son drove it while he was finishing high school. When he went to college, we planned to have Janice's son drive it to school, but I needed to take it to the repair shop because it sometimes wouldn't start. Early one Saturday morning as I drove it to the repair shop I was in a serious accident.

I was traveling about sixty-five miles per hour in the left freeway lane when the car suddenly shut off. I had no electrical power. I later learned the cause was an electrical ignition failure. Because I had no electrical power, I could not turn on the hazard lights to warn the other drivers behind me that I was slowing down. Because there was no left shoulder, I could not pull off that side of the freeway. A shoulder existed on the right side of the freeway, but because the traffic in the other lanes was speeding past so fast I wasn't able to attempt to steer across the other three lanes to safety. I just continued to go slower and slower.

At first there was no one behind me. However, as I tentatively watched in my rearview mirror, I noticed cars behind me in the distance approaching fast. The first car that came up from behind me soon realized how slowly I was traveling and swerved around me. However, the next car had even less time to avoid hitting me and narrowly avoided hitting me by switching lanes at the last possible moment. I could see that the third car was not going to be able to change lanes. It had even less time to react, and there was another car in next lane immediately to its right. By now my car had slowed to less than thirty miles per hour. I knew that I was going to get hit and I knew that the impact would be severe. Just before impact, I held tightly to both sides of the steering wheel and braced my head and back against the seat to prepare for the inevitable collision.

The driver in the car behind me had no time to react after the car in front of him swerved around me. His sedan rear-ended the back of our little convertible at about sixty-five or seventy miles per hour. The front end of the sedan was totaled, and the back end of our little convertible was completely demolished. The impact was so severe that the steering wheel in our convertible was bent forward about forty-five degrees on both sides where my hands had gripped the wheel.

While the other driver incurred whiplash-type injuries, miraculously I was not injured. When I was rear-ended in a car accident years before, the other driver in that accident hit me from behind traveling about thirty-five miles per hour when I was stopped at a stop sign. After that accident I required treatment and rehabilitation for about six months for soft tissue injuries to my neck and back. However, in this accident I wasn't hurt at all. I didn't even have a sore neck. God protected me.

Following the accident I learned that in recent years numerous injuries and deaths occurred across the country as the result of ignition failures. When I consider how God protected me from harm, I can only praise God for this miracle.

I believe that God will protect us and provide for our needs if we trust Him completely. We still may have hardship, we still may experience loss, and we still may become saddened by life's events. However, if you put all of your faith and trust in God and in His faithfulness, He will never leave you and He will be with you during the storm. Perhaps things in life won't turn out as you expect or plan, but remember God has a plan and a purpose for you.

I hope I have reached my goal in writing this story so that others might be helped by hearing His message. Humbly, I hope my story inspires you to reach out to Christ. If you are suffering from depression or PTSD, or if you are discouraged or angry, I hope that my story served to educate you about depression and PTSD. I also hope my story encouraged you to seek treatment so that you can overcome depression.

Sometimes, I hear people say they are angry at God for the tragedies or losses they experienced in their lives. They say they are angry at God because they reason that a loving and kind

God would not have allowed those tragedies or losses to occur. They conclude and decide that God is to blame, so they blame Him. Maybe there have been times where you have felt this way.

However, my belief is that these negative meanings are from Satan. I believe Satan wants you to believe these negative meanings and thoughts so you will help him achieve his goal, which is your separation from God.

When you have suffered from loss or tragedy, you may feel like the lyrics in the song "Worn" by Tenth Avenue North. Each time I hear the song, I cry because the lyrics describe what it feels to be depressed. I also cry because I am so humbled by the Lord's saving grace. Here are the touching lyrics:

> I'm tired. I'm worn.
> My heart is heavy
> From the work it takes
> To keep on breathing.
> I've made mistakes.
> I've let my hope fail.
> My soul feels crushed
> By the weight of this world.
> And I know that You can give me rest.
> So I cry out with all that I have left.
> Let me see redemption win.
> Let me know the struggle ends.
> That You can mend a heart
> That's frail and torn.
> I wanna know a song can rise
> From the ashes of a broken life.
> And all that's dead inside can be reborn.
> Cause I'm worn.
> I know I need to lift my eyes up.
> But I'm just too weak.
> Life just won't let up.
> And I know that You can give me rest.

So I cry out with all that I have left.
Let me see redemption win.
Let me know the struggle ends.
That You can mend a heart
That's frail and torn.
I wanna know a song can rise
From the ashes of a broken life.
And all that's dead inside can be reborn.
Cause I'm worn.
My prayers are wearing thin.
Yeah, I'm worn.
Even before the day begins.
Yeah, I'm worn.
I've lost my will to fight.
I'm worn.
So, heaven come and flood my eyes.
Let me see redemption win.
Let me know the struggle ends.
That You can mend a heart that's frail and torn.
I wanna know a song can rise
From the ashes of a broken life.
Cause all that's dead inside can be reborn.
Though I'm worn.
Yeah, I'm worn. (http://www.azlyrics.com/lyrics/
tenthavenuenorth/worn.html)[5]

While the lyrics are haunting, I encourage you to listen to the song. (http://www.youtube.com/watch?v=UUEy8nZvpdM)

I encourage you to watch the YouTube video. The moving melody captures the ache and pain of depression. This may be how you feel. You may feel like your spirit has been crushed. You may feel like you cannot carry the weight or bear the burden of a loss any longer. Sometimes I felt that way. Through tears I would cry out to God in prayer that my load was getting a little bit too heavy and that I needed His help. If you feel this way, know that God can heal that hurt or loss. God can restore your soul and renew your mind.

God is a kind, loving, and compassionate God. When bad things happen or when tragedy strikes or a loss is suffered, instinctively people want to assess blame and find fault. When the tragedy or loss is of a great magnitude, people sometimes blame God for allowing the tragedy or loss to happen or for not preventing it from happening. The blame and fault are leveled when those people can't comprehend the meaning behind the loss. They are conflicted and confused. Satan then uses that opportunity to provide the negative meaning that it is God who is to blame.

Sometimes a tragedy or a loss occurs to fulfill a greater purpose. When we don't immediately know or understand that meaning or purpose, when we are at a loss to understand a meaning for our loss, we become susceptible to accept Satan's negative meaning and blame God.

My message to those people suffering and hurting, and who may even be suffering from depression because of that tragedy or loss, is that I understand your loss is real, and I am deeply sorry for your loss. My message is that your suffering and pain is real and deeply felt. I don't pretend to know why such things happen, but I do know that God is in control and that He has a plan and a purpose. You may want to disagree with me, especially if your loss is great, such as in the case of the loss of a loved one.

However, my message also is that God is compassionate and knows and understands your loss, sadness, and pain. God knows and understands your loss because while we were still sinners, God sent His only son, Jesus Christ, to die on a cross for our sins. God allowed His own Son to be crucified and put to death for a greater plan and purpose:

> For God so loved the world that He gave His one and only
> Son, that whoever believes in Him shall not perish but have
> eternal life. (John 3:16)

God knows what it is to experience the loss of a loved one as God allowed His only Son, Jesus, who was blameless and perfect, to endure the crucifixion and death on the cross so each of us may be saved. Jesus's death and resurrection was that greater plan and purpose. God understands and knows your loss. God has compassion for your loss and can heal your loss. God wants you to have peace.

If God can lift me up, He also can lift you up. "And we know that in all things God works for the good of those who love Him, who have been called according to His purpose" (Romans 8:28). Even what others may intend for harm or evil, God can use for good (Genesis 50:20).

It doesn't matter where you've been or what you've done. It doesn't matter how bruised or broken you are. It doesn't matter what has happened to you in your life or what's been done to you or what loss you have experienced. Even if you are despondent and think you should end your life, stop and remember King David's words: "I have no refuge; no one cares for my life. I cry to you, O LORD; I say, 'You are my refuge'" (Psalm 142:4–5).

"He heals the brokenhearted and binds up their wounds" (Psalm 147:3).

If you feel you have no refuge, let God be your refuge, protection, and hope. Don't give up. Let God be your refuge. He can heal you. He can restore your soul. All you have to do is ask Him. Confess to Him. Seek Him. Trust in Him. Let Him. Believe Him. Accept Him. Know Him. Live for Him.

Just like He had a plan and a purpose for Peter, even after Peter denied knowing Christ three times, He has a plan and a purpose for you. It is not too late. Reach out to Him. He is reaching out to you. Take His hand. Accept Him. Let Him be your Architect.

It also doesn't matter how talented you are, how intelligent you are, how creative you are, how artistic you are, how brilliant you are, or how skilled you are. If you are living your life without Christ, you are living your life without real meaning and purpose. You may have success, fame, or wealth, but none of those things will last and none of those things will have any lasting power. Unless you have the right blueprint, all your works and achievements will lack meaning. All your money, success, and accolades will lack meaning. Without God, your life lacks true meaning.

God has blessed you with all those talents and skills for a greater purpose and meaning. God has a plan and a purpose and a blueprint for your life just for you. Let Him use you for His will. Take the challenge. Accept Him.

Let God be your Architect.

Epilogue

When I answered God's call to write this book, I didn't know anything about publishing a book, and I couldn't afford to hire a literary agent to promote the book and guide it through the publishing process. I soon learned that many publishers will only review a manuscript either written or recommended by a published author. My book satisfied neither condition. Undaunted, I sent the manuscript to about a dozen publishers, but the outlook was generally negative. I was told that if a publisher liked the book, I shouldn't expect to receive a response for six to nine months, and if a publisher didn't like the book, I wouldn't even receive a response. My impression was that my situation was the classic case of, "Don't call us, we'll call you."

As a result, I decided, after much prayer, to publish the book independently. Since I couldn't believe that God called me to write this book without providing for its publication, I believed God was leading me to publish the book independently. CreateSpace, a company affiliated with Amazon, formatted and printed the book, and I created a separate company called Brokenhearted Publishing to serve as the publisher. The book became available for sale at Amazon.com in June of 2014.

However, because neither CreateSpace nor Amazon provided any marketing services, book sales languished. Predictably, Satan suggested the obvious negative meanings. Satan ridiculed me for believing that I could help people. He reminded me that it is impossible for people to be helped by a book they will never read because they don't even know it exists.

Nevertheless, I sincerely believed that God wanted me to write this book to help people, and I reminded Satan that nothing is impossible with God. I applied each of the steps and exercised discernment to reject Satan's negative meanings. With a renewed mind, I was confident that God somehow would make sure that the book would get to those who needed it, and I prayed that God would reveal His plan. I didn't know how God would make this happen, but I expectantly waited on the Lord and trusted Him to provide whatever was necessary to complete this work to publication.

About nine months later, Tate Publishing, one of the publishers to whom I had sent a manuscript, informed me that it had reviewed the manuscript and wanted to publish the book. When I reviewed the publishing contract, I was pleased to learn that Tate Publishing not only agreed to publish the book, but that it also agreed to market the book. I had stepped out in faith and wrote this book, but my attempt at independently publishing the book proved unsuccessful. I lacked the skills and resources and qualifications needed to market the book. Nevertheless, God didn't need me to publish the book. Rather, God provided Tate Publishing. "The Lord will guide you always; He will satisfy your needs" (Isaiah 58:11).

While God called me and worked through me and inspired me to write this book, He didn't need me to do anything else. He didn't need my ability. He just needed my availability. When God calls us to follow Him or to be obedient to do something, we can't understand or know the endgame or result. Rather, we simply are to obey and trust and have faith in God to provide the rest. "God will meet all your needs according to his glorious riches in Christ Jesus" (Philippians 4:19). I give all of the praise and credit to God.

It now is August 2015, and as I write this epilogue, I am confronted with a dilemma. The project manager for Tate Publishing told me that the book is ready for its final review prior to its publication next month. I need to finish writing this epilogue now and submit it to Tate Publishing if it is to be included in the book. My dilemma is that the real estate development project still has not yet funded. While I have answered God's call to complete this project, it still has not funded more than five and a half years later.

I believe that God has been changing me and preparing me during these past five and a half years. He has renewed my mind and, time after time, repeatedly has shown me what life looks like when one places one's complete trust and faith in God. However, my faith and trust and hope in God are nothing of my own. It is my faith in God's faithfulness.

Accordingly, I believe that God wants me to demonstrate further what it means to step out in faith and act on faith. Just like when I answered God's call to write this book even though I didn't know how He would get it published, I answered God's call to work on this project even though I didn't know how He would get it funded. This is the act of faith—the acting out and stepping out on faith. It is obeying and acting in such a bold and confident way in faith that God will provide whatever is required to complete the work that He calls you to do.

All the heroes in the Bible exhibited such faith in their obedience. Yet it was their faith in God's faithfulness, and not in their works or in their following the law, which was credited as righteousness. "Against all hope, Abraham in hope believed.... Yet he did not waver through unbelief regarding the promise of God, being fully persuaded that God had power to do what He had promised" (Romans 4:18–21). "This righteousness from God comes through faith in Jesus Christ to all who believe" (Romans 3:22).

Such righteousness was not only just for Abraham, but it also is for each of us. "The words 'it was credited to him [Abraham]' were written not for him alone, but also for us, to whom God will credit righteousness—for us who believe in Him who raised Jesus our Lord from the dead. He was delivered over to death for our sins and was raised to life for our justification" (Romans 4:23–25). "I may gain Christ and be found in Him, not having a righteousness of my own that comes from the law, but that which is through faith in Christ—the righteousness that comes from God and is by faith" (Philippians 3:8–9).

Accordingly, I am boldly and confidently declaring that God will find a way to fund this project within the next thirty days before the book's publication deadline. I am submitting this epilogue to the publisher with that confident and prayerful expectation, and with the knowledge that this epilogue will be deleted and not become part of the book if the funding does not happen within the next thirty days, "being confident of this, that He who has begun a good work in you will carry it on to completion" (Philippians 1:6). The fact that you are reading this epilogue is evidence that God has in fact provided the funding for the project!

This is the same bold faith Elijah exhibited before the 450 Baal prophets. Elijah didn't simply place the wood on the stone altar and then ask God to light the wood on fire. Before he prayed to God, Elijah taunted the Baal prophets. He then instructed that the wood be so saturated with water that the water covered the ground and filled the trench sounding the altar. Elijah first acted out and stepped out in faith—in his faith in God's faithfulness.

Elijah then prayed expectantly and confidently to God, knowing that God would answer his prayer. God answered Elijah's prayer not only by setting the wood on fire, but also setting fire to the water, to the stones, and to the ground!

The centurion who approached Jesus also demonstrated such faith:

> When Jesus had entered Capernaum, a centurion came to him, asking for help. "Lord," he said, "my servant lies at home paralyzed and in terrible suffering."
>
> Jesus said to him, "I will go and heal him."
>
> The centurion replied, "Lord, I do not deserve to have you come under my roof. But just say the word, and my servant will be healed. For I myself am a man under authority, with soldiers under me. I tell this one, 'Go,' and he goes; and that one, 'Come,' and he comes. I say to my servant, 'Do this,' and he does it."
>
> When Jesus heard this, he was astonished and said to those following him,
>
> "I tell you the truth, I have not found anyone in Israel with such great faith...."
>
> Then Jesus said to the centurion, "Go! It will be done just as you believed it would." And his servant was healed at that very hour. (Matthew 8:5–13)

From where does such faith originate? How can one with such faith pray with such boldness, confidence, and expectation? Hope, trust, and faith are gifts of God's grace and mercy through Jesus's death on the cross and in His resurrection. "Since we have such a hope, we are very bold" (2 Corinthians 3:12). Faith is that belief in the unseen grounded in God's faithfulness. The Lord's compassions never fail, and they are renewed each morning. Great is His faithfulness (Lamentations 3:22–23). God will never leave you nor forsake you (Hebrews 13:5). Jesus Christ is the same yesterday, today, and forever (Hebrews 13:8).

I believe that we are all capable of such faith in God's faithfulness, in God's promises, and in God's Word. Such faith is more than believing God is who He says He is, and is more than knowing God and His Word. Faith is acting out on God's faithfulness and promises in assurance and dependence. With such faith, we can expect miracles. If one has such hope and trust and faith in the unseen and in God's faithfulness, such faith should be accompanied with the assurance and boldness and confidence in the expectation of realized and answered prayer. "Such confidence as this is ours through Christ before God. Not that we are competent in ourselves to claim anything for ourselves, but our competence comes from God. He has made us competent as ministers of a new covenant" (2 Corinthians 2:5). Without faith, it is impossible to please God (Hebrews 11:6).

How then can one develop such faith, especially while living in this culture and in this world? Such faith begins with the recognition that we are nothing without God:

> I am the vine; you are the branches. If a man remains in Me and I in him, he will bear much fruit; apart from Me you can do nothing. If anyone does not remain in Me, he is like a branch that is thrown away and withers; such branches are picked up, thrown into the fire and burned. If you remain in Me and My words remain in you, ask whatever you wish, and it will be given you. This is to My Father's glory, that you bear much fruit, showing yourselves to be My disciples. (John 15:5–8)

Such faith then is strengthened and deepened by conforming our will to God's will. I have observed many Christians exercise discernment in deciding what they should do by asking, "What would Jesus do?" They then would try to act accordingly. We can know what Jesus would do by reading and knowing the Word, but knowing what Jesus would do, and then trying to behave the same way as Jesus is often difficult to do. Only Jesus is perfect. We fail, make mistakes, and mess up. We are not perfect like Jesus.

I also have observed some Christians often say that we are to behave so our behavior will "reflect" Christ. In fact, the Bible says that we are to reflect the Lord's glory (2 Corinthians 3:18). Because Christ lives within us as Christians, we are to reflect Christ's glory that lives within us. However, because we are human, it is difficult for us to attempt to have our behavior reflect Christ's behavior. If our lives were to reflect Christ, our lives and our behavior would have the qualities of a perfectly flawless mirror so that they would reflect Christ perfectly. However, our lives are neither perfect nor flawless. Our mistakes, sins, and imperfections are revealed in broken lives. Each mistake is visible as a crack or blemish in our mirrorlike lives.

Have you ever seen your reflection in a mirror or surface that is cracked or blemished? The image looking back at you is tarnished and blemished. Have you ever seen your reflection in one of those carnival or fun-zone mirrors where the glass is wavy or distorted? The image gets distorted and does not accurately reflect a true representation. This is how it is when we exercise our own will instead of God's will. It becomes impossible to reflect Christ when we distort God's will, and instead what we reflect is our own will.

I also have observed some Christians say that the way to reflect Christ is to model our behavior after Christ's behavior, or to imitate Christ. However, I believe that this also is a weak substitute. Such an attempt to imitate Christ's behavior, just like our attempt to have our behavior reflect Christ's behavior, again depends on our own efforts or works. No matter how hard we may try, such a plan is flawed. Our abilities, efforts, behavior, and works always will fall short.

At first, our good intentions may seem to create a good appearance to others, and to others we may even look and act "holy." While such appearances and behavior may fool others, or even ourselves, eventually our efforts, behavior, and works cannot be sustained. Just like a Rolex "look-alike" or a knockoff designer handbag, our efforts, behavior, and works are nothing more than a cheap imitation of the real article. When we try to imitate Jesus, our behavior is neither real nor authentic. We can't imitate Jesus. We can't be perfect like Jesus.

So, what is the answer? How can we obtain such faith? "For it is by grace you have been saved, through faith—and this not from yourselves, it is the gift of God—not by works, so that no one can boast. For we are God's workmanship, created in Christ Jesus to do good works, which God prepared in advance for us to do" (Ephesians 2:8–10). The answer is that to achieve such faith, we have to remove our will and our works from this equation and become completely dependent on God. It is addition by subtraction.

Earlier in the book, I made an analogy of our works to a glass full of water. In that analogy, the water in the glass represented for each of us our will, our plans, and our works. As I said earlier in the book, when we overfill the glass with our works beyond capacity, it spills all over the place and we make a mess of our lives.

Now, consider again the glass half full of water. Instead of filling the glass (your life) the rest of the way with more of your works and your efforts and your plans, instead you can fill up the rest of your life with Christ. However, staying with this analogy, if you simply add Christ to your life, you will only realize a portion of God's grace and blessings. Yet, this often is what Christians do. This is what I did. I added Christ to my life, literally. My old life was still there. Although Christ was with me, I was still striving to execute my own plans, efforts, and works. When I prayed, I asked God to help me accomplish what I wanted to do. I was still focusing on my will instead of on God's will.

You will recall that earlier in the book, I discussed Peter's pronouncement to Christ that he was willing to die for Christ. When I concluded that all Christians would say that they also would be willing to die for Christ, I wondered that the more difficult question might be whether we are willing to live for Christ. When we continue to exercise our will and attempt to perform our works, we interfere with God's will.

Jesus said, "I tell you the truth, no one can see the kingdom of God unless he is born again" (John 3:3). We can't accept Christ into our lives and yet continue to live our old lives according to our will, our plans, and our works. "Therefore, if anyone is in Christ, he is a new creation; the old has gone, the new has come!" (2 Corinthians 5:17). It is impossible to be a new creation and at the same time hold on to our old self and our old ways. We cannot do our will and our works and at the same time attempt to do God's will or God's works.

In this sense, then, we need to pour out that half-full glass of water. We need to empty ourselves of our own will, our own ego, our own pride, and our own works. Before we truly can be born again, we need to put to death our old selves. Only in this sense then can we become a new creation in Christ. We need to empty ourselves and pour ourselves out so that God can fill us up and work in and through us completely. Such a death to our old selves was made possible by Christ's death and resurrection. "We were therefore buried with Him through baptism into death in order that, just as Christ was raised from the dead through the glory of the Father, we too may live a new life" (Romans 3:20).

We each are to be an empty vessel. We should pour out our half-full glass of water so that we can accept the full measure of Christ. Our attitude should be that, "O Lord, you are our Father. We are the clay, You are the potter; we are all the work of Your hand" (Isaiah 64:8). In this way, our behavior neither attempts to imitate nor reflect Christ's behavior. By dying to ourselves, we get out of our own way, and we get out of God's way. "I will instruct you and teach you in the way you should go; I will counsel you and watch over you. Do not be like the horse or the mule, which have no understanding but must be controlled by bit and bridle" (Psalm 32:8–9).

If we continue to lean on our own understanding, we will fail to learn what is God's will for us. If we continue to strive to accomplish our works, we will fail to be available for God to perform His work in and through us. If we continue to have faith and trust in our own abilities, we will fail to be able to trust in God completely. "For the sinful nature desires what is contrary to the Spirit, and the Spirit what is contrary to the sinful nature. They are in conflict with each other" (Galatians 5:17). "The Holy Spirit will teach you all things" (John 14:26).

We have to break our spirit—our will—and accept Christ's Spirit. "A broken spirit is a pleasing sacrifice to God" (Psalm 51:17). We need to let go and let God. Instead of continuing to do our own works and offering our works to God, we should allow God to work in and through us. "I will give you a new heart and put a new spirit in you" (Ezekiel 36:26). Instead of focusing on our works, we should let God's works be our focus and mission. "For it is God who works in you to will and act according to His good purpose" (Philippians 2:13).

In this sense, then, by putting to death our old self, we are living for Christ. In this way we can die for Christ and live for Christ. By putting to death our old self—dying for Christ—we live for Christ by letting him work through us. "Now if we died with Christ, we believe that we will also live with Him" (Romans 6:8). We certainly will live with Christ in eternity, but we also can more completely live with Him in this life here in this world. This is how we are born again.

"What counts is a new creation" (Galatians 6:15). "I have been crucified with Christ and I no longer live, but Christ lives in me. The life I live in the body, I live by faith in the Son of God, who loved me and gave Himself for me" (Galatians 2:20). "Those who belong to Christ Jesus have crucified the sinful nature with its passions and desires" (Galatians 5:24). The act of putting to death our old self and our will is our complete and total surrender and submission to Christ. God gave us free will, but it is this act of surrendering and sacrificing our will for God's will that sanctifies us and frees us to be able to have complete and total faith in God. This is the faith that pleases God (Romans 12:1–2).

One neither acquires nor realizes such sanctification immediately upon accepting Christ and being saved. Even Apostle Paul recognized that this sanctification is a process:

> Not that I have already obtained all this, or have already been made perfect, but I press on to take hold of that for which Christ Jesus took hold of me. Brothers, I do not consider myself yet to have taken hold of it. But one thing I do: Forgetting what is behind and straining toward what is ahead, I press on toward the goal to win the prize for which God has called me heavenward in Christ Jesus. (Philippians 3:12–14)

The sanctification process of dying your old self takes place over time as our faith becomes deeper and stronger, and requires that we adopt a renewed mind. We are to be like-minded as Christ, having the same love, being one in spirit and purpose (Philippians 2:2). "Your attitude [of humility] should be the same as that of Christ Jesus" (Philippians 2:5). We need to have a renewed mind to be able to discard our old self. "You were taught, with regard to your former way of life, to put off your old self, which is being corrupted by its deceitful desires; to be made new in the attitude of your minds; and to put on the new self, created to be like God in true righteousness and holiness" (Ephesians 4:22–24).

By having a renewed mind and being like-minded as Christ, with an attitude of humility, we develop a deeper faith and a closer relationship with God. Just as Jacob wrestled (Genesis 32:22–32), we wrestle with putting our old selves to death. Until we overcome that struggle of surrendering our will, our efforts at imitating Christ will continue to be but a poor reflection. "Now we see but a poor reflection as in a mirror; then we shall see face to face. Now I know in part; then I shall know fully, even as I am fully known" (1 Corinthians 13:12).

In these past five and a half years in which I have been working on the project, and in the process of writing this book, God has changed me. As I underwent my own sanctification process, God has renewed in me a new mind-set. Earlier in the book, I made a statement that God changed me from being in a place where I would ask God to give me strength to be able to do and accomplish my works, and that he took me to a new attitude where I would begin each day by asking God what He wanted me to do for him. However, even then, I was still focusing on my own works.

Now, over this past year, God has further changed me. He has continued to reshape and renew my mind. Now, instead of beginning each day asking God what he wants me to do for Him, I begin each day by giving Him thanks and by humbling myself and asking God to work in and through me so that His will can be done. He also has changed me and taught me the benefits and blessings gained by waiting on the Lord in faith. "Delight yourself in the Lord and He will give you the desires of your heart" (Psalm 37:4).

In this book I sincerely have tried to praise and honor God. "I will praise you, O Lord, with all my heart; I will tell of all your wonders" (Psalm 9:1). I conclude my story by hoping that it will benefit and encourage you in your own walk in faith, "For we walk by faith, not by sight" (2 Corinthians 5:7). God has promised that He will honor those who honor Him. "Those who honor me I will honor" (1 Samuel 2:30). Honor God, and He will honor you.

Let God be your architect.

Notes

Chapter 1

1. Laura Ingalls Wilder wrote a series of books between 1932 and 1943 recounting her childhood in the Midwest between 1869–1889 commonly known as *The Little House on the Prairie,* but the book by that name actually was her third book in the series. The setting for her eighth book, *These Happy Golden Years* (1943), in which Laura began teaching at a one-room schoolhouse, was the small town of Desmet, South Dakota, located about 120 miles from our family farm.

2. O'Connell, Rev. John P. *The Life Of Christ.* Catholic Press (1954).

3. In 1994, the name of Sioux Falls College was changed to the University of Sioux Falls, described as a Christian liberal arts university on its website. (https://www.usiouxfalls.edu/index.php?option=com_content&task=view&id=674&Itemid=109)

4. Mark 7:8.

5. Ephesians 2:8–10.

Chapter 2

1. Matthew 19:29.

2. Mark 10:29–30 states, "I tell you the truth," Jesus replied, "no one who has left home or brothers or sisters or mother or father or children or fields for me and the gospel will fail to receive a hundred times as much in this present age (homes, brothers, sisters, mothers, children and fields—and with them, persecutions) and in the age to come, eternal life."

3. Luke 18:29–30 states, "I tell you the truth," Jesus said to them, "no one who has left home or wife or brothers or parents or children for the sake of the kingdom of God will fail to receive many times as much in this age and, in the age to come, eternal life."

4. *Perry Mason* aired on television from 1957 to 1966 and was the longest running television show starring an attorney. *To Kill A Mockingbird* was written by Harper Lee, who received the Pulitzer Prize for fiction in 1961. The movie by the same name was released in 1962 and starred Gregory Peck, who received an Oscar for Best Actor.

Chapter 4

1. "Heaven has no rage like love to hatred turned, Nor hell a fury like a woman scorned." Congreve, William. *The Mourning Bride,* Act III, Scene VIII (1697).

2. 1 Kings 3:16–28.

3. 1 Kings 3:22.

4. 1 Kings 3:25.

5. 1 Kings 3:26.

6. 1 Kings 3:27.

Chapter 5

1. See, e.g., Levy, Clifford J. and Rashbaum, William K. "After The Attacks: The Airports; Bush And Top Aides Proclaim Policy Of 'Ending' States That Back Terror; Local Airports Shut After An Arrest." New York Times. (14 September 2001).

2. Id.

3. Holmes TH, Rahe RH. "The Social Readjustment Rating Scale". *J Psychosom Res* 11 (2): 213–8 (1967).

Chapter 6

1. In 1996, Congress passed the Mental Health Parity Act (MHPA), requiring that either the annual or lifetime dollar limits on mental health benefits cannot be lower than medical or surgical benefits offered by a group health plan that provided mental health coverage. However, the MHPA did not require insurers to provide mental health coverage, and it did not cover substance abuse and chemical dependency. Further, it also allowed insurers to seize upon loopholes to avoid paying claims. Insurers could circumvent coverage by creating a maximum number of provider visits or caps on the number of days an insurer would cover inpatient hospitalizations. In 2008, Congress finally passed legislation removing those loopholes.

2. Congress passed the Paul Wellstone and Pete Domenici Mental Health Parity and Addiction Equity Act of 2008 requiring group health insurance plans of fifty or more insured employees to provide coverage for mental illness (MI) and substance use disorders (SUD) on parity with

all other medical and surgical procedures covered by the insurance plan. While the 2008 Act did not require group health plans to provide coverage for MH and SUD benefits, it stated that when plans do provide coverage for MH and SUD benefits, then those MH and SUD benefits cannot be lower or have more limited coverage than those for the other medical and surgical benefits offered under the plan.

3. The United States Supreme Court upheld the constitutionality of the Patient Protection and Affordable Care Act in the case *National Federation of Independent Business v. Sebelius* (132 S.Ct. 2566 [2012]).

   On February 20, 2013, the Obama administration (Kathleen Sebelius, Secretary of Health and Human Services) announced a federal rule imposed under the Patient Protection and Affordable Care Act requiring health insurers to provide coverage for the treatment of mental illnesses, behavioral disorders, drug addiction, and alcohol abuse. (Pear, Robert. (2013, February 21). "New Federal Rule Requires Insurers to Offer Mental Health Coverage." *New York Times*, p. A16).

4. The first published use of the phrase "grace under pressure" was in an April 20, 1926, letter Hemingway wrote F. Scott Fitzgerald, reprinted in *Ernest Hemingway: Selected Letters 1917-1961* edited by Carlos Baker, pages 199–201.

   The phrase "grace under pressure" gained notoriety when Ernest Hemingway used it in an interview by Dorothy Parker, who was writing a profile article about Hemmingway. Parker asked Hemingway: "Exactly what do you mean by 'guts'?" Hemingway replied: "I mean, grace under pressure." The profile is titled "The Artist's

Reward," and it appeared in the *New Yorker* on November 30, 1929.

5. Kennedy, John F. *Profiles in Courage.* Harper & Brothers, New York, New York. (1956).

6. "For God is not the author of confusion, but of peace." 1 Corinthians 14:33.

7. "The God of peace will soon crush Satan under your feet" (Romans 16:20).

8. Ephesians 6:10–17.

9. John 14:6.

10. Philippians 3:9.

11. 1 John 5:4–5.

12. Hebrews 4:12.

13. James 4:7.

14. 2 Corinthians 10:3–5.

15. Matthew 4:4; Matthew 4:7; and Matthew 4:10.

16. Assisi, Francis. *The Writings of St. Francis of Assisi.* Translated by Paschal Robinson. "First Rule of the Friars Minor." (Rule 17, p. 50). The Dolphin Press, Philadelphia, Pennsylvania (1905).

17. Psalm 23:1–6.

18. Mark 4:37.

19. Mark 4:38.

20. Id.

21. Mark 4:39.

22. Mark: 4:41.

23. Psalm 107: 28–29.

24. Job 38:11.

25. Mark 1:31–33.

26. Mark 1:41.

27. Mark 2:10–11.

28. Matthew 8:25.

29. Ephesians 6:12.

30. Matthew 26:47–50. At Luke 22: 3–4 it is said, "Then Satan entered Judas, called Iscariot, one of the Twelve. And Judas went to the chief priests and the officers of the temple guard and discussed with them how he might betray Jesus."

31. Matthew 27:4.

32. Matthew 27:4–5.

33. Id.

34. Matthew 26:59–74.

35. Matthew 26:75. At Luke 22: 61 it is said that just after the rooster crowed, "The Lord turned and looked straight at Peter. Then Peter remembered the word the Lord had spoken to him: 'Before the rooster crows today, you will disown me three times.'"

36. Luke 24:12.

37. John 21:1–7.

38. John 21:15–18.

39. Luke 22:31–32.

40. Hebrews 10:16–17 (*see also* Hebrews 8:12).

41. Psalm 51:3; Psalm 51:7.

42. Isaiah 43:25. *See also* Jeremiah 31:34; Acts 3:19.

43. Psalm 103:12.

44. 2 Corinthians 5:17–19.

45. Isaiah 1:18–20.

46. John 8:31–32.

47. Romans 8:31.

48. Taylor DJ, Lichstein KL, Durrence HH, Reidel BW, Bush AJ. "Epidemiology of insomnia, depression, and anxiety." *Sleep* (11); pp. 1457-64 (2005).

49. Ohayon, Maurice. "The effects of breathing-related sleep disorders on mood disturbances in the general population." *Journal of Clinical Psychiatry.* 2003 Oct; 64(10): 1195-200; quiz, 1274-6.

50. Matthew 11:28–30.

51. Psalm 139:23.

52. 1 Corinthians 14:33.

53. Exodus 33:14.

54. James 5:16.

55. Psalm 91:14–16.

56. Luke 4:18; *see* Isaiah 61:1.

57. Psalm 147:3.

58. 2 Corinthians 5:19.

59. Matthew 18:21–22. In the translation of The New King James Version of the Bible it is stated, "seventy times seven."

60. 1 Chronicles 29:3–5.

61. Matthew 18:33.

62. Matthew 6:9–13.

63. Matthew 18:25.

64. Matthew 18:23.

65. Matthew 18:34.

66. Matthew 18:35.

67. Romans 16:20.

68. Joshua 10:24.

69. Joshua 10:25.

70. Joshua 1:9.

71. 1 Thessalonians 5:16–18.

72. Deuteronomy 34:1–8.

73. Deuteronomy 31:1–8.

74. Mark 4:40.

75. Matthew 4:10–11.

76. "The original authorship of the poem is disputed, with dozens of people claiming to have penned it. Rachel Aviv in a *Poetry Foundation* article discusses the various claims and suggests that the source of this poem is the opening paragraph of Charles Haddon Spurgeon's 1880 sermon 'The Education of the Sons of God.'" http://en.wikipedia. org/wiki/Footprints_(poem)
Aviv, Rachel. "Enter Sandman: Who wrote footprints?". *Poetry Foundation*. Retrieved 2008-08-05.
Spurgeon, Charles Haddon. "The Education of the Sons of God" (PDF). *Metropolitan Tabernacle*, Newington (10 June 1880).

77. Psalm 37:23–24.

78. Ephesians 6:10.

Chapter 7

1. http://www.notable-quotes.com/e/epictetus_quotes.html

2. Nabi, Hermann; Kimimaki, Mika; Batty, G. David; Shipley, Martin J.; Britton, Annie; Brunner, Eric J.; Vahtera, Jussi; Lemongne, Cedric; Elbaz, Alexis; Singh-Manoux, Archana. "Increased risk of coronary heart disease among individuals reporting adverse impact of stress on their health: the Whitehall II prospective cohort study." *European Heart Journal.* Oxford University Press (June 26, 2013).

3. http://www.escardio.org/about/press/press-releases/pr-13/Pages/effect-of-stress.aspx.

4. http://www.nlm.nih.gov/medlineplus/news/fullstory 138222.html.

5. http://news.yahoo.com/blogs/power-players-abc-news/patrick-kennedy-members-congress-battle-mental-illness-families-105658057.html

6. http://www.forbes.com/sites/melaniehaiken/2013/02/05/22-the-number-of-veterans-who-now-commit-suicide-every-day/.

7. Id.

8. Id.

9. Colin, Chris. "How Dogs Can Help Veterans Overcome PTSD: New research finds that 'man's best friend' could be lifesavers for veterans of the wars in Iraq and Afghanistan." *Smithsonian.* (July-August 2012). http://www.smithsonianmag.com/science-nature/How-Dogs-Can-Help-Veterans-Overcome-PTSD-160281185.html

10. Yount, Rick A. "Testimony of Rick A. Yount before Congressional Subcommittee." August 26, 2013.
http://veterans.house.gov/prepared-statement/prepared-statement-rick-yount-director-paws-purple-hearts.
The Paws for Purple Hearts is a program of Bergin University of Canine Studies in Santa Rosa, CA. Bergin University was awarded a one year $245,000 contract by Walter Reed Army Medical Center in September 2010 to provide a Patient Service Dog Training Program from September 28, 2010, through September 27, 2011.
PPH was inspired by the success of a therapeutic service-dog training program Yount started in 2006 at Morgantown, West Virginia to help at-risk teens develop social skills while providing them with a rewarding career path. Yount's *Golden Rule Assistance Dog Program* (GRAD) was offered to public school dropouts through Morgantown's Alternative Learning Center. Several GRAD-trained assistance dogs were placed with disabled veterans.

11. "Myth: Reframing Mental Illness as a 'Brain Disease' Reduces Stigma." Canadian Foundation For Healthcare Improvement. (04/06/2012).

12. Id.

13. Id.

14. World Health Organization. "Leprosy Fact Sheet N°101." (September 2012).
http://www.who.int/mediacentre/factsheets/fs101/en/.

15. Numbers 12:10–16.

16. 2 Kings 5:1–27.

17. World Health Organization. "Leprosy Fact Sheet N°101." (September 2012).

http://www.who.int/mediacentre/factsheets/fs101/en/

18. Id.

19. Id.

20. Matthew 11:5; Luke 17:12.

21. U.S. Department of Health and Human Services. "National Hansen's Disease (Leprosy) Program." http://www.hrsa.gov/hansensdisease/.

22. "VOX POPULI: Poems of Kazuko To reflect pain, isolation of leprosy." Asahi Shimbun. (August 30, 2013). *Vox Populi* ("Voice of the People") Vox Dei is a daily column that runs on Page 1 of the vernacular Asahi Shimbun. http://ajw.asahi.com/article/views/ AJ201308300037

23. Id.

24. Id.

25. Id.

26. Id.

27. Matthew 8:3; Mark 1:41; Luke 5:13; Matthew 11:5; Luke 17:12.

Chapter 8

1. Matthew 21:21–22.

2. 1 Corinthians 13: 2.

3. James 2:26.

4. Matthew 21:21–22.

5. 1 Corinthians 13:2.

6. James 2:26.

7. Joshua 3:13; Joshua 3:14–17.

8. 1 Kings 18:27–29.

9. 1 Kings 18:33–35.

10. 1 Kings 18:38.

11. 2 Corinthians 12:9–10.

12. I give credit for this expression of faith to Pastor Mark Batterson, author of *In a Pit with a Lion on A Snowy Day*.

13. Batterson, Mark. *In a Pit with a Lion on a Snowy Day* (p. 144). Multnomah Books. Colorado Springs, Colorado (2006).

14. Batterson, Mark. *In a Pit with A Lion on a Snowy Day*. Multnomah Books. Colorado Springs, Colorado (2006).

15. Batterson, Mark. *The Circle Maker*. Zondervan. Grand Rapids, MI. (2011).

16. Matthew 22:37.

17. Matthew 26:35.

18. 2 Corinthians 3:12.

19. 2 Corinthians 2:17.

20. 2 Corinthians 5:20.

21. Id.

22. Galatians 4:9.

23. John 4:48.

24. John 20:29.

25. Philippians 4:19.

26. Romans 8:31.

Conclusion

1. 1 Samuel 2:30 ("Those who honor me I will honor.").

2. Ekman, Paul. *Telling Lies: Clues to Deceit in the Marketplace, Politics, and Marriage* (p. 66). W. W. Norton & Company. New York, NY. (1992).

3. Graham, Billy. "Billy Graham: My Heart Aches For America."
Billy Graham Evangelistic Association.
(July 24, 2012)
http://www.billygraham.org/articlepage.asp?articleid=8813

4. Rogers, Edward B.; Stanford, Matthew; Garland, Diana R. "The effects of mental illness on families within faith communities." *Mental Health, Religion & Culture.* (May 2011)
Stanford, Matthew; Philpott, David. "Baptist senior pastors' knowledge and perceptions of mental illness." *Mental Health, Religion & Culture.* (March 2011)
Stanford, Matthew; McAlister, Kandace R. "Perceptions of Serious Mental Illness in the Local Church." *Journal of Religion, Disability & Health.* (2008)
Stanford, Matthew. "Demon or disorder: A survey of attitudes toward mental illness in the Christian church." *Mental Health, Religion & Culture.* (May 2007)

5. Consult the band's website at www.tenthavenuenorth.com.

CPSIA information can be obtained
at www.ICGtesting.com
Printed in the USA
LVOW04s2057120816

500060LV00016B/276/P